FREE Test Taking Tips Video/DVD Offer

To better serve you, we created videos covering test taking tips that we want to give you for FREE. **These videos cover world-class tips that will help you succeed on your test.**

We just ask that you send us feedback about this product. Please let us know what you thought about it—whether good, bad, or indifferent.

To get your **FREE videos**, you can use the QR code below or email freevideos@studyguideteam.com with "Free Videos" in the subject line and the following information in the body of the email:

    a. The title of your product

    b. Your product rating on a scale of 1-5, with 5 being the highest

    c. Your feedback about the product

If you have any questions or concerns, please don't hesitate to contact us at info@studyguideteam.com.

Thank you!

TExES Math 7-12 Study Guide (235) and 2 Practice Exams [4th Edition]

Lydia Morrison

Copyright © 2024 by TPB Publishing

All rights reserved. No part of this publication may be reproduced, distributed, or transmitted in any form or by any means, including photocopying, recording, or other electronic or mechanical methods, without the prior written permission of the publisher, except in the case of brief quotations embodied in critical reviews and certain other noncommercial uses permitted by copyright law.

Written and edited by TPB Publishing.

TPB Publishing is not associated with or endorsed by any official testing organization. TPB Publishing is a publisher of unofficial educational products. All test and organization names are trademarks of their respective owners. Content in this book is included for utilitarian purposes only and does not constitute an endorsement by TPB Publishing of any particular point of view.

Interested in buying more than 10 copies of our product? Contact us about bulk discounts:
bulkorders@studyguideteam.com

ISBN 13: 9781637758748

Table of Contents

Welcome *1*
  FREE Videos/DVD OFFER 1
Quick Overview *2*
Test-Taking Strategies *3*
Introduction *7*
Study Prep Plan for the TExES Math 7-12 Test *9*
Number Concepts *13*
  Number and Quantity 13
  Practice Quiz 42
  Answer Explanations 43
Patterns and Algebra *44*
  Practice Quiz 89
  Answer Explanations 90
Geometry and Measurement *91*
  Practice Quiz 136
  Answer Explanations 138
Probability and Statistics *139*
  Practice Quiz 166
  Answer Explanations 168
Mathematical Processes and Perspectives *170*
  Practice Quiz 174
  Answer Explanations 175
Mathematical Learning, Instruction and Assessment *176*

Practice Quiz 181
Answer Explanations 182

Practice Test #1 .... *183*

Number Concepts 183
Patterns and Algebra 185
Geometry and Measurement 193
Probability and Statistics 197
Mathematical Processes and Perspectives 199
Mathematical Learning, Instruction and Assessment 201

Answer Explanations #1 .... *204*

Number Concepts 204
Patterns and Algebra 206
Geometry and Measurement 211
Probability and Statistics 215
Mathematical Processes and Perspectives 218
Mathematical Learning, Instruction and Assessment 218

Practice Test #2 .... *221*

Number Concepts 221
Patterns and Algebra 223
Geometry and Measurement 231
Probability and Statistics 237
Mathematical Processes and Perspectives 240
Mathematical Learning, Instruction, and Assessment 242

Answer Explanations #2 .... *244*

Number Concepts 244
Patterns and Algebra 246

Table of Contents

Geometry and Measurements 251

Probability and Statistics 253

Mathematical Processes and Perspectives 255

Mathematical Learning, Instruction, and Assessment 256

Welcome

Dear Reader,

Welcome to your new Test Prep Books study guide! We are pleased that you chose us to help you prepare for your exam. There are many study options to choose from, and we appreciate you choosing us. Studying can be a daunting task, but we have designed a smart, effective study guide to help prepare you for what lies ahead.

Whether you're a parent helping your child learn and grow, a high school student working hard to get into your dream college, or a nursing student studying for a complex exam, we want to help give you the tools you need to succeed. We hope this study guide gives you the skills and the confidence to thrive, and we can't thank you enough for allowing us to be part of your journey.

In an effort to continue to improve our products, we welcome feedback from our customers. We look forward to hearing from you. Suggestions, success stories, and criticisms can all be communicated by emailing us at info@studyguideteam.com.

Sincerely,
Test Prep Books Team

FREE Videos/DVD OFFER

Doing well on your exam requires both knowing the test content and understanding how to use that knowledge to do well on the test. We offer completely FREE test taking tip videos. **These videos cover world-class tips that you can use to succeed on your test.**

To get your **FREE videos**, you can use the QR code below or email freevideos@studyguideteam.com with "Free Videos" in the subject line and the following information in the body of the email:

    a. The title of your product
    b. Your product rating on a scale of 1-5, with 5 being the highest
    c. Your feedback about the product

If you have any questions or concerns, please don't hesitate to contact us at info@studyguideteam.com.

Quick Overview

As you draw closer to taking your exam, effective preparation becomes more and more important. Thankfully, you have this study guide to help you get ready. Use this guide to help keep your studying on track and refer to it often.

This study guide contains several key sections that will help you be successful on your exam. The guide contains tips for what you should do the night before and the day of the test. Also included are test-taking tips. Knowing the right information is not always enough. Many well-prepared test takers struggle with exams. These tips will help equip you to accurately read, assess, and answer test questions.

A large part of the guide is devoted to showing you what content to expect on the exam and to helping you better understand that content. In this guide are practice test questions so that you can see how well you have grasped the content. Then, answer explanations are provided so that you can understand why you missed certain questions.

Don't try to cram the night before you take your exam. This is not a wise strategy for a few reasons. First, your retention of the information will be low. Your time would be better used by reviewing information you already know rather than trying to learn a lot of new information. Second, you will likely become stressed as you try to gain a large amount of knowledge in a short amount of time. Third, you will be depriving yourself of sleep. So be sure to go to bed at a reasonable time the night before. Being well-rested helps you focus and remain calm.

Be sure to eat a substantial breakfast the morning of the exam. If you are taking the exam in the afternoon, be sure to have a good lunch as well. Being hungry is distracting and can make it difficult to focus. You have hopefully spent lots of time preparing for the exam. Don't let an empty stomach get in the way of success!

When travelling to the testing center, leave earlier than needed. That way, you have a buffer in case you experience any delays. This will help you remain calm and will keep you from missing your appointment time at the testing center.

Be sure to pace yourself during the exam. Don't try to rush through the exam. There is no need to risk performing poorly on the exam just so you can leave the testing center early. Allow yourself to use all of the allotted time if needed.

Remain positive while taking the exam even if you feel like you are performing poorly. Thinking about the content you should have mastered will not help you perform better on the exam.

Once the exam is complete, take some time to relax. Even if you feel that you need to take the exam again, you will be well served by some down time before you begin studying again. It's often easier to convince yourself to study if you know that it will come with a reward!

Test-Taking Strategies

1. Predicting the Answer

When you feel confident in your preparation for a multiple-choice test, try predicting the answer before reading the answer choices. This is especially useful on questions that test objective factual knowledge. By predicting the answer before reading the available choices, you eliminate the possibility that you will be distracted or led astray by an incorrect answer choice. You will feel more confident in your selection if you read the question, predict the answer, and then find your prediction among the answer choices. After using this strategy, be sure to still read all of the answer choices carefully and completely. If you feel unprepared, you should not attempt to predict the answers. This would be a waste of time and an opportunity for your mind to wander in the wrong direction.

2. Reading the Whole Question

Too often, test takers scan a multiple-choice question, recognize a few familiar words, and immediately jump to the answer choices. Test authors are aware of this common impatience, and they will sometimes prey upon it. For instance, a test author might subtly turn the question into a negative, or he or she might redirect the focus of the question right at the end. The only way to avoid falling into these traps is to read the entirety of the question carefully before reading the answer choices.

3. Looking for Wrong Answers

Long and complicated multiple-choice questions can be intimidating. One way to simplify a difficult multiple-choice question is to eliminate all of the answer choices that are clearly wrong. In most sets of answers, there will be at least one selection that can be dismissed right away. If the test is administered on paper, the test taker could draw a line through it to indicate that it may be ignored; otherwise, the test taker will have to perform this operation mentally or on scratch paper. In either case, once the obviously incorrect answers have been eliminated, the remaining choices may be considered. Sometimes identifying the clearly wrong answers will give the test taker some information about the correct answer. For instance, if one of the remaining answer choices is a direct opposite of one of the eliminated answer choices, it may well be the correct answer. The opposite of obviously wrong is obviously right! Of course, this is not always the case. Some answers are obviously incorrect simply because they are irrelevant to the question being asked. Still, identifying and eliminating some incorrect answer choices is a good way to simplify a multiple-choice question.

4. Don't Overanalyze

Anxious test takers often overanalyze questions. When you are nervous, your brain will often run wild, causing you to make associations and discover clues that don't actually exist. If you feel that this may be a problem for you, do whatever you can to slow down during the test. Try taking a deep breath or counting to ten. As you read and consider the question, restrict yourself to the particular words used by the author. Avoid thought tangents about what the author *really* meant, or what he or she was *trying* to say. The only things that matter on a multiple-choice test are the words that are actually in the question. You must avoid reading too much into a multiple-choice question, or supposing that the writer meant something other than what he or she wrote.

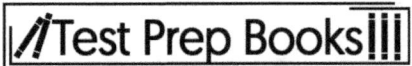

5. No Need for Panic

It is wise to learn as many strategies as possible before taking a multiple-choice test, but it is likely that you will come across a few questions for which you simply don't know the answer. In this situation, avoid panicking. Because most multiple-choice tests include dozens of questions, the relative value of a single wrong answer is small. As much as possible, you should compartmentalize each question on a multiple-choice test. In other words, you should not allow your feelings about one question to affect your success on the others. When you find a question that you either don't understand or don't know how to answer, just take a deep breath and do your best. Read the entire question slowly and carefully. Try rephrasing the question a couple of different ways. Then, read all of the answer choices carefully. After eliminating obviously wrong answers, make a selection and move on to the next question.

6. Confusing Answer Choices

When working on a difficult multiple-choice question, there may be a tendency to focus on the answer choices that are the easiest to understand. Many people, whether consciously or not, gravitate to the answer choices that require the least concentration, knowledge, and memory. This is a mistake. When you come across an answer choice that is confusing, you should give it extra attention. A question might be confusing because you do not know the subject matter to which it refers. If this is the case, don't

eliminate the answer before you have affirmatively settled on another. When you come across an answer choice of this type, set it aside as you look at the remaining choices. If you can confidently assert that one of the other choices is correct, you can leave the confusing answer aside. Otherwise, you will need to take a moment to try to better understand the confusing answer choice. Rephrasing is one way to tease out the sense of a confusing answer choice.

7. Your First Instinct

Many people struggle with multiple-choice tests because they overthink the questions. If you have studied sufficiently for the test, you should be prepared to trust your first instinct once you have carefully and completely read the question and all of the answer choices. There is a great deal of research suggesting that the mind can come to the correct conclusion very quickly once it has obtained all of the relevant information. At times, it may seem to you as if your intuition is working faster even than your reasoning mind. This may in fact be true. The knowledge you obtain while studying may be retrieved from your subconscious before you have a chance to work out the associations that support it. Verify your instinct by working out the reasons that it should be trusted.

8. Key Words

Many test takers struggle with multiple-choice questions because they have poor reading comprehension skills. Quickly reading and understanding a multiple-choice question requires a mixture of skill and experience. To help with this, try jotting down a few key words and phrases on a piece of scrap paper. Doing this concentrates the process of reading and forces the mind to weigh the relative importance of the question's parts. In selecting words and phrases to write down, the test taker thinks about the question more deeply and carefully. This is especially true for multiple-choice questions that are preceded by a long prompt.

9. Subtle Negatives

One of the oldest tricks in the multiple-choice test writer's book is to subtly reverse the meaning of a question with a word like *not* or *except*. If you are not paying attention to each word in the question, you can easily be led astray by this trick. For instance, a common question format is, "Which of the following is...?" Obviously, if the question instead is, "Which of the following is not...?," then the answer will be quite different. Even worse, the test makers are aware of the potential for this mistake and will include one answer choice that would be correct if the question were not negated or reversed. A test taker who misses the reversal will find what he or she believes to be a correct answer and will be so confident that he or she will fail to reread the question and discover the original error. The only way to avoid this is to practice a wide variety of multiple-choice questions and to pay close attention to each and every word.

10. Reading Every Answer Choice

It may seem obvious, but you should always read every one of the answer choices! Too many test takers fall into the habit of scanning the question and assuming that they understand the question because they recognize a few key words. From there, they pick the first answer choice that answers the question they believe they have read. Test takers who read all of the answer choices might discover that one of the latter answer choices is actually *more* correct. Moreover, reading all of the answer choices can remind you of facts related to the question that can help you arrive at the correct answer. Sometimes, a misstatement or incorrect detail in one of the latter answer choices will trigger your memory of the subject and will enable you to find the right answer. Failing to read all of the answer choices is like not reading all of the items on a restaurant menu: you might miss out on the perfect choice.

11. Spot the Hedges

One of the keys to success on multiple-choice tests is paying close attention to every word. This is never truer than with words like *almost*, *most*, *some*, and *sometimes*. These words are called "hedges" because they indicate that a statement is not totally true or not true in every place and time. An absolute statement will contain no hedges, but in many subjects, the answers are not always straightforward or absolute. There are always exceptions to the rules in these subjects. For this reason,

you should favor those multiple-choice questions that contain hedging language. The presence of qualifying words indicates that the author is taking special care with his or her words, which is certainly important when composing the right answer. After all, there are many ways to be wrong, but there is only one way to be right! For this reason, it is wise to avoid answers that are absolute when taking a multiple-choice test. An absolute answer is one that says things are either all one way or all another. They often include words like *every*, *always*, *best*, and *never*. If you are taking a multiple-choice test in a subject that doesn't lend itself to absolute answers, be on your guard if you see any of these words.

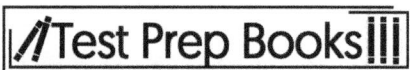

12. Long Answers

In many subject areas, the answers are not simple. As already mentioned, the right answer often requires hedges. Another common feature of the answers to a complex or subjective question are qualifying clauses, which are groups of words that subtly modify the meaning of the sentence. If the question or answer choice describes a rule to which there are exceptions or the subject matter is complicated, ambiguous, or confusing, the correct answer will require many words in order to be expressed clearly and accurately. In essence, you should not be deterred by answer choices that seem excessively long. Oftentimes, the author of the text will not be able to write the correct answer without offering some qualifications and modifications. Your job is to read the answer choices thoroughly and completely and to select the one that most accurately and precisely answers the question.

13. Restating to Understand

Sometimes, a question on a multiple-choice test is difficult not because of what it asks but because of how it is written. If this is the case, restate the question or answer choice in different words. This process serves a couple of important purposes. First, it forces you to concentrate on the core of the question. In order to rephrase the question accurately, you have to understand it well. Rephrasing the question will concentrate your mind on the key words and ideas. Second, it will present the information to your mind in a fresh way. This process may trigger your memory and render some useful scrap of information picked up while studying.

14. True Statements

Sometimes an answer choice will be true in itself, but it does not answer the question. This is one of the main reasons why it is essential to read the question carefully and completely before proceeding to the answer choices. Too often, test takers skip ahead to the answer choices and look for true statements. Having found one of these, they are content to select it without reference to the question above. The savvy test taker will always read the entire question before turning to the answer choices. Then, having settled on a correct answer choice, he or she will refer to the original question and ensure that the selected answer is relevant. The mistake of choosing a correct-but-irrelevant answer choice is especially common on questions related to specific pieces of objective knowledge.

15. No Patterns

One of the more dangerous ideas that circulates about multiple-choice tests is that the correct answers tend to fall into patterns. These erroneous ideas range from a belief that B and C are the most common right answers, to the idea that an unprepared test-taker should answer "A-B-A-C-A-D-A-B-A." It cannot be emphasized enough that pattern-seeking of this type is exactly the WRONG way to approach a multiple-choice test. To begin with, it is highly unlikely that the test maker will plot the correct answers according to some predetermined pattern. The questions are scrambled and delivered in a random order. Furthermore, even if the test maker was following a pattern in the assignation of correct answers, there is no reason why the test taker would know which pattern he or she was using. Any attempt to discern a pattern in the answer choices is a waste of time and a distraction from the real work of taking the test. A test taker would be much better served by extra preparation before the test than by reliance on a pattern in the answers.

Introduction

Function of the Test

The Texas Examination of Educator Standards (TExES) Mathematics 7-12 test is one of dozens of TExES tests used as part of the certification process for teachers in the state of Texas. Texas law requires every person seeking certification as an educator in Texas to pass comprehensive examinations appropriate to the area in which they wish to teach. The TExES tests have been developed gradually since 2002 as the means by which prospective educators can meet this requirement.

The TExES tests are intended to identify individuals who have the appropriate level of knowledge to teach in Texas public schools. They are governed by the Texas State Board for Educator Certification and the Texas Education Agency. These state agencies have contracted with Educational Testing Service (ETS) to assist in development and deployment of the tests. All TExES tests are based on Texas Essential Knowledge and Skills, the required curriculum for all Texas public school students.

The TExES Mathematics 7-12 test evaluates prospective teachers' skills and preparedness for teaching 7th through 12th grade math. The test is not used for purposes other than determining whether the test taker qualifies for certification. Understandably, it is almost exclusively taken in Texas, by individuals seeking employment as public educators in Texas. In the 2015-2016 year, the TExES Math 7-12 test was taken by 2,446 test takers, of whom 58% passed.

Test Administration

Prospective exam candidates must first get approval to take the test from their Educator Preparation Program (EPP). Once a candidate receives approval from their EPP, he or she can register to take the test through ETS, either online or by phone.

The test is administered by computer at test centers throughout Texas and at selected test centers in states bordering Texas and elsewhere. The test takes five hours, and may be taken in either a morning or afternoon testing session. Candidates taking multiple TExES tests may take tests in both sessions in one day.

As with all computer-based TExES tests, Texas law requires that a test taker who does not pass the TExES Math 7-12 exam must wait 45 days before retaking the test. A test taker may attempt the test for a maximum of five total administrations (the original plus four retakes).

In accordance with the Americans with Disabilities Act, individuals with documented disabilities can receive testing accommodations. Such individuals must register for their test through ETS and have their desired accommodations approved prior to the testing day.

Test Format

Test takers should arrive at their computer testing center with an admission ticket and appropriate identification. After signing in at the test center, test takers are given the opportunity to secure personal belongings in a locker and then they are assigned a computer. The test consists of 100 multiple-choice

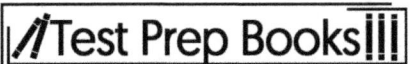

questions. The questions cover six domains of knowledge in the field of Math instruction. These domains, and the approximate percentage of the test content they comprise, are as follows:

Domain	Approximate Percentage of Test
Number Concepts	14%
Patterns and Algebra	33%
Geometry and Measurement	19%
Probability and Statistics	14%
Mathematical Processes and Perspectives	10%
Mathematics Learning, Instruction, and Assessment	10%

Scoring

All TExES tests are criterion-referenced, meaning they are designed to measure each performance against a reference baseline rather than in relation to other test takers. Raw scores are based on the number of multiple-choice questions answered correctly, with no penalty for guessing incorrectly, along with scores given by two scorers for the constructed-response questions. The raw score is then scaled to enable comparison between results on different forms of the test. Scaled scores range from 100 to 300, with a passing score set at 240. The average score in the 2015-2016 year was 239.89, almost precisely at the passing score.

Score reports include both the pass/fail result and the test taker's raw score information broken down by subject matter within the test, for the purpose of aiding preparation for a potential retake attempt. Scores are posted within seven days of the test date.

Recent/Future Developments

The limit of a maximum five total attempts to pass was instituted effective September 1, 2015. All attempts taken before that date count as one total attempt. No other substantial recent or prospective changes have been announced.

Study Prep Plan for the TExES Math 7-12 Test

1 **Schedule** - Use one of our study schedules below or come up with one of your own.

2 **Relax** - Test anxiety can hurt even the best students. There are many ways to reduce stress. Find the one that works best for you.

3 **Execute** - Once you have a good plan in place, be sure to stick to it.

One Week Study Schedule

Day 1	Number Concepts
Day 2	Patterns and Algebra
Day 3	Geometry and Measurement
Day 4	Probability and Statistics
Day 5	Mathematical Processes and Perspectives
Day 6	Practice Test #1
Day 7	Take Your Exam!

Two Week Study Schedule

Day 1	Number Concepts	Day 8	Using Coordinate Geometry to...
Day 2	Deductive Reasoning	Day 9	Probability and Statistics
Day 3	Patterns and Algebra	Day 10	Making Inferences and Justifying Conclusions...
Day 4	Operations with Polynomials	Day 11	Mathematical Processes and Perspectives
Day 5	Geometry and Measurement	Day 12	Practice Test #1
Day 6	Classification of Angles	Day 13	Practice Test #2
Day 7	Circle Theorems	Day 14	Take Your Exam!

Study Prep Plan for the TExES Math 7-12 Test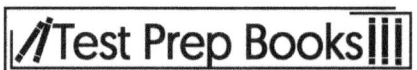

One Month Study Schedule

Day 1	Number Concepts	Day 11	Trigonometric Identities	Day 21	Probability and Statistics
Day 2	Strategies and Algorithms to…	Day 12	Behavior of a Function	Day 22	Describing a Set of Data
Day 3	Rational Expressions and Real Numbers	Day 13	Geometry and Measurement	Day 23	Independence and Conditional Probability
Day 4	Properties Involving Algebraic Expressions	Day 14	Effects of Changes to Dimensions on Area…	Day 24	Making Inferences and Justifying Conclusions…
Day 5	Determining the Reasonableness of…	Day 15	Classification of Angles	Day 25	Statistical Processes
Day 6	Patterns and Algebra	Day 16	Using Geometry Software	Day 26	Mathematical Processes and Perspectives
Day 7	Common Functions	Day 17	Circle Theorems	Day 27	Mathematical Learning, Instruction and….
Day 8	Polynomial Identities	Day 18	Applying Geometric Concepts to Rea…	Day 28	Practice Test #1
Day 9	Systems of Equations	Day 19	Using Coordinate Geometry to…	Day 29	Practice Test #2
Day 10	Operations with Polynomials	Day 20	Vectors	Day 30	Take Your Exam!

Build your own prep plan by visiting:

testprepbooks.com/prep

As you study for your test, we'd like to take the opportunity to remind you that you are capable of great things! With the right tools and dedication, you truly can do anything you set your mind to. The fact that you are holding this book right now shows how committed you are. In case no one has told you lately, you've got this! Our intention behind including this coloring page is to give you the chance to take some time to engage your creative side when you need a little brain-break from studying. As a company, we want to encourage people like you to achieve their dreams by providing good quality study materials for the tests and certifications that improve careers and change lives. As individuals, many of us have taken such tests in our careers, and we know how challenging this process can be. While we can't come alongside you and cheer you on personally, we can offer you the space to recall your purpose, reconnect with your passion, and refresh your brain through an artistic practice. We wish you every success, and happy studying!

Number Concepts

Number and Quantity

Base-10 Numerals, Number Names, and Expanded Form

Numbers used in everyday life are constituted in a base-10 system. Each digit in a number, depending on its location, represents some multiple of 10, or quotient of 10 when dealing with decimals. Each digit to the left of the decimal point represents a higher multiple of 10. Each digit to the right of the decimal point represents a quotient of a higher multiple of 10 for the divisor. For example, consider the number 7,631.42. The digit one represents simply the number one. The digit 3 represents 3×10. The digit 6 represents $6 \times 10 \times 10$ (or 6×100). The digit 7 represents $7 \times 10 \times 10 \times 10$ (or $7 \times 1,000$). The digit 4 represents $4 \div 10$. The digit 2 represents $(2 \div 10) \div 10$, or $2 \div (10 \times 10)$ or $2 \div 100$.

A number is written in expanded form by expressing it as the sum of the value of each of its digits. The expanded form in the example above, which is written with the highest value first down to the lowest value, is expressed as:
$$7,000 + 600 + 30 + 1 + .4 + .02$$

When verbally expressing a number, the integer part of the number (the numbers to the left of the decimal point) resembles the expanded form without the addition between values. In the above example, the numbers read "seven thousand six hundred thirty-one." When verbally expressing the decimal portion of a number, the number is read as a whole number, followed by the place value of the furthest digit (non-zero) to the right. In the above example, 0.42 is read "forty-two hundredths." Reading the number 7,631.42 in its entirety is expressed as "seven thousand six hundred thirty-one and forty-two hundredths." The word *and* is used between the integer and decimal parts of the number.

Composing and Decomposing Multi-Digit Numbers

Composing and decomposing numbers aids in conceptualizing what each digit of a multi-digit number represents. The standard, or typical, form in which numbers are written consists of a series of digits representing a given value based on their place value. Consider the number 592.7. This number is composed of 5 hundreds, 9 tens, 2 ones, and 7 tenths.

Composing a number requires adding the given numbers for each place value and writing the numbers in standard form. For example, composing 4 thousands, 5 hundreds, 2 tens, and 8 ones consists of adding as follows: $4,000 + 500 + 20 + 8$, to produce 4,528 (standard form).

Decomposing a number requires taking a number written in standard form and breaking it apart into the sum of each place value. For example, the number 83.17 is decomposed by breaking it into the sum of 4 values (for each of the 4 digits): 8 tens, 3 ones, 1 tenth, and 7 hundredths. The decomposed or "expanded" form of 83.17 is:
$$80 + 3 + .1 + .07$$

Place Value of a Given Digit

The number system that is used consists of only ten different digits or characters. However, this system is used to represent an infinite number of values. The place value system makes this infinite number of values possible. The position in which a digit is written corresponds to a given value. Starting from the decimal point (which is implied, if not physically present), each subsequent place value to the left represents a value greater than the one before it. Conversely, starting from the decimal point, each subsequent place value to the right represents a value less than the one before it.

The names for the place values to the left of the decimal point are as follows:

...	Billions	Hundred-Millions	Ten-Millions	Millions	Hundred-Thousands	Ten-Thousands	Thousands	Hundreds	Tens	Ones

*Note that this table can be extended infinitely further to the left.

The names for the place values to the right of the decimal point are as follows:

Decimal Point (.)	Tenths	Hundredths	Thousandths	Ten-Thousandths	...

*Note that this table can be extended infinitely further to the right.

When given a multi-digit number, the value of each digit depends on its place value. Consider the number 682,174.953. Referring to the chart above, it can be determined that the digit 8 is in the ten-thousands place. It is in the fifth place to the left of the decimal point. Its value is 8 ten-thousands or 80,000. The digit 5 is two places to the right of the decimal point. Therefore, the digit 5 is in the hundredths place. Its value is 5 hundredths or $\frac{5}{100}$ (equivalent to .05).

Base-10 System

Value of Digits

In accordance with the base-10 system, the value of a digit increases by a factor of ten each place it moves to the left. For example, consider the number 7. Moving the digit one place to the left (70), increases its value by a factor of 10:

$$7 \times 10 = 70$$

Moving the digit two places to the left (700) increases its value by a factor of 10 twice:

$$7 \times 10 \times 10 = 700$$

Moving the digit three places to the left (7,000) increases its value by a factor of 10 three times ($7 \times 10 \times 10 \times 10 = 7,000$), and so on.

Conversely, the value of a digit decreases by a factor of ten each place it moves to the right. (Note that multiplying by $\frac{1}{10}$ is equivalent to dividing by 10). For example, consider the number 40. Moving the digit one place to the right (4) decreases its value by a factor of 10:

$$40 \div 10 = 4$$

Moving the digit two places to the right (0.4), decreases its value by a factor of 10 twice ($40 \div 10 \div 10 = 0.4$) or:

$$40 \times \frac{1}{10} \times \frac{1}{10} = 0.4$$

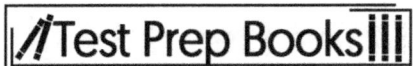

Moving the digit three places to the right (0.04) decreases its value by a factor of 10 three times ($40 \div 10 \div 10 \div 10 = 0.04$) or ($40 \times \frac{1}{10} \times \frac{1}{10} \times \frac{1}{10} = 0.04$), and so on.

Exponents to Denote Powers of 10

The value of a given digit of a number in the base-10 system can be expressed utilizing powers of 10. A power of 10 refers to 10 raised to a given exponent such as $10^0, 10^1, 10^2, 10^3$, etc. For the number 10^3, 10 is the base and 3 is the exponent. A base raised by an exponent represents how many times the base is multiplied by itself. Therefore, $10^1 = 10$, $10^2 = 10 \times 10 = 100$, $10^3 = 10 \times 10 \times 10 = 1,000$, $10^4 = 10 \times 10 \times 10 \times 10 = 10,000$, etc. Any base with a zero exponent equals one.

Powers of 10 are utilized to decompose a multi-digit number without writing all the zeroes. Consider the number 872,349. This number is decomposed to:

$$800,000 + 70,000 + 2,000 + 300 + 40 + 9$$

When utilizing powers of 10, the number 872,349 is decomposed to:

$$(8 \times 10^5) + (7 \times 10^4) + (2 \times 10^3) + (3 \times 10^2) + (4 \times 10^1) + (9 \times 10^0)$$

The power of 10 by which the digit is multiplied corresponds to the number of zeroes following the digit when expressing its value in standard form. For example, 7×10^4 is equivalent to 70,000 or 7 followed by four zeros.

Comparing, Classifying, and Ordering Rational Numbers

A **rational number** is any number that can be written as a fraction or ratio. Within the set of rational numbers, several subsets exist that are referenced throughout the mathematics topics. Counting numbers are the first numbers learned as a child. Counting numbers consist of 1,2,3,4, and so on. Whole numbers include all counting numbers and zero (0,1,2,3,4,…). Integers include counting numbers, their opposites, and zero (…, -3, -2, -1, 0, 1, 2, 3, …). Rational numbers are inclusive of integers, fractions, and decimals that terminate, or end (1.7, 0.04213) or repeat ($0.136\bar{5}$).

When comparing or ordering numbers, the numbers should be written in the same format (decimal or fraction), if possible. For example, $\sqrt{49}$, 7.3, and $\frac{15}{2}$ are easier to order if each one is converted to a decimal, such as 7, 7.3, and 7.5 (converting fractions and decimals is covered in the following section). A number line is used to order and compare the numbers. Any number that is to the right of another number is greater than that number. Conversely, a number positioned to the left of a given number is less than that number.

Structure of the Number System

The mathematical number system is made up of two general types of numbers: real and complex. *Real numbers* are both *irrational* and *rational numbers.*, while *complex numbers* are those composed of both a real number and an imaginary one. Imaginary numbers are the result of taking the square root of -1, and $\sqrt{-1} = i$.

The real number system is often explained using a Venn diagram similar to the one below. After a number has been labeled as a real number, further classification occurs when considering the other groups in this diagram. If a number is a never-ending, non-repeating decimal, it falls in the irrational

Number Concepts

category. Otherwise, it is rational. More information on these types of numbers is provided in the previous section. Furthermore, if a number does not have a fractional part, it is classified as an integer, such as -2, 75, or zero. Whole numbers are an even smaller group that only includes positive integers and zero. The last group of natural numbers is made up of only positive integers, such as 2, 56, or 12.

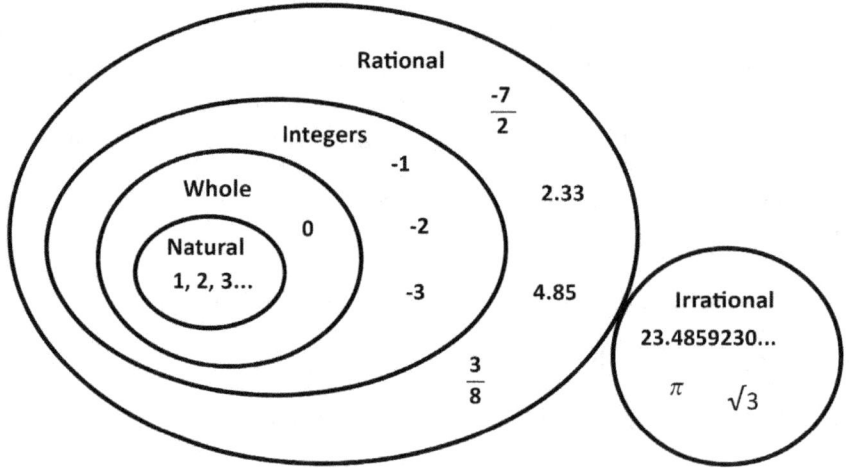

Real numbers can be compared and ordered using the number line. If a number falls to the left on the real number line, it is less than a number on the right. For example, $-2 < 5$ because -2 falls to the left of zero, and 5 falls to the right. Numbers to the left of zero are negative while those to the right are positive.

Complex numbers are made up of the sum of a real number and an imaginary number. Some examples of complex numbers include $6 + 2i$, $5 - 7i$, and $-3 + 12i$. Adding and subtracting complex numbers is similar to collecting like terms. The real numbers are added together, and the imaginary numbers are added together.

For example, if the problem asks to simplify the expression $6 + 2i - 3 + 7i$, the 6 and -3 are combined to make 3, and the $2i$ and $7i$ combine to make $9i$. Multiplying and dividing complex numbers is similar to working with exponents. One rule to remember when multiplying is that $i * i = -1$. For example, if a problem asks to simplify the expression $4i(3 + 7i)$, the $4i$ should be distributed throughout the 3 and the $7i$. This leaves the final expression $12i - 28$. The 28 is negative because $i * i$ results in a negative number. The last type of operation to consider with complex numbers is the conjugate. The *conjugate* of a complex number is a technique used to change the complex number into a real number. For example, the conjugate of $4 - 3i$ is $4 + 3i$. Multiplying $(4 - 3i)(4 + 3i)$ results in $16 + 12i - 12i + 9$, which has a final answer of:

$$16 + 9 = 25$$

The order of operations—PEMDAS—simplifies longer expressions with real or imaginary numbers. Each operation is listed in the order of how they should be completed in a problem containing more than one operation. Parenthesis can also mean grouping symbols, such as brackets and absolute value. Then, exponents are calculated. Multiplication and division should be completed from left to right, and addition and subtraction should be completed from left to right.

Number Concepts

Simplification of another type of expression occurs when radicals are involved. As explained previously, root is another word for radical. For example, the following expression is a radical that can be simplified: $\sqrt{24x^2}$. First, the number must be factored out to the highest perfect square. Any perfect square can be taken out of a radical. Twenty-four can be factored into 4 and 6, and 4 can be taken out of the radical. $\sqrt{4} = 2$ can be taken out, and 6 stays underneath. If $x > 0$, x can be taken out of the radical because it is a perfect square. The simplified radical is $2x\sqrt{6}$. An approximation can be found using a calculator.

There are also properties of numbers that are true for certain operations. The *commutative* property allows the order of the terms in an expression to change while keeping the same final answer. Both addition and multiplication can be completed in any order and still obtain the same result. However, order does matter in subtraction and division. The *associative* property allows any terms to be "associated" by parentheses and retain the same final answer. For example,

$$(4 + 3) + 5 = 4 + (3 + 5)$$

Both addition and multiplication are associative; however, subtraction and division do not hold this property. The *distributive* property states that:

$$a(b + c) = ab + ac$$

It is a property that involves both addition and multiplication, and the *a* is distributed onto each term inside the parentheses.

Integers can be factored into prime numbers. To *factor* is to express as a product. For example, $6 = 3 \cdot 2$, and $6 = 6 \cdot 1$. Both are factorizations, but the expression involving the factors of 3 and 2 is known as a *prime factorization* because it is factored into a product of two *prime numbers*—integers which do not have any factors other than themselves and 1. A *composite number* is a positive integer that can be divided into at least one other integer other than itself and 1, such as 6. Integers that have a factor of 2 are even, and if they are not divisible by 2, they are odd. Finally, a *multiple* of a number is the product of that number and a counting number—also known as a *natural number*. For example, some multiples of 4 are 4, 8, 12, 16, etc.

Properties of Rational and Irrational Numbers

All real numbers can be separated into two groups: rational and irrational numbers. *Rational numbers* are any numbers that can be written as a fraction, such as $\frac{1}{3}, \frac{7}{4}$, and -25. Alternatively, *irrational numbers* are those that cannot be written as a fraction, such as numbers with never-ending, non-repeating decimal values. Many irrational numbers result from taking roots, such as $\sqrt{2}$ or $\sqrt{3}$. An irrational number may be written as 34.5684952.... The ellipsis (...) represents the line of numbers after the decimal that does not repeat and is never-ending.

When rational and irrational numbers interact, there are different types of number outcomes. For example, when adding or multiplying two rational numbers, the result is a rational number. No matter what two fractions are added or multiplied together, the result can always be written as a fraction. The following expression shows two rational numbers multiplied together:

$$\frac{3}{8} * \frac{4}{7} = \frac{12}{56}$$

Number Concepts

The product of these two fractions is another fraction that can be simplified to $\frac{3}{14}$.

As another interaction, rational numbers added to irrational numbers will always result in irrational numbers. No part of any fraction can be added to a never-ending, non-repeating decimal to make a rational number. The same result is true when multiplying a rational and irrational number. Taking a fractional part of a never-ending, non-repeating decimal will always result in another never-ending, non-repeating decimal. An example of the product of rational and irrational numbers is shown in the following expression: $2 * \sqrt{7}$.

The last type of interaction concerns two irrational numbers, where the sum or product may be rational or irrational depending on the numbers being used. The following expression shows a rational sum from two irrational numbers:

$$\sqrt{3} + (6 - \sqrt{3}) = 6$$

The product of two irrational numbers can be rational or irrational. A rational result can be seen in the following expression:

$$\sqrt{2} * \sqrt{8} = \sqrt{2 * 8} = \sqrt{16} = 4$$

An irrational result can be seen in the following:

$$\sqrt{3} * \sqrt{2} = \sqrt{6}$$

The order of operations—PEMDAS—simplifies longer expressions with real or imaginary numbers. Each operation is listed in the order of how they should be completed in a problem containing more than one operation. Parentheses can also mean grouping symbols, such as brackets and absolute value. Then, exponents are calculated. Multiplication and division should be completed from left to right, and addition and subtraction should be completed from left to right. The following graphic shows step-by-step how an expression is simplified using the order of operations:

$$25 \div (8 - 3)^2 - 1$$

$$25 \div (5)^2 - 1$$

$$25 \div 25 - 1$$

$$1 - 1$$

$$0$$

Simplification of another type of expression occurs when radicals are involved. As explained previously, root is another word for radical. For example, the following expression is a radical that can be simplified: $\sqrt{24x^2}$. First, the number must be factored out to the highest perfect square. Any perfect square can be taken out of a radical. Twenty-four can be factored into 4 and 6, and 4 can be taken out of the radical. $\sqrt{4} = 2$ can be taken out, and 6 stays underneath. If $x > 0$, x can be taken out of the radical because it is a perfect square. The simplified radical is $2x\sqrt{6}$. An approximation can be found using a calculator.

There are also properties of numbers that are true for certain operations. The *commutative* property allows the order of the terms in an expression to change while keeping the same final answer. Both addition and multiplication can be completed in any order and still obtain the same result. However,

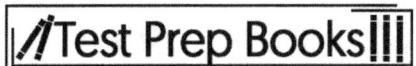

Number Concepts

order does matter in subtraction and division. The *associative* property allows any terms to be "associated" by parentheses and retain the same final answer. For example:

$$(4 + 3) + 5 = 4 + (3 + 5)$$

Both addition and multiplication are associative; however, subtraction and division do not hold this property. The *distributive* property states that:

$$a(b + c) = ab + ac$$

It is a property that involves both addition and multiplication, and the *a* is distributed onto each term inside the parentheses.

Integers can be factored into prime numbers. To *factor* is to express as a product. For example, $6 = 3 \cdot 2$, and $6 = 6 \cdot 1$. Both are factorizations, but the expression involving the factors of 3 and 2 is known as a *prime factorization* because it is factored into a product of two *prime numbers*—integers which do not have any factors other than themselves and 1. A *composite number* is a positive integer that can be divided into at least one other integer other than itself and 1, such as 6. Integers that have a factor of 2 are even, and if they are not divisible by 2, they are odd. Finally, a *multiple* of a number is the product of that number and a counting number—also known as a *natural number*. For example, some multiples of 4 are 4, 8, 12, 16, etc.

Strategies and Algorithms to Perform Operations on Rational Numbers

A rational number is any number that can be written in the form of a ratio or fraction. Integers can be written as fractions with a denominator of 1 ($5 = \frac{5}{1}$; $-342 = \frac{-342}{1}$; etc.). Decimals that terminate and/or repeat can also be written as fractions ($47 = \frac{47}{100}$; $.\overline{33} = \frac{1}{3}$). For more on converting decimals to fractions, see the section *Converting Between Fractions, Decimals,* and *Percent.*

When adding or subtracting fractions, the numbers must have the same denominators. In these cases, numerators are added or subtracted, and denominators are kept the same. For example, $\frac{2}{7} + \frac{3}{7} = \frac{5}{7}$ and:

$$\frac{4}{5} - \frac{3}{5} = \frac{1}{5}$$

If the fractions to be added or subtracted do not have the same denominator, a common denominator must be found. This is accomplished by changing one or both fractions to a different but equivalent fraction. Consider the example $\frac{1}{6} + \frac{4}{9}$. First, a common denominator must be found. One method is to find the least common multiple (LCM) of the denominators 6 and 9. This is the lowest number that both 6 and 9 will divide into evenly. In this case the LCM is 18. Both fractions should be changed to equivalent fractions with a denominator of 18. To obtain the numerator of the new fraction, the old numerator is multiplied by the same number by which the old denominator is multiplied. For the fraction $\frac{1}{6}$, 6 multiplied by 3 will produce a denominator of 18. Therefore, the numerator is multiplied by 3 to produce the new numerator:

$$\left(\frac{1 \times 3}{6 \times 3} = \frac{3}{18}\right)$$

Number Concepts

For the fraction $\frac{4}{9}$, multiplying both the numerator and denominator by 2 produces $\frac{8}{18}$. Since the two new fractions have common denominators, they can be added:

$$\left(\frac{3}{18} + \frac{8}{18} = \frac{11}{18}\right)$$

When multiplying or dividing rational numbers, these numbers may be converted to fractions and multiplied or divided accordingly. When multiplying fractions, all numerators are multiplied by each other and all denominators are multiplied by each other.
For example, $\frac{1}{3} \times \frac{6}{5} = \frac{1 \times 6}{3 \times 5} = \frac{6}{15}$ and:

$$\frac{-1}{2} \times \frac{3}{1} \times \frac{11}{100} = \frac{-1 \times 3 \times 11}{2 \times 1 \times 100} = \frac{-33}{200}$$

When dividing fractions, the problem is converted by multiplying by the reciprocal of the divisor. This is done by changing division to multiplication and "flipping" the second fraction, or divisor. For example, $\frac{1}{2} \div \frac{3}{5} \to \frac{1}{2} \times \frac{5}{3}$ and $\frac{5}{1} \div \frac{1}{3} \to \frac{5}{1} \times \frac{3}{1}$. To complete the problem, the rules for multiplying fractions should be followed.

Note that when adding, subtracting, multiplying, and dividing mixed numbers (ex. $4\frac{1}{2}$), it is easiest to convert these to improper fractions (larger numerator than denominator). To do so, the denominator is kept the same. To obtain the numerator, the whole number is multiplied by the denominator and added to the numerator. For example, $4\frac{1}{2} = \frac{9}{2}$ and $7\frac{2}{3} = \frac{23}{3}$. Also, note that answers involving fractions should be converted to the simplest form.

Converting Between Fractions, Decimals, and Percent

To convert a fraction to a decimal, the numerator is divided by the denominator. For example, $\frac{3}{8}$ can be converted to a decimal by dividing 3 by 8 ($\frac{3}{8} = 0.375$). To convert a decimal to a fraction, the decimal point is dropped, and the value is written as the numerator. The denominator is the place value farthest to the right with a digit other than zero. For example, to convert .48 to a fraction, the numerator is 48, and the denominator is 100 (the digit 8 is in the hundredths place). Therefore:

$$0.48 = \frac{48}{100}$$

Fractions should be written in the simplest form, or reduced. To reduce a fraction, the numerator and denominator are divided by the largest common factor. In the previous example, 48 and 100 are both divisible by 4. Dividing the numerator and denominator by 4 results in a reduced fraction of $\frac{12}{25}$.

To convert a decimal to a percent, the number is multiplied by 100. To convert .13 to a percent, .13 is multiplied by 100 to get 13 percent. To convert a fraction to a percent, the fraction is converted to a decimal and then multiplied by 100. For example, $\frac{1}{5}$ = .20 and .20 multiplied by 100 produces 20 percent.

To convert a percent to a decimal, the value is divided by 100. For example, 125 percent is equal to 1.25 ($\frac{125}{100}$). To convert a percent to a fraction, the percent sign is dropped, and the value is written as the numerator with a denominator of 100. For example, 80% = $\frac{80}{100}$. This fraction can be reduced ($\frac{80}{100} = \frac{4}{5}$).

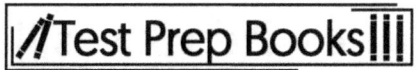

Properties of Exponents

Exponents are used in mathematics to express a number or variable multiplied by itself a certain number of times. For example, x^3 means x is multiplied by itself three times. In this expression, x is called the *base*, and 3 is the *exponent*. Exponents can be used in more complex problems when they contain fractions and negative numbers.

Fractional exponents can be explained by looking first at the inverse of exponents, which are *roots*. Given the expression x^2, the square root can be taken, $\sqrt{x^2}$, cancelling out the 2 and leaving x by itself, if x is positive. Cancellation occurs because $\sqrt{x}$ can be written with exponents, instead of roots, as $x^{\frac{1}{2}}$. The numerator of 1 is the exponent, and the denominator of 2 is called the root (which is why it's referred to as *square root*). Taking the square root of x^2 is the same as raising it to the $\frac{1}{2}$ power. Written out in mathematical form, it takes the following progression:

$$\sqrt{x^2} = (x^2)^{\frac{1}{2}} = x$$

From properties of exponents, $2 \cdot \frac{1}{2} = 1$ is the actual exponent of x. Another example can be seen with $x^{\frac{4}{7}}$. The variable x, raised to four-sevenths, is equal to the seventh root of x to the fourth power: $\sqrt[7]{x^4}$. In general, $x^{\frac{1}{n}} = \sqrt[n]{x}$ and $x^{\frac{m}{n}} = \sqrt[n]{x^m}$.

Negative exponents also involve fractions. Whereas y^3 can also be rewritten as $\frac{y^3}{1}$, y^{-3} can be rewritten as $\frac{1}{y^3}$. A negative exponent means the exponential expression must be moved to the opposite spot in a fraction to make the exponent positive. If the negative appears in the numerator, it moves to the denominator. If the negative appears in the denominator, it is moved to the numerator. In general, $a^{-n} = \frac{1}{a^n}$, and a^{-n} and a^n are reciprocals.

Take, for example, the following expression:

$$\frac{a^{-4}b^2}{c^{-5}}$$

Since a is raised to the negative fourth power, it can be moved to the denominator. Since c is raised to the negative fifth power, it can be moved to the numerator. The b variable is raised to the positive second power, so it does not move. The simplified expression is as follows:

$$\frac{b^2 c^5}{a^4}$$

In mathematical expressions containing exponents and other operations, the order of operations must be followed. *PEMDAS* states that exponents are calculated after any parentheses and grouping symbols but before any multiplication, division, addition, and subtraction.

Scientific Notation

Scientific Notation is used to represent numbers that are either very small or very large. For example, the distance to the sun is approximately 150,000,000,000 meters. Instead of writing this number with so many zeros, it can be written in scientific notation as $1.5 * 10^{11}$ meters. The same is true for very small

Number Concepts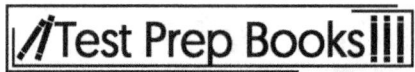

numbers, but the exponent becomes negative. If the mass of a human cell is 0.000000000001 kilograms, that measurement can be easily represented by $1.0 * 10^{-12}$ kilograms. In both situations, scientific notation makes the measurement easier to read and understand. Each number is translated to an expression with one digit in the tens place times an expression corresponding to the zeros.

When two measurements are given and both involve scientific notation, it is important to know how these interact with each other:

- In addition and subtraction, the exponent on the ten must be the same before any operations are performed on the numbers. For example, $(1.3 * 10^4) + (3.0 * 10^3)$ cannot be added until one of the exponents on the ten is changed. The $3.0 * 10^3$ can be changed to $0.3 * 10^4$, then the 1.3 and 0.3 can be added. The answer comes out to be $1.6 * 10^4$.

- For multiplication, the first numbers can be multiplied and then the exponents on the tens can be added. Once an answer is formed, it may have to be converted into scientific notation again depending on the change that occurred.
  - The following is an example of multiplication with scientific notation:

$$(4.5 * 10^3) * (3.0 * 10^{-5}) = 13.5 * 10^{-2}$$

    Since this answer is not in scientific notation, the decimal is moved over to the left one unit, and 1 is added to the ten's exponent. This results in the final answer: $1.35 * 10^{-1}$.

- For division, the first numbers are divided, and the exponents on the tens are subtracted. Again, the answer may need to be converted into scientific notation form, depending on the type of changes that occurred during the problem.

- *Order of magnitude* relates to scientific notation and is the total count of powers of 10 in a number. For example, there are 6 orders of magnitude in 1,000,000. If a number is raised by an order of magnitude, it is multiplied times 10. Order of magnitude can be helpful in estimating results using very large or small numbers. An answer should make sense in terms of its order of magnitude.
  - For example, if area is calculated using two dimensions with 6 orders of magnitude, because area involves multiplication, the answer should have around 12 orders of magnitude. Also, answers can be estimated by rounding to the largest place value in each number. For example, 5,493,302 * 2,523,100 can be estimated by 5 * 3 = 15 with 12 orders of magnitude.

Representing Rational Numbers and Their Operations

Concrete Models
Concrete objects are used to develop a tangible understanding of operations of rational numbers. Tools such as tiles, blocks, beads, and hundred charts are used to model problems. For example, a hundred chart (10×10) and beads can be used to model multiplication. If multiplying 5 by 4, beads are placed across 5 rows and down 4 columns producing a product of 20. Similarly, tiles can be used to model division by splitting the total into equal groups. If dividing 12 by 4, 12 tiles are placed one at a time into 4 groups. The result is 4 groups of 3. This is also an effective method for visualizing the concept of remainders.

Representations of objects can be used to expand on the concrete models of operations. Pictures, dots, and tallies can help model these concepts. Utilizing concrete models and representations creates a foundation upon which to build an abstract understanding of the operations.

Rational Numbers on a Number Line

A number line typically consists of integers (…3, 2, 1, 0, -1, -2, -3…), and is used to visually represent the value of a rational number. Each rational number has a distinct position on the line determined by comparing its value with the displayed values on the line. For example, if plotting -1.5 on the number line below, it is necessary to recognize that the value of -1.5 is .5 less than -1 and .5 greater than -2. Therefore, -1.5 is plotted halfway between -1 and -2.

Number lines can also be useful for visualizing sums and differences of rational numbers. Adding a value indicates moving to the right (values increase to the right), and subtracting a value indicates moving to the left (numbers decrease to the left). For example, $-3 - 2$ is displayed by starting at -3 and moving to the left 2 spaces, if the number line is in increments of 1. This will result in an answer of -5.

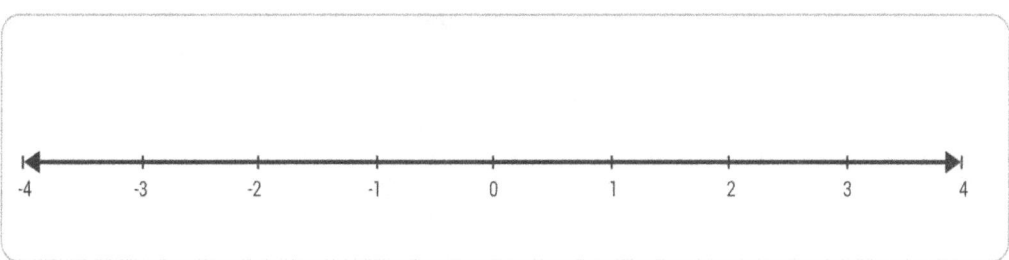

Multiplication and Division Problems

Multiplication and division are inverse operations that can be represented by using rectangular arrays, area models, and equations. Rectangular arrays include an arrangement of rows and columns that correspond to the factors and display product totals.

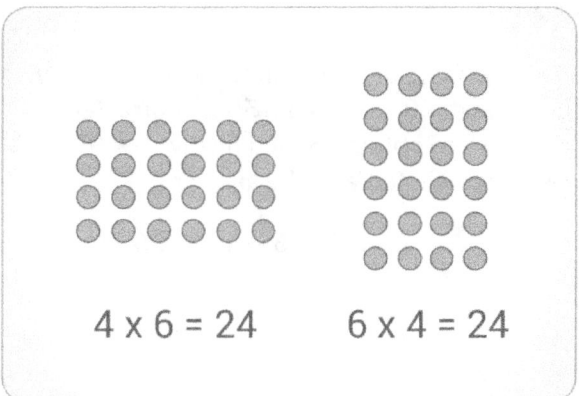

Another method of multiplication can be done with the use of an *area model*. An area model is a rectangle that is divided into rows and columns that match up to the number of place values within each number. Take the example 29×65. These two numbers can be split into simpler numbers:

$$29 = 25 + 4 \text{ and } 65 = 60 + 5$$

Number Concepts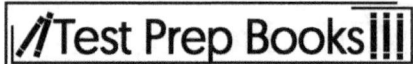

The products of those 4 numbers are found within the rectangle and then summed up to get the answer. The entire process is:

$$(60 \times 25) + (5 \times 25) + (60 \times 4) + (5 \times 4) = 1,500 + 240 + 125 + 20 = 1,885.$$

Here is the actual area model:

	25	4
60	60x25 1,500	60x4 240
5	5x25 125	5x4 20

```
   1,500
     240
     125
 +    20
 -------
   1,885
```

Dividing a number by a single digit or two digits can be turned into repeated subtraction problems. An area model can be used throughout the problem that represents multiples of the divisor. For example, the answer to 8580 ÷ 55 can be found by subtracting 55 from 8580 one at a time and counting the total number of subtractions necessary.

However, a simpler process involves using larger multiples of 55. First, $100 \times 55 = 5,500$ is subtracted from 8,580, and 3,080 is leftover. Next, $50 \times 55 = 2,750$ is subtracted from 3,080 to obtain 380. $5 \times 55 = 275$ is subtracted from 330 to obtain 55, and finally, $1 \times 55 = 55$ is subtracted from 55 to obtain zero. Therefore, there is no remainder, and the answer is:

$$100 + 50 + 5 + 1 = 156$$

Here is a picture of the area model and the repeated subtraction process:

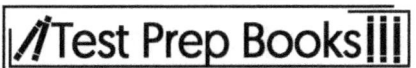

Rational Expressions and Real Numbers

A fraction, or ratio, wherein each part is a polynomial, defines *rational expressions*. Some examples include: $\frac{2x+6}{x}$, $\frac{1}{x^2-4x+8}$, and $\frac{z^2}{x+5}$. Exponents on the variables are restricted to whole numbers, which means roots and negative exponents are not included in rational expressions.

Rational expressions can be transformed by factoring. For example, the expression $\frac{x^2-5x+6}{(x-3)}$ can be rewritten by factoring the numerator to obtain:

$$\frac{(x-3)(x-2)}{(x-3)}$$

Therefore, the common binomial $(x-3)$ can cancel so that the simplified expression is:

$$\frac{(x-2)}{1} = (x-2)$$

Additionally, other rational expressions can be rewritten to take on different forms. Some may be factorable in themselves, while others can be transformed through arithmetic operations. Rational expressions are closed under addition, subtraction, multiplication, and division by a nonzero expression. *Closed* means that if any one of these operations is performed on a rational expression, the result will still be a rational expression. The set of all real numbers is another example of a set closed under all four operations.

Adding and subtracting rational expressions is based on the same concepts as adding and subtracting simple fractions. For both concepts, the denominators must be the same for the operation to take place. For example, here are two rational expressions:

$$\frac{x^3-4}{(x-3)} + \frac{x+8}{(x-3)}$$

Since the denominators are both $(x-3)$, the numerators can be combined by collecting like terms to form:

$$\frac{x^3 + x + 4}{(x-3)}$$

If the denominators are different, they need to be made common (the same) by using the Least Common Denominator (LCD). Each denominator needs to be factored, and the LCD contains each factor that appears in any one denominator the greatest number of times it appears in any denominator. The original expressions need to be multiplied times a form of 1, which will turn each denominator into the LCD. This process is like adding fractions with unlike denominators. It is also important when working with rational expressions to define what value of the variable makes the denominator zero. For this particular value, the expression is undefined.

Multiplication of rational expressions is performed like multiplication of fractions. The numerators are multiplied; then, the denominators are multiplied. The final fraction is then simplified. The expressions are simplified by factoring and cancelling out common terms. In the following example, $\frac{x^2}{(x-4)} * \frac{x^2-x-12}{2}$, the numerator of the second expression can be factored first to simplify the expression before multiplying. It turns into $\frac{x^2}{(x-4)} * \frac{(x-4)(x+3)}{2}$, where the $(x-4)$ cancels out on the top and bottom, leaving $\frac{x^2}{1} * \frac{(x+3)}{2}$. Then multiplication is performed, resulting in:

$$\frac{x^3 + 3x^2}{2}$$

Dividing rational expressions is similar to the division of fractions, where division turns into multiplying by a reciprocal. Therefore, given $\frac{x^2-3x+7}{x-4} \div \frac{x^2-5x+3}{x-4}$, the expression is rewritten as a multiplication problem:

$$\frac{x^2 - 3x + 7}{x - 4} * \frac{x - 4}{x^2 - 5x + 3}$$

The $x - 4$ cancels out, leaving:

$$\frac{x^2 - 3x + 7}{x^2 - 5x + 3}$$

The final answers should always be completely simplified. If a function is composed of a rational expression, the zeros of the graph can be found from setting the polynomial in the numerator as equal to zero and solving. The values that make the denominator equal to zero will either exist on the graph as a hole or a vertical asymptote.

Equations and Inequalities

The sum of a number and 5 is equal to -8 times the number. To find this unknown number, a simple equation can be written to represent the problem. Key words such as difference, equal, and times are used to form the following equation with one variable:

$$n + 5 = -8n$$

When solving for n, opposite operations are used. First, n is subtracted from $-8n$ across the equals sign, resulting in $5 = -9n$. Then, -9 is divided on both sides, leaving $n = -\frac{5}{9}$. This solution can be graphed on the number line with a dot as shown below:

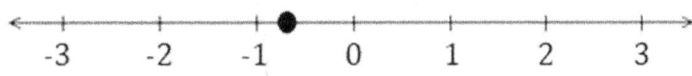

If the problem were changed to say, "The sum of a number and 5 is greater than -8 times the number," then an inequality would be used instead of an equation. Using key words again, *greater than* is represented by the symbol >. The inequality $n + 5 > -8n$ can be solved using the same techniques, resulting in $n < -\frac{5}{9}$. The only time solving an inequality differs from solving an equation is when a negative number is either multiplied times or divided by each side of the inequality. The sign must be switched in this case. For this example, the graph of the solution changes to the following graph because the solution represents all real numbers less than $-\frac{5}{9}$. Not included in this solution is $-\frac{5}{9}$ because it is a *less than* symbol, not *equal to*.

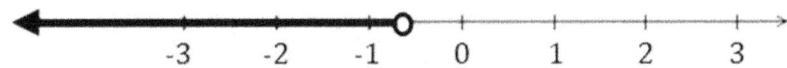

Equations and inequalities in two variables represent a relationship. Jim owns a car wash and charges $40 per car. The rent for the facility is $350 per month. An equation can be written to relate the number of cars Jim cleans to the money he makes per month. Let x represent the number of cars and y represent the profit Jim makes each month from the car wash. The equation $y = 40x - 350$ can be used to show Jim's profit or loss. Since this equation has two variables, the coordinate plane can be used to show the relationship and predict profit or loss for Jim. The following graph shows that Jim must wash at least nine cars to pay the rent, where $x = 9$. Anything nine cars and above yield a profit shown in the value on the y-axis.

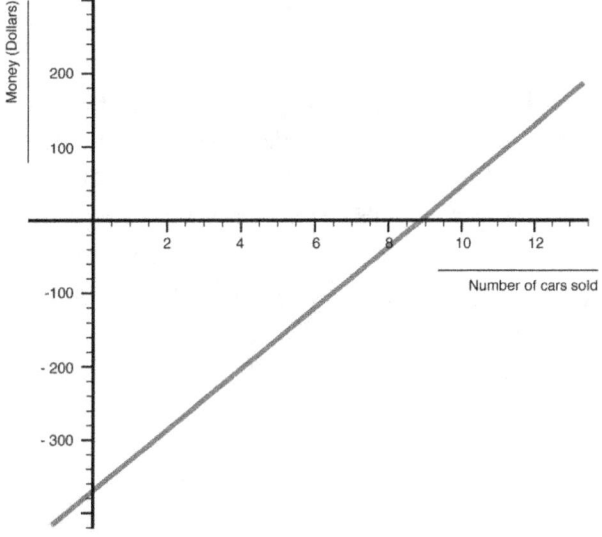

Number Concepts

With a single equation in two variables, the solutions are limited only by the situation the equation represents. When two equations or inequalities are used, more constraints are added. For example, in a system of linear equations, there is often—although not always—only one answer. The point of intersection of two lines is the solution. For a system of inequalities, there are infinitely many answers.

The intersection of two solution sets gives the solution set of the system of inequalities. In the following graph, the darker shaded region is where two inequalities overlap. Any set of x and y found in that region satisfies both inequalities. The line with the positive slope is solid, meaning the values on that line are included in the solution. The line with the negative slope is dotted, so the coordinates on that line are not included.

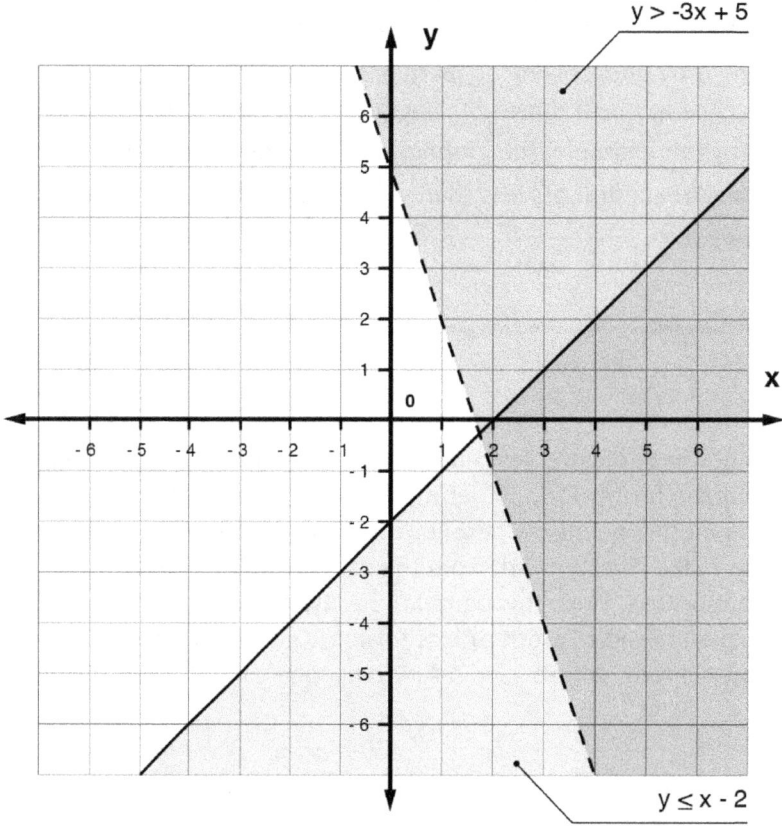

Formulas with two variables are equations used to represent a specific relationship. For example, the formula $d = rt$ represents the relationship between distance, rate, and time. If Bob travels at a rate of 35 miles per hour on his road trip from Westminster to Seneca, the formula $d = 35t$ can be used to represent his distance traveled in a specific length of time. Formulas can also be used to show different roles of the variables, transformed without any given numbers. Solving for r, the formula becomes $\frac{d}{t} = r$. The t is moved over by division so that *rate* is a function of distance and time.

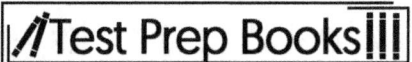

Number Concepts

Deductive Reasoning

When arriving at a conclusion using definitions, rules, or properties, the process used is deductive reasoning. In algebra, the associative, commutative, and distributive properties are used to justify algebraic steps. Both addition and multiplication are associative and commutative, and the distributive property states that:

$$a(b + c) = ab + ac$$

An example of deductive reasoning is to use such properties to show that $(xy)z = (zy)x$. First, the commutative property of multiplication is used to show that:

$$(xy)z = z(xy) = z(yx)$$

Then, the associative property of multiplication is used to show that:

$$z(yx) = (zy)x$$

Properties of Rational and Irrational Numbers

All real numbers can be separated into two groups: rational and irrational numbers. *Rational numbers* are any numbers that can be written as a fraction, such as $\frac{1}{3}, \frac{7}{4}$, and -25. Alternatively, *irrational numbers* are those that cannot be written as a fraction, such as numbers with never-ending, non-repeating decimal values. Many irrational numbers result from taking roots, such as $\sqrt{2}$ or $\sqrt{3}$. An irrational number may be written as 34.5684952…. The ellipsis (…) represents the line of numbers after the decimal that does not repeat and is never-ending.

When rational and irrational numbers interact, there are different types of number outcomes. For example, when adding or multiplying two rational numbers, the result is a rational number. No matter what two fractions are added or multiplied together, the result can always be written as a fraction. The following expression shows two rational numbers multiplied together:

$$\frac{3}{8} * \frac{4}{7} = \frac{12}{56}$$

The product of these two fractions is another fraction that can be simplified to $\frac{3}{14}$.

As another interaction, rational numbers added to irrational numbers will always result in irrational numbers. No part of any fraction can be added to a never-ending, non-repeating decimal to make a rational number. The same result is true when multiplying a rational and irrational number. Taking a fractional part of a never-ending, non-repeating decimal will always result in another never-ending, non-repeating decimal. An example of the product of rational and irrational numbers is shown in the following expression: $2 * \sqrt{7}$.

The last type of interaction concerns two irrational numbers, where the sum or product may be rational or irrational depending on the numbers being used. The following expression shows a rational sum from two irrational numbers:

$$\sqrt{3} + (6 - \sqrt{3}) = 6$$

Number Concepts

The product of two irrational numbers can be rational or irrational. A rational result can be seen in the following expression:

$$\sqrt{2} * \sqrt{8} = \sqrt{2*8} = \sqrt{16} = 4$$

An irrational result can be seen in the following:

$$\sqrt{3} * \sqrt{2} = \sqrt{6}$$

Complex Numbers as Solutions

Complex numbers may result from solving polynomial equations using the quadratic equation. Since complex numbers result from taking the square root of a negative number, the number found under the radical in the quadratic formula—called the *determinant*—tells whether or not the answer will be real or complex. If the determinant is negative, the roots are complex. Even though the coefficients of the polynomial may be real numbers, the roots are complex.

Solving polynomials by factoring is an alternative to using the quadratic formula. For example, in order to solve $x^2 - b^2 = 0$ for x, it needs to be factored. It factors into:

$$(x + b)(x - b) = 0$$

The solution set can be found by setting each factor equal to zero, resulting in $x = \pm b$. When b^2 is negative, the factors are complex numbers. For example, $x^2 + 64 = 0$ can be factored into:

$$(x + 8i)(x - 8i) = 0$$

The two roots are then found to be $x = \pm 8i$.

When dealing with polynomials and solving polynomial equations, it is important to remember the fundamental theorem of algebra. When given a polynomial with a degree of n, the theorem states that there will be n roots. These roots may or may not be complex. For example, the following polynomial equation of degree 2 has two complex roots:

$$x^2 + 1 = 0$$

The factors of this polynomial are $(x + i)$ and $(x - i)$, resulting in the roots $x = i, -i$. As seen on the graph below, imaginary roots occur when the graph does not touch the x-axis.

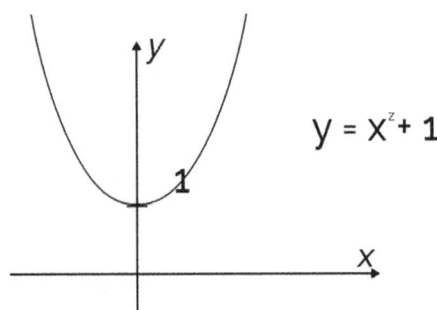

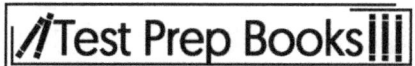

When a graphing calculator is permitted, the graph can always confirm the number and types of roots of the polynomial.

A polynomial identity is a true equation involving polynomials. For example, $x^2 - 5x + 6 = (x - 3)(x - 2)$, which can be proved through multiplication by the FOIL method and factoring. This idea can be extended to involve complex numbers. Because,

$$i^2 = -1, x^3 + 9x = x(x^2 + 9) = x(x + 3i)(x - 3i)$$

This identity can also be proven through FOIL and factoring.

Properties of Complex Numbers

Given a complex number $a + bi$, its *complex conjugate* is $a - bi$. For example, the complex conjugate of $4 + 3i$ is $4 - 3i$. It is the number with equal real part and opposite imaginary part. The absolute value of a complex number $a + bi$, also known as its *magnitude* or *modulus* is $\sqrt{a^2 + b^2}$. It is equal to the distance from the origin to the corresponding point in the complex plane. A multiplicative inverse of any number is what one multiplies by to obtain a product of 1. In other words, it is the reciprocal. For a complex number $a + bi$, its *multiplicative inverse* is $\frac{1}{a+bi}$, which can be rewritten once rationalized as:

$$\frac{a}{a^2 + b^2} - \frac{b}{a^2 + b^2}i$$

The complex numbers form a field, which means that two complex numbers can be added together and multiplied times one another and either result is still a complex number. Also, for any complex number $a + bi$, its additive inverse $-a - bi$ is also a complex number. Finally, every nonzero complex number has a multiplicative inverse that is a complex number. Addition can be performed using the same process as vector addition. In this case, addition is done component-wise. In component form, $(a + bi) + (c + di) = (a + c) + (b + d)i$, in which the real part and imaginary part are considered separate components.

Representing Complex Numbers

Given the situation, the format in which a complex number is used is important. When given as $a + bi$, it is written in its algebraic, rectangular, or Cartesian form, and it relates to an ordered pair (a, b) in the complex plane with a real (horizontal) and imaginary (vertical) axis. A complex number that is completely imaginary lies on the vertical axis. Its vector form is found similarly by writing its real and imaginary parts into vector form $< a, b >$. Polar form of a complex number is necessary if there is desire to use complex numbers in the real number system by using polar coordinates. In this case, $z = a + bi = r(\cos \theta + i \sin \theta)$, where r represents the absolute value of z and $\theta = \tan^{-1}\left(\frac{b}{a}\right)$. The ordered pair (r, θ) represent the polar coordinates. Finally, a complex number can be represented in exponential form, and Euler's formula $e^{i\theta} = \cos \theta + i \sin \theta$ is necessary. With this formula, the complex number's exponential form is $z = re^{i\theta}$. Also, it is true that $a = r \cos \theta$ and $b = r \sin \theta$.

Complex Number Operations

Complex number operations can be performed using geometric representations of the numbers themselves. In terms of addition, two complex numbers can be added by adding the real parts together separately from the imaginary parts. This operation can be performed within the ordered pairs. Multiplication can be thought of using polar coordinates. Its magnitude r, which is the distance from the point to the origin in the complex plane, and its argument θ, which is the angle from the horizontal axis to the line segment connecting the origin and the point itself, can be used. Two complex numbers can be multiplied by one another by multiplying their magnitudes together and adding their arguments together. Therefore, the product of the complex number with magnitude r_1 and argument θ_1 with the complex number with magnitude r_2 and argument θ_2 is the complex number with magnitude $r_1 r_2$ and argument $\theta_1 + \theta_2$.

Basic Concepts of Number Theory

Prime and Composite Numbers

Whole numbers are classified as either prime or composite. A prime number can only be divided evenly by itself and one. For example, the number 11 can only be divided evenly by 11 and one; therefore, 11 is a prime number. A helpful way to visualize a prime number is to use concrete objects and try to divide them into equal piles. If dividing 11 coins, the only way to divide them into equal piles is to create 1 pile of 11 coins or to create 11 piles of 1 coin each. Other examples of prime numbers include 2, 3, 5, 7, 13, 17, and 19.

A composite number is any whole number that is not a prime number. A composite number is a number that can be divided evenly by one or more numbers other than itself and one. For example, the number 6 can be divided evenly by 2 and 3. Therefore, 6 is a composite number. If dividing 6 coins into equal piles, the possibilities are 1 pile of 6 coins, 2 piles of 3 coins, 3 piles of 2 coins, or 6 piles of 1 coin. Other examples of composite numbers include 4, 8, 9, 10, 12, 14, 15, 16, 18, and 20.

To determine if a number is a prime or composite number, the number is divided by every whole number greater than one and less than its own value. If it divides evenly by any of these numbers, then the number is composite. If it does not divide evenly by any of these numbers, then the number is prime. For example, when attempting to divide the number 5 by 2, 3, and 4, none of these numbers divide evenly. Therefore, 5 must be a prime number.

Factors and Multiples of Numbers

The factors of a number are all integers that can be multiplied by another integer to produce the given number. For example, 2 is multiplied by 3 to produce 6. Therefore, 2 and 3 are both factors of 6. Similarly, $1 \times 6 = 6$ and $2 \times 3 = 6$, so 1, 2, 3, and 6 are all factors of 6. Another way to explain a factor is to say that a given number divides evenly by each of its factors to produce an integer. For example, 6 does not divide evenly by 5. Therefore, 5 is not a factor of 6.

Multiples of a given number are found by taking that number and multiplying it by any other whole number. For example, 3 is a factor of 6, 9, and 12. Therefore, 6, 9, and 12 are multiples of 3. The multiples of any number are an infinite list. For example, the multiples of 5 are 5, 10, 15, 20, and so on. This list continues without end. A list of multiples is used in finding the least common multiple, or LCM, for fractions when a common denominator is needed. The denominators are written down and their multiples listed until a common number is found in both lists. This common number is the LCM.

Prime factorization breaks down each factor of a whole number until only prime numbers remain. All composite numbers can be factored into prime numbers. For example, the prime factors of 12 are 2, 2, and 3:

$$2 \times 2 \times 3 = 12$$

To produce the prime factors of a number, the number is factored, and any composite numbers are continuously factored until the result is the product of prime factors only. A factor tree, such as the one below, is helpful when exploring this concept.

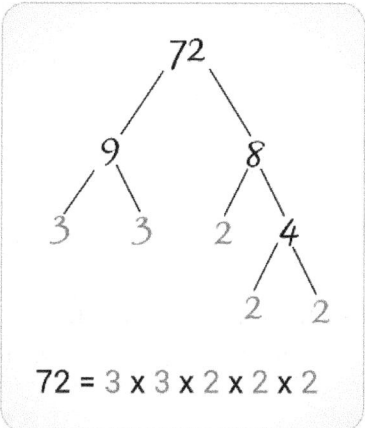

Number Relationships

The set of natural numbers can be separated into a variety of different types such as odds, evens, perfect squares, cubes, primes, composite, Fibonacci, etc. Number theory concepts can be used to prove relationships between these subsets of natural numbers. One of the main goals of number theory is to discover relationships between different subsets and prove that they are true. For example, some number theory proofs involve showing that the sum of two odd numbers is even and the sum of two even numbers is even.

Properties Involving Algebraic Expressions

Properties such as associativity and commutativity that hold among operations between real numbers also hold between algebraic expressions. Addition and multiplication are associative and commutative; therefore, addition and multiplication can be completed in any order inside an algebraic expression. This is helpful when it comes to solving equations. The addition and multiplication principles state that anything can be added to or multiplied by both sides of an equation to maintain equality. This process is helpful when it comes to isolating the variable. The only time there might be an issue is multiplying times a rational expression with a variable in the denominator. One must make sure that the denominator cannot equal zero. Therefore, it would not be appropriate to multiply both sides of the equation $x^2 = 1$ by $\frac{1}{x}$ to solve for x. The solution $x = 0$ would be lost.

Matrices

Matrices can be used to represent linear equations, solve systems of equations, and manipulate data to simulate change. Matrices consist of numerical entries in both rows and columns. The following matrix A is a 3 × 4 matrix because it has three rows and four columns:

$$A = \begin{bmatrix} 3 & 2 & -5 & 3 \\ 3 & 6 & 2 & -5 \\ -1 & 3 & 7 & 0 \end{bmatrix}$$

Number Concepts

Matrices can be added or subtracted only if they have the same dimensions. For example, the following matrices can be added by adding corresponding matrix entries:

$$\begin{bmatrix} 3 & 4 \\ 2 & -6 \end{bmatrix} + \begin{bmatrix} -1 & 4 \\ 4 & 2 \end{bmatrix} = \begin{bmatrix} 2 & 8 \\ 6 & -4 \end{bmatrix}$$

Multiplication can also be used to manipulate matrices. *Scalar multiplication* involves multiplying a matrix by a constant. Each matrix entry needs to be multiplied by the constant. The following example shows a 3 × 2 matrix being multiplied by the constant 6:

$$6 \times \begin{bmatrix} 3 & 4 \\ 2 & -6 \\ 1 & 0 \end{bmatrix} = \begin{bmatrix} 18 & 24 \\ 12 & -36 \\ 6 & 0 \end{bmatrix}$$

Matrix multiplication of two matrices involves finding multiple dot products. The *dot product* of a row and column is the sum of the products of each corresponding row and column entry. In the following example, a 2 × 2 matrix is multiplied by a 2 × 2 matrix. The dot product of the first row and column is:

$$(2 \times 1) + (1 \times 2) = (2) + (2) = 4$$

$$\begin{bmatrix} 2 & 1 \\ 3 & 5 \end{bmatrix} \times \begin{bmatrix} 1 & 4 \\ 2 & 0 \end{bmatrix} = \begin{bmatrix} 4 & 8 \\ 13 & 12 \end{bmatrix}$$

The same process is followed to find the other three values in the solution matrix. Matrices can only be multiplied if the number of columns in the first matrix equals the number of rows in the second matrix. The previous example is also an example of square matrix multiplication because they are both square matrices. A *square matrix* has the same number of rows and columns. For square matrices, the order in which they are multiplied does matter. Therefore, matrix multiplication does not satisfy the commutative property. It does, however, satisfy the associative and distributive properties.

Another transformation of matrices can be found by using the *identity matrix*—also referred to as the "*I*" *matrix*. The identity matrix is similar to the number one in normal multiplication. The identity matrix is a square matrix with ones in the diagonal spots and zeros everywhere else. The identity matrix is also the result of multiplying a matrix by its inverse. This process is similar to multiplying a number by its reciprocal.

The *zero matrix* is also a matrix acting as an additive identity. The zero matrix consists of zeros in every entry. It does not change the values of a matrix when using addition.

The *inverse of a matrix* is useful for solving complex systems of equations. Not all matrices have an inverse, but this can be checked by finding the *determinant* of the matrix. If the determinant of the matrix is 0, it is not invertible. Additionally, only square matrices are invertible. To find the determinant of any matrix, each value of the first row is multiplied by the determinant of submatrix consisting of all except the row and column for that value. The results of multiplication are alternatingly subtracted and added for 3 × 3 or larger matrices. The determinant of a matrix can be represented with straight bars (such as $|A|$) or the function $\det(A)$, where A is a matrix.

Using the *square 2 x 2 matrix*, the determinant is: $|A| = \begin{vmatrix} a & b \\ c & d \end{vmatrix} = ad - bc$

The absolute value of the determinant of matrix A is equal to the area of a parallelogram with vertices $(0, 0)$, (a, b), (c, d), and $(a + c, b + d)$.

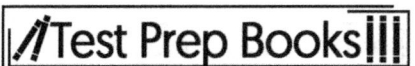

For example, the determinant of the matrix $\begin{bmatrix} -5 & 1 \\ 3 & 4 \end{bmatrix}$ is:

$$-5(4) - 1(3) = -20 - 3 = -23$$

Using a 3 x 3 matrix $\begin{bmatrix} a & b & c \\ d & e & f \\ g & h & i \end{bmatrix}$, the determinant is $a(ei - fh) - b(di - fg) + c(dh - eg)$.

For example, the determinant of the matrix $A = \begin{bmatrix} 2 & 0 & 1 \\ -1 & 3 & 2 \\ 2 & -2 & -1 \end{bmatrix}$ is:

$$|A| = 2\big(3(-1) - 2(-2)\big) - 0\big(-1(-1) - 2(2)\big) + 1\big(-1(-2) - 3(2)\big)$$

$$|A| = 2(-3 + 4) - 0(1 - 4) + 1(2 - 6)$$

$$|A| = 2(1) - 0(-3) + 1(-4)$$

$$|A| = 2 - 0 - 4 = -2$$

The pattern continues for larger square matrices. For a matrix with real values, this can then be simplified to a real number. If the determinant is non-zero, the square matrix can be inversed.

One way to find an inverse matrix is to use the *matrix of minors*. A *minor* is the determinant of the submatrix found by excluding the row and column of that minor. The matrix formed by all the minors would be M. To use the previous example, the minor of the first row and column is:

$$M_a = ei - fh = 3(-1) - 2(-2) = -3 + 4 = 1$$

When dealing with larger matrices it can be inconvenient to letter the items in a matrix. Another way to refer to them is by the numbers of rows and columns in the matrix. The position of any given value in some matrix A is at row i and column j is thus $A_{i,j}$. Using the previous example, $ie - fh$ was the minor of the first matrix item, which would be $M_{1,1} = A_{2,2}A_{3,3} - A_{2,3}A_{3,2}$. The following matrix shows all the minors:

$$M = \begin{bmatrix} 1 & -3 & -4 \\ 2 & -4 & -4 \\ -3 & 5 & 6 \end{bmatrix}$$

The next step to finding the inverse is to find the *cofactor matrix* from the matrix of minors. This is simply negating every other item in the matrix, in a checkerboard-like pattern. This is done the same for matrices of all sizes. The cofactors of M are:

$$\begin{bmatrix} 1 & 3 & -4 \\ -2 & -4 & 4 \\ -3 & -5 & 6 \end{bmatrix}$$

The last steps to finding the inverse are to transpose the matrix of cofactors and divide it by the determinant of the original matrix, $|A|$. *Transposing* a matrix means turning the rows into columns and

Number Concepts

vice versa. For example, the third item of the first row would become the third item of the first column. This turns the previous cofactor matrix into an *adjoint matrix*:

$$\begin{bmatrix} 1 & -2 & -3 \\ 3 & -4 & -5 \\ -4 & 4 & 6 \end{bmatrix}$$

Dividing the transposed matrix by the determinant of our original matrix gives the inverse of matrix A:

$$A^{-1} = \frac{1}{|A|} \times \begin{bmatrix} 1 & -2 & -3 \\ 3 & -4 & -5 \\ -4 & 4 & 6 \end{bmatrix} = \frac{1}{-2} \times \begin{bmatrix} 1 & -2 & -3 \\ 3 & -4 & -5 \\ -4 & 4 & 6 \end{bmatrix} = \begin{bmatrix} -\frac{1}{2} & 1 & \frac{3}{2} \\ -\frac{3}{2} & 2 & \frac{5}{2} \\ 2 & -2 & -3 \end{bmatrix}$$

Given a system of linear equations, a matrix can be used to represent the entire system. Operations can then be performed on the matrix to solve the system. The following system offers an example:

$$x + y + z = 4$$

$$y + 3z = -2$$

$$2x + y - 2z = 12$$

There are three variables and three equations. The coefficients in the equations can be used to form a 3 x 3 matrix:

$$\begin{bmatrix} 1 & 1 & 1 \\ 0 & 1 & 3 \\ 2 & 1 & -2 \end{bmatrix}$$

The number of rows equals the number of equations, and the number of columns equals the number of variables. The numbers on the right side of the equations can be turned into a 3 x 1 matrix. That matrix is shown here:

$$\begin{bmatrix} 4 \\ -2 \\ 12 \end{bmatrix}$$

Such a matrix can also be referred to as a *vector*. The variables are represented in a matrix of their own:

$$\begin{bmatrix} x \\ y \\ z \end{bmatrix}$$

The system can be represented by the following matrix equation:

$$\begin{bmatrix} 1 & 1 & 1 \\ 0 & 1 & 3 \\ 2 & 1 & -2 \end{bmatrix} \begin{bmatrix} x \\ y \\ z \end{bmatrix} = \begin{bmatrix} 4 \\ -2 \\ 12 \end{bmatrix}$$

Simply, this is written as $AX = B$. By using the inverse of a matrix, the solution can be found: $X = A^{-1}B$. Once the inverse of A is found, it is then multiplied by B to find the solution to the system: $x = 12, y = -8,$ and $z = 2$.

Ratios and Proportions

Ratios are used to show the relationship between two quantities. The ratio of oranges to apples in the grocery store may be 3 to 2. That means that for every 3 oranges, there are 2 apples. This comparison can be expanded to represent the actual number of oranges and apples, such as 36 oranges to 24 apples. Another example may be the number of boys to girls in a math class. If the ratio of boys to girls is given as 2 to 5, that means there are 2 boys to every 5 girls in the class. Ratios can also be compared if the units in each ratio are the same. The ratio of boys to girls in the math class can be compared to the ratio of boys to girls in a science class by stating which ratio is higher and which is lower.

Rates are used to compare two quantities with different units. *Unit rates* are the simplest form of rate. With unit rates, the denominator in the comparison of two units is one. For example, if someone can type at a rate of 1,000 words in 5 minutes, then their unit rate for typing is $\frac{1,000}{5} = 200$ words in one minute or 200 words per minute. Any rate can be converted into a unit rate by dividing to make the denominator one. 1,000 words in 5 minutes has been converted into the unit rate of 200 words per minute.

Ratios and rates can be used together to convert rates into different units. For example, if someone is driving 50 kilometers per hour, that rate can be converted into miles per hour by using a ratio known as the *conversion factor*. Since the given value contains kilometers and the final answer needs to be in miles, the ratio relating miles to kilometers needs to be used. There are 0.62 miles in 1 kilometer. This, written as a ratio and in fraction form, is $\frac{0.62 \text{ miles}}{1 \text{ km}}$. To convert 50km/hour into miles per hour, the following conversion needs to be set up:

$$\frac{50 \text{ km}}{\text{hour}} \times \frac{0.62 \text{ miles}}{1 \text{ km}} = 31 \text{ miles per hour}$$

The ratio between two similar geometric figures is called the *scale factor*. For example, a problem may depict two similar triangles, A and B. The scale factor from the smaller triangle A to the larger triangle B is given as 2 because the length of the corresponding side of the larger triangle, 16, is twice the corresponding side on the smaller triangle, 8. This scale factor can also be used to find the value of a missing side, x, in triangle A. Since the scale factor from the smaller triangle (A) to larger one (B) is 2, the larger corresponding side in triangle B (given as 25) can be divided by 2 to find the missing side in A (x = 12.5). The scale factor can also be represented in the equation $2A = B$ because two times the lengths of A gives the corresponding lengths of B. This is the idea behind similar triangles.

Much like a scale factor can be written using an equation like $2A = B$, a *relationship* is represented by the equation $Y = kX$. X and Y are proportional because as values of X increase, the values of Y also increase. A relationship that is inversely proportional can be represented by the equation $Y = \frac{k}{X}$, where the value of Y decreases as the value of x increases and vice versa.

Proportional reasoning can be used to solve problems involving ratios, percentages, and averages. Ratios can be used in setting up proportions and solving them to find unknowns. For example, if a student completes an average of 10 pages of math homework in 3 nights, how long would it take the student to complete 22 pages? Both ratios can be written as fractions. The second ratio would contain

Number Concepts

the unknown. The following proportion represents this problem, where x is the unknown number of nights:

$$\frac{10 \text{ pages}}{3 \text{ nights}} = \frac{22 \text{ pages}}{x \text{ nights}}$$

Solving this proportion entails cross-multiplying and results in the following equation: $10x = 22*3$. Simplifying and solving for x results in the exact solution: $x = 6.6 \; nights$. The result would be rounded up to 7 because the homework would actually be completed on the 7th night.

The following problem uses ratios involving percentages:

If 20% of the class is girls and 30 students are in the class, how many girls are in the class?

To set up this problem, it is helpful to use the common proportion: $\frac{\%}{100} = \frac{is}{of}$. Within the proportion, % is the percentage of girls, 100 is the total percentage of the class, *is* is the number of girls, and *of* is the total number of students in the class. Most percentage problems can be written using this language. To solve this problem, the proportion should be set up as $\frac{20}{100} = \frac{x}{30}$, and then solved for x. Cross-multiplying results in the equation $20*30 = 100x$, which results in the solution $x = 6$. There are 6 girls in the class.

Ratios can be used to solve problems that concern length, volume, and other units. For example, a problem may ask for the volume of a cone to be found that has a radius, $r = 7m$ and a height, $h = 16m$. Referring to the formulas provided on the test, the volume of a cone is given as: $V = \pi r^2 \frac{h}{3}$, where r is the radius, and h is the height. Plugging $r = 7$ and $h = 16$ into the formula, the following is obtained:

$$V = \pi(7^2)\frac{16}{3}$$

Therefore, the volume of the cone is found to be approximately 821m³. Sometimes, answers in different units are sought. If this problem wanted the answer in liters, 821m³ would need to be converted. Using the equivalence statement 1m³ = 1,000L, the following ratio would be used to solve for liters:

$$821m^3 \times \frac{1,000L}{1m^3}$$

Cubic meters in the numerator and denominator cancel each other out, and the answer is converted to 821,000 liters, or $8.21*10^5$ L.

Other conversions can also be made between different given and final units. If the temperature in a pool is 30°C, what is the temperature of the pool in degrees Fahrenheit? To convert these units, an equation is used relating Celsius to Fahrenheit. The following equation is used:

$$T_{°F} = 1.8 T_{°C} + 32$$

Plugging in the given temperature and solving the equation for T yields the result:

$$T_{°F} = 1.8(30) + 32 = 86°F$$

Units in both the metric system and U.S. customary system are widely used.

Counting Techniques

There are many counting techniques that can help solve problems involving counting possibilities. For example, the *Addition Principle* states that if there are m choices from Group 1 and n choices from Group 2, then $n + m$ is the total number of choices possible from Groups 1 and 2. For this to be true, the groups can't have any choices in common. The *Multiplication Principle* states that if Process 1 can be completed n ways and Process 2 can be completed m ways, the total number of ways to complete both Process 1 and Process 2 is $n \times m$. For this rule to be used, both processes must be independent of each other. Counting techniques also involve permutations. A *permutation* is an arrangement of elements in a set for which order must be considered. For example, if three letters from the alphabet are chosen, ABC and BAC are two different permutations. The multiplication rule can be used to determine the total number of possibilities. If each letter can't be selected twice, the total number of possibilities is:

$$26 \times 25 \times 24 = 15{,}600$$

A formula can also be used to calculate this total. In general, the notation $P(n, r)$ represents the number of ways to arrange r objects from a set of n and, the formula is:

$$P(n, r) = \frac{n!}{(n-r)!}$$

In the previous example,

$$P(26, 3) = \frac{26!}{23!} = 15{,}600$$

Contrasting permutations, a *combination* is an arrangement of elements in which order doesn't matter. In this case, ABC and BAC are the same combination. In the previous scenario, there are six permutations that represent each single combination. Therefore, the total number of possible combinations is:

$$15{,}600 \div 6 = 2{,}600$$

In general, $C(n, r)$ represents the total number of combinations of n items selected r at a time where order doesn't matter. Another way to represent the combinations of r items selected out of a set of n items is $\binom{n}{r}$. The formula for select combinations of items is:

$$\binom{n}{r} = C(n, r) = \frac{n!}{(n-r)!\, r!}$$

Therefore, the following relationship exists between permutations and combinations:

$$C(n, r) = \frac{P(n, r)}{r!} = \frac{P(n, r)}{P(r, r)}$$

Determining the Reasonableness of Results

When solving math word problems, the solution obtained should make sense within the given scenario. The step of checking the solution will reduce the possibility of a calculation error or a solution that may be *mathematically* correct but not applicable in the real world. Consider the following scenarios:

Number Concepts

A problem states that Lisa got 24 out of 32 questions correct on a test and asks to find the percentage of correct answers. To solve the problem, a student divided 32 by 24 to get 1.33, and then multiplied by 100 to get 133 percent. By examining the solution within the context of the problem, the student should recognize that getting all 32 questions correct will produce a perfect score of 100 percent. Therefore, a score of 133 percent with 8 incorrect answers does not make sense, and the calculations should be checked.

A problem states that the maximum weight on a bridge cannot exceed 22,000 pounds. The problem asks to find the maximum number of cars that can be on the bridge at one time if each car weighs 4,000 pounds. To solve this problem, a student divided 22,000 by 4,000 to get an answer of 5.5. By examining the solution within the context of the problem, the student should recognize that although the calculations are mathematically correct, the solution does not make sense. Half of a car on a bridge is not possible, so the student should determine that a maximum of 5 cars can be on the bridge at the same time.

Mental Math Estimation

Once a result is determined to be logical within the context of a given problem, the result should be evaluated by its nearness to the expected answer. This is performed by approximating given values to perform mental math. Numbers should be rounded to the nearest value possible to check the initial results.

Consider the following example: A problem states that a customer is buying a new sound system for their home. The customer purchases a stereo for $435, 2 speakers for $67 each, and the necessary cables for $12. The customer chooses an option that allows him to spread the costs over equal payments for 4 months. How much will the monthly payments be?

After making calculations for the problem, a student determines that the monthly payment will be $145.25. To check the accuracy of the results, the student rounds each cost to the nearest ten (440 + 70 + 70 + 10) and determines that the total is approximately $590. Dividing by 4 months gives an approximate monthly payment of $147.50. Therefore, the student can conclude that the solution of $145.25 is very close to what should be expected.

When rounding, the place-value that is used in rounding can make a difference. Suppose the student had rounded to the nearest hundred for the estimation. The result (400 + 100 + 100 + 0 = 600; 600 ÷ 4 = 150) will show that the answer is reasonable but not as close to the actual value as rounding to the nearest ten.

Precision and Accuracy

Precision and accuracy are used to describe groups of measurements. *Precision* describes a group of measures that are very close together, regardless of whether the measures are close to the true value. *Accuracy* describes how close the measures are to the true value.

Since accuracy refers to the closeness of a value to the true measurement, the level of accuracy depends on the object measured and the instrument used to measure it. This will vary depending on the situation. If measuring the mass of a set of dictionaries, kilograms may be used as the units. In this case, it is not vitally important to have a high level of accuracy. If the measurement is a few grams away from the true value, the discrepancy might not make a big difference in the problem.

Number Concepts

In a different situation, the level of accuracy may be more significant. Pharmacists need to be sure they are very accurate in their measurements of medicines that they give to patients. In this case, the level of accuracy is vitally important and not something to be estimated. In the dictionary situation, the measurements were given as whole numbers in kilograms. In the pharmacist's situation, the measurements for medicine must be taken to the milligram and sometimes further, depending on the type of medicine.

When considering the accuracy of measurements, the error in each measurement can be shown as absolute and relative. *Absolute error* tells the actual difference between the measured value and the true value. The *relative error* tells how large the error is in relation to the true value. There may be two problems where the absolute error of the measurements is 10 grams. For one problem, this may mean the relative error is very small because the measured value is 14,990 grams, and the true value is 15,000 grams. Ten grams in relation to the true value of 15,000 is small: 0.06%. For the other problem, the measured value is 290 grams, and the true value is 300 grams. In this case, the 10-gram absolute error means a high relative error because the true value is smaller. The relative error is 10/300 = 0.03, or 3%.

Practice Quiz

1. At the store, Jan spends $90 on apples and oranges. Apples cost $1 each and oranges cost $2 each. If Jan buys the same number of apples as oranges, how many oranges did she buy?
   a. 20
   b. 25
   c. 30
   d. 35

2. A train traveling 50 miles per hour takes a trip lasting 3 hours. If a map has a scale of 1 inch per 10 miles, how many inches apart are the train's starting point and ending point on the map?
   a. 14
   b. 12
   c. 13
   d. 15

3. A traveler takes an hour to drive to a museum, spends 3 hours and 30 minutes there, and takes half an hour to drive home. What percentage of their time was spent driving?
   a. 15%
   b. 30%
   c. 40%
   d. 60%

4. $52.3 \times 10^{-3} =$
   a. 0.00523
   b. 0.0523
   c. 0.523
   d. 523

5. If $\frac{5}{2} \div \frac{1}{3} = n$, then n is between:
   a. 5 and 7
   b. 1 and 3
   c. 9 and 11
   d. 7 and 9

See answers on the next page.

Answer Explanations

1. C: The best way to solve this problem is by using a system of equations. We know that Jan bought $90 worth of apples ($a$) and oranges ($o$) at $1 and $2 respectively. That means our first equation is:

$$1(a) + 2(o) = 90$$

We also know that she bought an equal number of apples and oranges, which gives us our second equation: $a = o$. We can then replace a with o in the first equation to give:

$$1(o) + 2(o) = 90 \text{ or } 3(o) = 90$$

Which yields:

$$o = 30$$

Thus, Jan bought 30 oranges (and 30 apples).

2. D: First, the train's journey in the real world is:

$$3 \text{ h} \times 50 \frac{\text{mi}}{\text{h}} = 150 \text{ mi}$$

On the map, 1 inch corresponds to 10 miles, so that is equivalent to:

$$150 \text{ mi} \times \frac{1 \text{ in}}{10 \text{ mi}} = 15 \text{ in}$$

Therefore, the start and end points are 15 inches apart on the map.

3. B: The total trip time is 1 + 3.5 + 0.5 = 5 hours. The total time driving is 1 + 0.5 = 1.5 hours. So, the fraction of time spent driving is $\frac{1.5}{5}$ or $\frac{3}{10}$. To convert this to a percentage, multiply the top and bottom by 10 to make the denominator 100. We find $\frac{3}{10} \times \frac{10}{10} = \frac{30}{100}$. Since the denominator is 100, the numerator is our percentage: 30%.

4. B: Multiplying by 10^{-3} means moving the decimal point three places to the left and putting in zeros as necessary.

5. D: $\frac{5}{2} \div \frac{1}{3} = \frac{5}{2} \times \frac{3}{1} = \frac{15}{2} = 7.5$.

Patterns and Algebra

Number Patterns

Given a sequence of numbers, a mathematical rule can be defined that represents the numbers if a pattern exists within the set. For example, consider the sequence of numbers 1, 4, 9, 16, 25, etc. This set of numbers represents the positive integers squared, and an explicitly defined sequence that represents this set is $f_n = n^2$. An important mathematical concept is recognizing patterns in sequences and translating the patterns into an explicit formula. Once the pattern is recognized and the formula is defined, the sequence can be extended easily. For example, the next three numbers in the sequence are 36, 49, and 64.

Predicting Values

In a similar sense, patterns can be used to make conjectures, predictions, and generalizations. If a pattern is recognized in a set of numbers, values can be predicted that aren't originally provided. For example, if an experiment results in the sequence of numbers 1, 4, 9, 16, and 25, where 1 represents the first trial, 2 represents the second trial, etc., one expects the tenth trial to result in a value of 100 because that value is equal to the square of the trial number.

Recursively Defined Functions

Similar to recursively defined sequences, recursively defined functions are not explicitly defined in terms of a variable. A recursive function builds on itself and consists of a smaller argument, such as $f(0)$ or $f(1)$ and the actual definition of the function. For example, a recursively defined function is the following:

$$f(0) = 3$$

$$f(n) = f(n-1) + 2n$$

Contrasting an explicitly defined function, a recursively defined function must be evaluated in order. The first five terms of this function are $f(0) = 3, f(1) = 5, f(2) = 9, f(3) = 15,$ and $f(4) = 23$. Some recursively defined functions have an explicit counterpart and, like sequences, they can be used to model real-life applications. The Fibonacci numbers can also be thought of as a recursively defined function if $f(n) = f_n$.

Closed-Form Functions

A *closed-form function* can be evaluated using a finite number of operations such as addition, subtraction, multiplication, and division. An example of a function that's not a closed-form function is one involving an infinite sum. For example, $y = \sum_{n=1}^{\infty} x$ isn't a closed-form function because it consists of a sum of infinitely many terms. Many recursively defined functions can be expressed as a closed-form expression. To convert to a closed-form expression, a formula must be found for the nth term. This means that the recursively defined sequence must be converted to its explicit formula.

Mathematical Induction

Proving by induction involves proving a statement about a number n by first proving it is true for $n = 1$ (the base case), then assuming it is true for $n = k$ (the assumption), and finally, by showing it is true for $n = k + 1$ (the induction step). An example is shown by proving that the sum of the first n positive

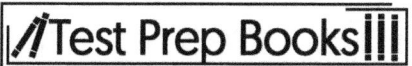

Patterns and Algebra

integers equals $\frac{n(n+1)}{2}$. The base case is shown by plugging $n = 1$ into the formula and showing a true statement. The assumption is made that the statement $1 + 2 + \cdots k = \frac{k(k+1)}{2}$ is true, and then the goal is to show that:

$$1 + 2 + \cdots k + (k + 1) = \frac{(k+1)(k+2)}{2}$$

This equation can be showing by plugging in the assumption and then finding a common denominator.

Sequences and Series

A *sequence* is an enumerated set of numbers, and each term or member is defined by the number that exists within the sequence. It can have either a finite or infinite number of terms, and a sequence is written as $\{a_n\}$, where a_n is the nth term of the sequence. An example of an infinite sequence is $\left\{\frac{n+1}{n^2}\right\}_{n=1}^{\infty}$. Its first three terms are found by evaluating at n=1, 2, and 3 to get 2, $\frac{3}{4}$, and $\frac{4}{9}$. Limits of infinite sequences, if they exist, can be found in a similar manner as finding infinite limits of functions. n needs to be treated as a variable, and then $\lim_{n \to \infty} \frac{n+1}{n^2}$ can be evaluated, resulting in 0.

An infinite series is the sum of an infinite sequence. For example, $\sum_{n=1}^{\infty} \frac{n+1}{n^2}$ is the infinite series of the sequence given above. Partial sums are sums of a finite number of terms. For example, s_{10} represents the sum of the first 10 terms, and in general, s_n represents the sum of the first n terms. An infinite series can either converge or diverge. If the sum of an infinite series is a finite number, the series is said to *converge*. Otherwise, it *diverges*. In the general infinite series $\sum a_n$, If $\lim_{n \to \infty} a_n \neq 0$ or does not exist, the series diverges. However, if $\lim_{n \to \infty} a_n = 0$, the series does not necessarily converge.

Several tests exist that determine whether a series converges:

- The Absolute Convergence Test states that if $\sum |a_n|$ converges, then $\sum a_n$ converges.

- The Integral Test states that if $f(n) = a_n$ is a positive, continuous, decreasing function, then $\sum a_n$ is convergent if and only if $\int_1^{\infty} f(x)dx$ is convergent. The geometric series $\sum ar^{n-1}$ is convergent if $|r| < 1$ and its sum is equal to $\frac{a}{1-r}$. If $|r| \geq 1$, the geometric series is divergent.

- The Limit Comparison Tests compares two infinite series $\sum a_n$ and $\sum b_n$ with positive terms. If $\sum b_n$ converges and $a_n \leq b_n$ for all n, then $\sum a_n$ converges. If $\sum b_n$ diverges and $a_n \geq b_n$ for all n, then $\sum a_n$ diverges. If $\lim_{n \to \infty} \frac{a_n}{b_n} = c$, where c is a finite, positive number, then either both series converge or diverge.

- The Alternating Series Test states that if $b_{n+1} \geq b_n$ for all n and $\lim_{n \to \infty} b_n = 0$, then the series $\sum (-1)^{n-1} b_n$.

Patterns and Algebra

- The Ratio Test states that if the limit of the ratio of consecutive terms a_{n+1}/a_n is less than 1, then the series is convergent. If the ratio is greater than 1, the series is divergent. If the limit is equal to 1, the test is inconclusive.

- The Root Test states that if $\lim_{n \to \infty} \sqrt[n]{|a_n|} < 1$, the series converges. If the same limit is greater than 1, the series diverges, and if the limit equals 1, the test is inconclusive.

Interest

One exponential formula that is commonly used is $A = Pe^{rt}$. This is the formula for **continually compounded interest**. A is the value of the investment after the time, t, in years. P is the initial amount of the investment, r is the interest rate, and e is the constant equal to approximately 2.718. Given an initial amount of $200 and a time of 3 years, if interest is compounded continuously at a rate of 6%, the total investment value can be found by plugging each value into the formula. The invested value at the end is $239.44. In more complex problems, the final investment may be given, and the rate may be the unknown. In this case, the formula becomes $239.44 = 200e^{r3}$. Solving for r requires isolating the exponential expression on one side by dividing by 200, yielding the equation $1.20 = e^{r3}$. Taking the natural log of both sides results in $\ln(1.2) = r3$. Using a calculator to evaluate the logarithmic expression, $r = 0.06 = 6\%$.

When considering the economic value of an investment and neglecting inflation, the future value, F, of a present value of P dollars, invested for n years at a fixed interest rate, r%, is given by the **single payment compound amount factor** as:

$F = P(1 + {}^r\!/_{100})^n$, which is often solved in tables titled "(F/P, i%, n)."

Inversely, the **single payment present worth factor (SPPWF)** states that the present value, P, of a future value of F dollars, n years from now at the same rates is:

$P = F(1 + {}^r\!/_{100})^{-n}$, often solved in "(P/F, i%, n)" tables.

Any future costs over any amount of time can be expressed in current dollars by applying the SPPWF equation as shown in the following example, worked out in the table below.

Consider seven equal annual payments of $5 million each, and determine the net present value of the payments for interest rates of 4 and 8 percent:

Year, n	Future Cost	Present Value: 4% Interest	Present Value: 8% Interest
0	$5,000,000	$5,000,000	$5,000,000
1	$5,000,000	$4,807,692	$4,629,630
2	$5,000,000	$4,622,781	$4,286,694
3	$5,000,000	$4,444,982	$3,969,161
4	$5,000,000	$4,274,021	$3,675,149
5	$5,000,000	$4,109,636	$3,402,916
6	$5,000,000	$3,951,573	$3,150,848
7	$5,000,000	$3,799,589	$2,917,452
Total	$40,000,000	$35,010,274	$31,031,850

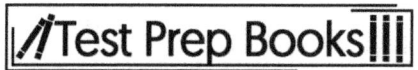

Functions

A *function* is defined as a relationship between inputs and outputs where there is only one output value for a given input. As an example, the following function is in function notation:

$$f(x) = 3x - 4$$

The $f(x)$ represents the output value for an input of x. If $x = 2$, the equation becomes:

$$f(2) = 3(2) - 4 = 6 - 4 = 2$$

The input of 2 yields an output of 2, forming the ordered pair $(2, 2)$. The following set of ordered pairs corresponds to the given function: $(2, 2), (0, -4), (-2, -10)$. The set of all possible inputs of a function is its *domain*, and all possible outputs is called the *range*. By definition, each member of the domain is paired with only one member of the range.

Functions can also be defined recursively. In this form, they are not defined explicitly in terms of variables. Instead, they are defined using previously-evaluated function outputs, starting with either $f(0)$ or $f(1)$. An example of a recursively-defined function is:

$$f(1) = 2, f(n) = 2f(n-1) + 2n, n > 1$$

The domain of this function is the set of all integers.

Domain and Range

The domain and range of a function can be found visually by its plot on the coordinate plane. In the function $f(x) = x^2 - 3$, for example, the domain is all real numbers because the parabola stretches as far left and as far right as it can go, with no restrictions. This means that any input value from the real number system will yield an answer in the real number system. For the range, the inequality $y \geq -3$ would be used to describe the possible output values because the parabola has a minimum at $y = -3$. This means there will not be any real output values less than -3 because -3 is the lowest value it reaches on the y-axis.

These same answers for domain and range can be found by observing a table. The table below shows that from input values $x = -1$ to $x = 1$, the output results in a minimum of -3. On each side of $x = 0$, the numbers increase, showing that the range is all real numbers greater than or equal to -3.

x (domain/input)	y (range/output)
-2	1
-1	-2
0	-3
-1	-2
2	1

Function Behavior

Typically, a function is denoted as an equation with an independent variable and dependent variable such as:

$$f(x) = x^2 + x - 2$$

Patterns and Algebra

In this case, it could define a concrete model and the variables could have meaning and units attached. However, a function can be represented in many other fashions. A table of variables, graphs, diagrams, verbal descriptions, and symbols, are other ways in which functions are represented.

For example, consider the sets $A = \{1, 2, 3, 4, 5\}$ and $B = \{1, 2, 3, 4, 5\}$. The following are equivalent variations of a rule for a function $f: A \rightarrow B$: the set of ordered pairs $\{(1,5), (2, 2), (3, 1), (4, 1), (5, 5)\}$ and the table:

x	1	2	3	4	5
f(x)	5	2	3	1	5

Both represent a function that takes each member of the domain and pairs it to exactly one member of the range. However, there is not an explicit formula given for the rule.

Different types of functions behave in different ways. A function is defined to be increasing over a subset of its domain if for all $x_1 \geq x_2$ in that interval, $f(x_1) \geq f(x_2)$. Also, a function is decreasing over an interval if for all $x_1 \geq x_2$ in that interval, $f(x_1) \leq f(x_2)$. A point in which a function changes from increasing to decreasing can also be labeled as the *maximum value* of a function if it is the largest point the graph reaches on the y-axis. A point in which a function changes from decreasing to increasing can be labeled as the minimum value of a function if it is the smallest point the graph reaches on the y-axis. Maximum values are also known as *extreme values*. The graph of a continuous function does not have any breaks or jumps in the graph. This description is not true of all functions. A radical function, for example, $f(x) = \sqrt{x}$, has a restriction for the domain and range because there are no real negative inputs or outputs for this function. The domain can be stated as $x \geq 0$, and the range is $y \geq 0$.

A piecewise-defined function also has a different appearance on the graph. In the following function, there are three equations defined over different intervals. It is a function because there is only one y-value for each x-value, passing the Vertical Line Test. The domain is all real numbers less than or equal to 6. The range is all real numbers greater than zero. From left to right, the graph decreases to zero, then increases to almost 4, and then jumps to 6. From input values greater than 2, the input decreases just below 8 to 4, and then stops.

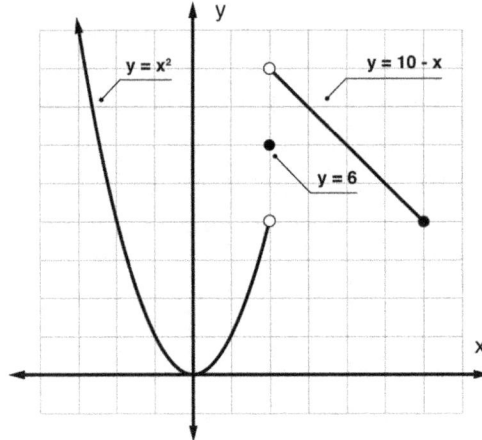

Logarithmic and exponential functions also have different behavior than other functions. These two types of functions are inverses of each other. The *inverse* of a function can be found by switching the place of x and y, and solving for y. When this is done for the exponential equation, $y = 2^x$, the function $y = \log_2 x$ is found.

The general form of a *logarithmic function* is $y = \log_b x$, which says b raised to the y power equals x.

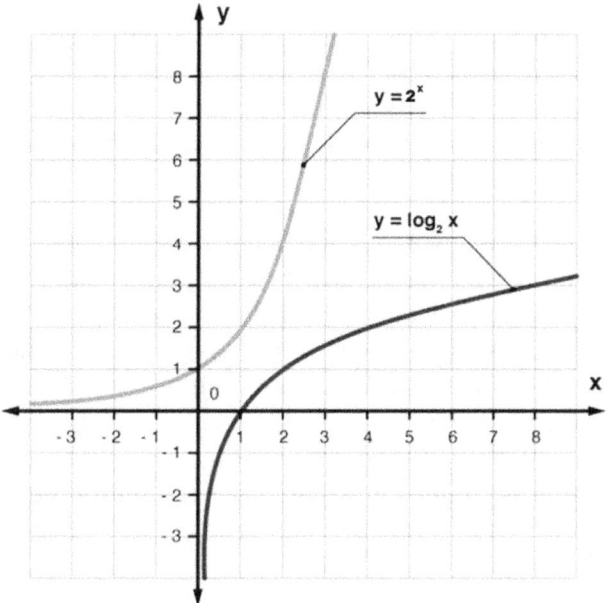

The thick black line on the graph above represents the logarithmic function $y = \log_2 x$. This curve passes through the point $(1, 0)$, just as all log functions do, because any value $b^0 = 1$. The graph of this logarithmic function starts very close to zero, but does not touch the y-axis. The output value will never be zero by the definition of logarithms. The thinner gray line seen above represents the exponential function $y = 2^x$. The behavior of this function is opposite the logarithmic function because the graph of an inverse function is the graph of the original function flipped over the line $y = x$. The curve passes through the point $(0, 1)$ because any number raised to the zero power is one. This curve also gets very close to the x-axis but never touches it because an exponential expression never has an output of zero. The x-axis on this graph is called a horizontal asymptote. An *asymptote* is a line that represents a boundary for a function. It shows a value that the function will get close to, but never reach.

Functions can also be described as being even, odd, or neither. If $f(-x) = f(x)$, the function is even. For example, the function $f(x) = x^2 - 2$ is even. Plugging in $x = 2$ yields an output of $y = 2$. After changing the input to $x = -2$, the output is still $y = 2$. The output is the same for opposite inputs. Another way to observe an even function is by the symmetry of the graph. If the graph is symmetrical about the axis, then the function is even. If the graph is symmetric about the origin, then the function is odd. Algebraically, if $f(-x) = -f(x)$, the function is odd.

Also, a function can be described as periodic if it repeats itself in regular intervals. Common periodic functions are trigonometric functions. For example, $y = \sin x$ is a periodic function with period 2π because it repeats itself every 2π units along the x-axis.

Common Functions

Three common functions used to model different relationships between quantities are linear, quadratic, and exponential functions. Linear functions are the simplest of the three, and the independent variable x has an exponent of 1. Written in the most common form, $y = mx + b$, the coefficient of x indicates how fast the function grows at a constant rate, and the b-value denotes the starting point. A quadratic function has an exponent of 2 on the independent variable x. Standard form for this type of function is $y = ax^2 + bx + c$, and the graph is a parabola. These type functions grow at a changing rate. An exponential function has an independent variable in the exponent $y = ab^x$. The graph of these types of functions is described as *growth* or *decay*, based on whether the base, b, is greater than or less than 1. These functions are different from quadratic functions because the base stays constant. A common base is base e.

The following three functions model a linear, quadratic, and exponential function respectively: $y = 2x$, $y = x^2$, and $y = 2^x$. Their graphs are shown below. The first graph, modeling the linear function, shows that the growth is constant over each interval. With a horizontal change of 1, the vertical change is 2. It models constant positive growth. The second graph shows the quadratic function, which is a curve that is symmetric across the y-axis. The growth is not constant, but the change is mirrored over the axis. The last graph models the exponential function, where the horizontal change of 1 yields a vertical change that increases more and more with each iteration of horizontal change. The exponential graph gets very close to the x-axis, but never touches it, meaning there is an asymptote there. The y-value can never be zero because the base of 2 can never be raised to an input value that yields an output of zero.

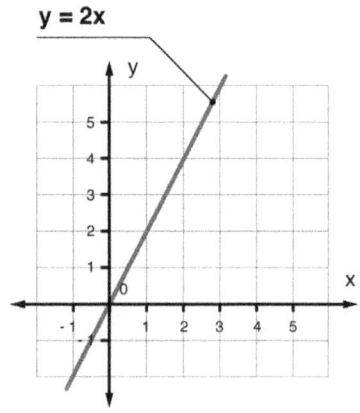
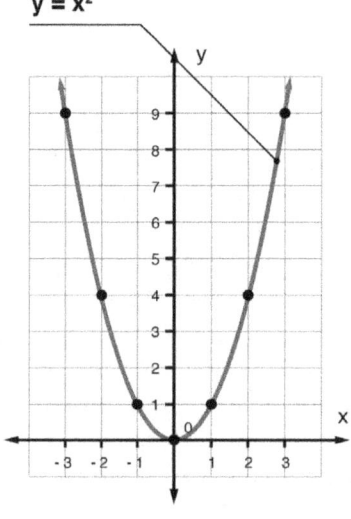
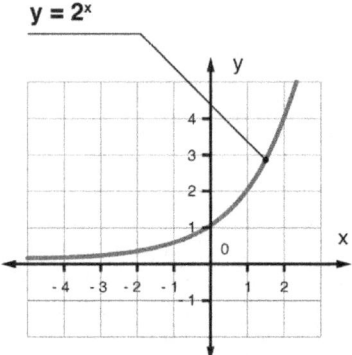

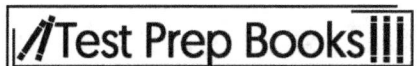

The three tables below show specific values for three types of functions. The third column in each table shows the change in the y-values for each interval. The first table shows a constant change of 2 for each equal interval, which matches the slope in the equation $y = 2x$. The second table shows an increasing change, but it also has a pattern. The increase is changing by 2 more each time, so the change is quadratic. The third table shows the change as factors of the base, 2. It shows a continuing pattern of factors of the base.

y = 2x		
x	y	Δy
1	2	
2	4	2
3	6	2
4	8	2
5	10	2

y = x²		
x	y	Δy
1	1	
2	4	3
3	9	5
4	16	7
5	25	9

y = 2ˣ		
x	y	Δy
1	2	
2	4	2
3	8	4
4	16	8
5	32	16

Given a table of values, the type of function can be determined by observing the change in y over equal intervals. For example, the tables below model two functions. The changes in interval for the x-values is 1 for both tables. For the first table, the y-values increase by 5 for each interval. Since the change is constant, the situation can be described as a linear function. The equation would be:

$$y = 5x + 3$$

For the second table, the change for y is 20, 100, and 500, respectively. The increases are multiples of 5, meaning the situation can be modeled by an exponential function. The equation below models this situation:

$$y = 5^x + 3$$

y = 5x + 3	
x	y
1	8
2	13
3	18
4	23

y = 5ˣ + 3	
x	y
1	8
2	28
3	128
4	628

Quadratic equations can be used to model real-world area problems. For example, a farmer may have a rectangular field that he needs to sow with seed. The field has length $x + 8$ and width $2x$. The formula for area should be used: $A = lw$. Therefore,

$$A = (x + 8) * 2x = 2x^2 + 16x$$

Patterns and Algebra

The possible values for the length and width can be shown in a table, with input x and output A. If the equation was graphed, the possible area values can be seen on the y-axis for given x-values.

Exponential growth and decay can be found in real-world situations. For example, if a piece of notebook paper is folded 25 times, the thickness of the paper can be found. To model this situation, a table can be used. The initial point is one-fold, which yields a thickness of 2 papers. For the second fold, the thickness is 4. Since the thickness doubles each time, the table below shows the thickness for the next few folds. Notice the thickness changes by the same factor each time. Since this change for a constant interval of folds is a factor of 2, the function is exponential. The equation for this is $y = 2^x$. For twenty-five folds, the thickness would be 33,554,432 papers.

x (folds)	y (paper thickness)
0	1
1	2
2	4
3	8
4	16
5	32

One exponential formula that is commonly used is the *interest formula*: $A = Pe^{rt}$. In this formula, interest is compounded continuously. A is the value of the investment after the time, t, in years. P is the initial amount of the investment, r is the interest rate, and e is the constant equal to approximately 2.718. Given an initial amount of $200 and a time of 3 years, if interest is compounded continuously at a rate of 6%, the total investment value can be found by plugging each value into the formula. The invested value at the end is $239.44. In more complex problems, the final investment may be given, and the rate may be the unknown. In this case, the formula becomes $239.44 = 200e^{r3}$. Solving for r requires isolating the exponential expression on one side by dividing by 200, yielding the equation $1.20 = e^{r3}$. Taking the natural log of both sides results in $\ln(1.2) = r3$. Using a calculator to evaluate the logarithmic expression, $r = 0.06 = 6\%$.

When working with logarithms and exponential expressions, it is important to remember the relationship between the two. In general, the logarithmic form is $y = \log_b x$ for an exponential form $b^y = x$. Logarithms and exponential functions are inverses of each other.

Transformations as Functions

A *function* is when a translation, reflection, or rotation (i.e., transformation) occurs in the coordinate plane. The original points are the *inputs* of the function, and the resulting points are the *outputs* of the function. For instance, if a shape is shifted to the right 4 units in the coordinate plane, the original x variable becomes $x + 4$. If a shape is reflected over the y-axis, all x coordinates are negated. For instance, if the original shape reaches the line $x = 4$, the resulting shape would reach the line $x = -4$.

Building a Function

Functions can be built out of the context of a situation. For example, the relationship between the money paid for a gym membership and the months that someone has been a member can be described

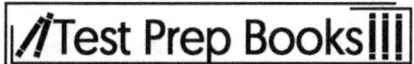

through a function. If the one-time membership fee is $40 and the monthly fee is $30, then the function can be written:

$$f(x) = 30x + 40$$

The x-value represents the number of months the person has been part of the gym, while the output is the total money paid for the membership. The table below shows this relationship. It is a representation of the function because the initial cost is $40 and the cost increases each month by $30.

x (months)	y (money paid to gym)
0	40
1	70
2	100
3	130

Functions can also be built from existing functions. For example, a given function $f(x)$ can be transformed by adding a constant, multiplying by a constant, or changing the input value by a constant. The new function $g(x) = f(x) + k$ represents a vertical shift of the original function. In $f(x) = 3x - 2$, a vertical shift 4 units up would be:

$$g(x) = 3x - 2 + 4 = 3x + 2$$

Multiplying the function times a constant k represents a vertical stretch, based on whether the constant is greater than or less than 1. The function $g(x) = kf(x) = 4(3x - 2) = 12x - 8$ represents a stretch. Changing the input x by a constant forms the function $g(x) = f(x + k) = 3(x + 4) - 2 = 3x + 12 - 2 = 3x + 10$, and this represents a horizontal shift to the left 4 units. If $(x - 4)$ was plugged into the function, it would represent a horizontal shift.

A composition function can also be formed by plugging one function into another. In function notation, this is written:

$$(f \circ g)(x) = f(g(x))$$

For two functions $f(x) = x^2$ and $g(x) = x - 3$, the composition function becomes:

$$f(g(x)) = (x - 3)^2 = x^2 - 6x + 9$$

The composition of functions can also be used to verify if two functions are inverses of each other.

Given the two functions $f(x) = 2x + 5$ and $g(x) = \frac{x-5}{2}$, the composition function can be found $(f \circ g)(x)$. Solving this equation yields:

$$f(g(x)) = 2\left(\frac{x-5}{2}\right) + 5 = x - 5 + 5 = x$$

It also is true that $g(f(x)) = x$. Since the composition of these two functions gives a simplified answer of x, this verifies that $f(x)$ and $g(x)$ are inverse functions. The domain of $f(g(x))$ is the set of all x-values in the domain of $g(x)$ such that $g(x)$ is in the domain of $f(x)$. Basically, both $f(g(x))$ and $g(x)$ have to be defined.

Patterns and Algebra

To build an inverse of a function, $f(x)$ needs to be replaced with y, and the x and y values need to be switched. Then, the equation can be solved for y. For example, given the equation $y = e^{2x}$, the inverse can be found by rewriting the equation $x = e^{2y}$. The natural logarithm of both sides is taken down, and the exponent is brought down to form the equation $\ln(x) = \ln(e)2y$. $\ln(e)=1$, which yields the equation $\ln(x) = 2y$. Dividing both sides by 2 yields the inverse equation:

$$\frac{\ln(x)}{2} = y = f^{-1}(x)$$

The domain of an inverse function is the range of the original function, and the range of an inverse function is the domain of the original function. Therefore, an ordered pair (x, y) on either a graph or a table corresponding to $f(x)$ means that the ordered pair (y, x) exists on the graph of $f^{-1}(x)$. Basically, if $f(x) = y$, then $f^{-1}(y) = x$. For a function to have an inverse, it must be one-to-one. That means it must pass the *Horizontal Line Test*, and if any horizontal line passes through the graph of the function twice, a function is not one-to-one. The domain of a function that is not one-to-one can be restricted to an interval in which the function is one-to-one, to be able to define an inverse function.

Functions can also be formed from combinations of existing functions. Given $f(x)$ and $g(x)$, $f + g$, $f - g$, fg, and $\frac{f}{g}$ can be built. The domains of $f + g$, $f - g$, and fg are the intersection of the domains of f and g. The domain of $\frac{f}{g}$ is the same set, excluding those values that make $g(x) = 0$. For example, if $f(x) = 2x + 3$ and $g(x) = x + 1$, then $\frac{f}{g} = \frac{2x+3}{x+1}$, and its domain is all real numbers except -1.

Rate of Change

Rate of change for any line calculates the steepness of the line over a given interval. Rate of change is also known as the slope or rise/run. The rates of change for nonlinear functions vary depending on the interval being used for the function. The rate of change over one interval may be zero, while the next interval may have a positive rate of change. The equation plotted on the graph below, $y = x^2$, is a quadratic function and non-linear.

The average rate of change from points $(0, 0)$ to $(1, 1)$ is 1 because the vertical change is 1 over the horizontal change of 1. For the next interval, $(1, 1)$ to $(2, 4)$, the average rate of change is 3 because the slope is $\frac{3}{1}$.

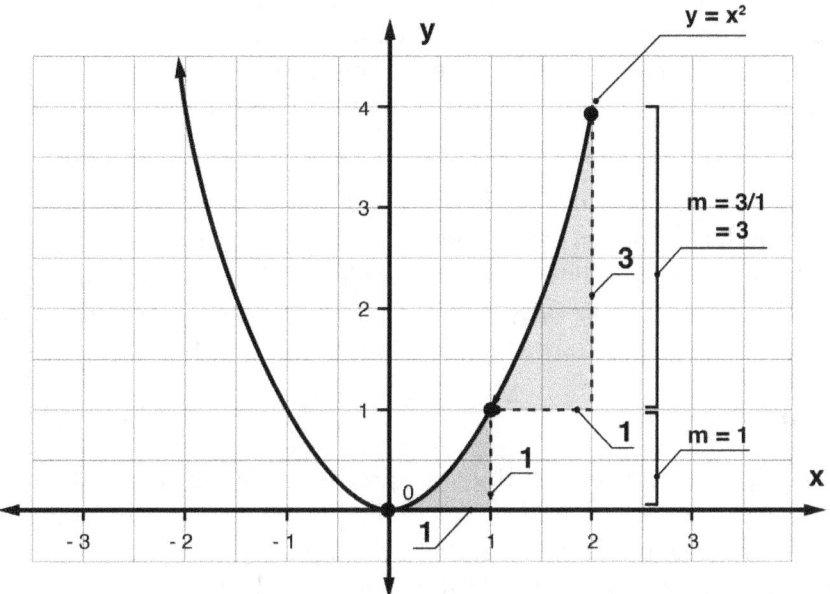

The rate of change for a linear function is constant and can be determined based on a few representations. One method is to place the equation in slope-intercept form: $y = mx + b$. Thus, m is the slope, and b is the y-intercept. In the graph below, the equation is $y = x + 1$, where the slope is 1 and the y-intercept is 1. For every vertical change of 1 unit, there is a horizontal change of 1 unit. The x-intercept is -1, which is the point where the line crosses the x-axis.

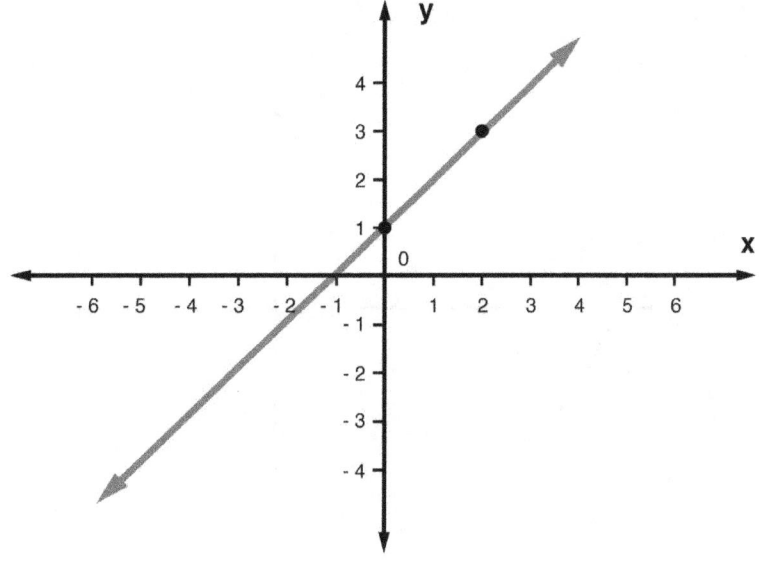

Patterns and Algebra

Solving Line Problems

Two lines are parallel if they have the same slope and a different intercept. Two lines are perpendicular if the product of their slope equals -1. Parallel lines never intersect unless they are the same line, and perpendicular lines intersect at a right angle. If two lines aren't parallel, they must intersect at one point. Determining equations of lines based on properties of parallel and perpendicular lines appears in word problems. To find an equation of a line, both the slope and a point the line goes through are necessary. Therefore, if an equation of a line is needed that's parallel to a given line and runs through a specified point, the slope of the given line and the point are plugged into the point-slope form of an equation of a line.

Secondly, if an equation of a line is needed that's perpendicular to a given line running through a specified point, the negative reciprocal of the slope of the given line and the point are plugged into the point-slope form. Also, if the point of intersection of two lines is known, that point will be used to solve the set of equations. Therefore, to solve a system of equations, the point of intersection must be found. If a set of two equations with two unknown variables has no solution, the lines are parallel.

Zeros of Polynomials

Finding the zeros of polynomial functions is the same process as finding the solutions of polynomial equations. These are the points at which the graph of the function crosses the x-axis. As stated previously, factors can be used to find the zeros of a polynomial function. The degree of the function shows the number of possible zeros. If the highest exponent on the independent variable is 4, then the degree is 4, and the number of possible zeros is 4. If there are complex solutions, the number of roots is less than the degree.

Given the function $y = x^2 + 7x + 6$, y can be set equal to zero, and the polynomial can be factored. The equation turns into $0 = (x + 1)(x + 6)$, where $x = -1$ and $x = -6$ are the zeros. Since this is a quadratic equation, the shape of the graph will be a parabola. Knowing that zeros represent the points where the parabola crosses the x-axis, the maximum or minimum point is the only other piece needed to sketch a rough graph of the function. By looking at the function in standard form, the coefficient of x is positive; therefore, the parabola opens *up*. Using the zeros and the minimum, the following rough sketch of the graph can be constructed:

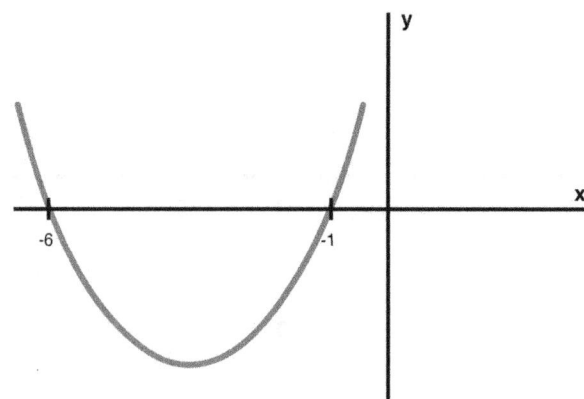

Finding the Zeros of a Function

The zeros of a function are the points where its graph crosses the x-axis. At these points, $y = 0$. One way to find the zeros is to analyze the graph. If given the graph, the x-coordinates can be found where the line crosses the x-axis. Another way to find the zeros is to set $y = 0$ in the equation and solve for x. Depending on the type of equation, this could be done by using opposite operations, by factoring the equation, by completing the square, or by using the quadratic formula. If a graph does not cross the x-axis, then the function may have complex roots.

Polynomial Identities

Difference of squares refers to a binomial composed of the difference of two squares. For example, $a^2 - b^2$ is a difference of squares. It can be written $(a)^2 - (b)^2$, and it can be factored into $(a - b)(a + b)$. Recognizing the difference of squares allows the expression to be rewritten easily because of the form it takes. For some expressions, factoring consists of more than one step. When factoring, it's important to always check to make sure that the result cannot be factored further. If it can, then the expression should be split further. If it cannot be, the factoring step is complete, and the expression is completely factored.

A sum and difference of cubes is another way to factor a polynomial expression. When the polynomial takes the form of addition or subtraction of two terms that can be written as a cube, a formula is given. The following graphic shows the factorization of a difference of cubes:

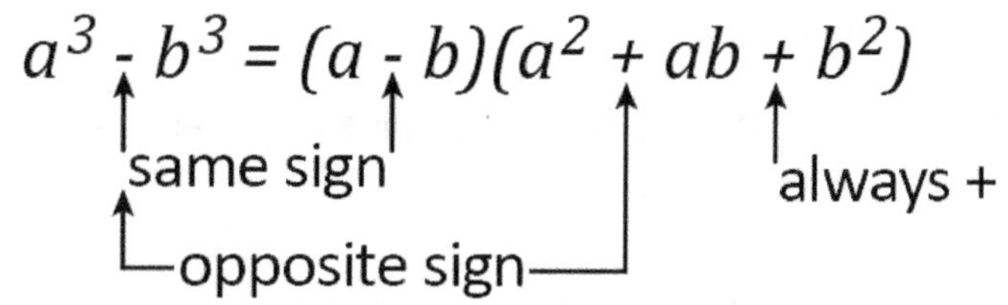

$$a^3 - b^3 = (a - b)(a^2 + ab + b^2)$$

- same sign
- opposite sign
- always +

This form of factoring can be useful in finding the zeros of a function of degree 3. For example, when solving $x^3 - 27 = 0$, this rule needs to be used. $x^3 - 27$ is first written as the difference two cubes, $(x)^3 - (3)^3$ and then factored into $(x - 3)(x^2 + 3x + 9)$. This expression may not be factored any further. Each factor is then set equal to zero. Therefore, one solution is found to be $x = 3$, and the other two solutions must be found using the quadratic formula. A sum of squares would have a similar process. The formula for factoring a sum of squares is:

$$a^3 + b^3 = (a + b)(a^2 - ab + b^2)$$

The opposite of factoring is multiplying. Multiplying a square of a binomial involves the following rules: $(a + b)^2 = a^2 + 2ab + b^2$ and:

$$(a - b)^2 = a^2 - 2ab + b^2$$

The binomial theorem for expansion can be used when the exponent on a binomial is larger than 2, and the multiplication would take a long time. The binomial theorem is given as:

$$(a+b)^n = \sum_{k=0}^{n} \binom{n}{k} a^{n-k} b^k \text{ where } \binom{n}{k} = \frac{n!}{k!\,(n-k)!}$$

The *Remainder Theorem* can be helpful when evaluating polynomial functions $P(x)$ for a given value of x. A polynomial can be divided by $(x - a)$, if there is a remainder of 0. This also means that $P(a) = 0$ and $(x - a)$ is a factor of $P(x)$. In a similar sense, if P is evaluated at any other number b, $P(b)$ is equal to the remainder of dividing: $P(x)$ by $(x - b)$.

Rewriting Expressions

Algebraic expressions are made up of numbers, variables, and combinations of the two, using mathematical operations. Expressions can be rewritten based on their factors. For example, the expression $6x + 4$ can be rewritten as $2(3x + 2)$ because 2 is a factor of both $6x$ and 4. More complex expressions can also be rewritten based on their factors. The expression $x^4 - 16$ can be rewritten as:

$$(x^2 - 4)(x^2 + 4)$$

This is a different type of factoring, where a difference of squares is factored into a sum and difference of the same two terms. With some expressions, the factoring process is simple and only leads to a different way to represent the expression. With others, factoring and rewriting the expression leads to more information about the given problem.

In the following quadratic equation, factoring the binomial leads to finding the zeros of the function:

$$x^2 - 5x + 6 = y$$

This equation factors into $(x - 3)(x - 2) = y$, where 2 and 3 are found to be the zeros of the function when y is set equal to zero. The zeros of any function are the x-values where the graph of the function on the coordinate plane crosses the x-axis.

Factoring an equation is a simple way to rewrite the equation and find the zeros, but factoring is not possible for every quadratic. Completing the square is one way to find zeros when factoring is not an option. The following equation cannot be factored:

$$x^2 + 10x - 9 = 0$$

The first step in this method is to move the constant to the right side of the equation, making it:

$$x^2 + 10x = 9$$

Then, the coefficient of x is divided by 2 and squared. This number is then added to both sides of the equation, to make the equation still true. For this example, $\left(\frac{10}{2}\right)^2 = 25$ is added to both sides of the equation to obtain:

$$x^2 + 10x + 25 = 9 + 25$$

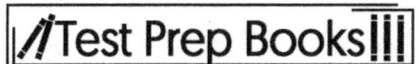

Patterns and Algebra

This expression simplifies to $x^2 + 10x + 25 = 34$, which can then be factored into:

$$(x+5)^2 = 34$$

Solving for x then involves taking the square root of both sides and subtracting 5. This leads to two zeros of the function:

$$x = \pm\sqrt{34} - 5$$

Depending on the type of answer the question seeks, a calculator may be used to find exact numbers.

Given a quadratic equation in standard form— $ax^2 + bx + c = 0$—the sign of a tells whether the function has a minimum value or a maximum value. If $a > 0$, the graph opens up and has a minimum value. If $a < 0$, the graph opens down and has a maximum value. Depending on the way the quadratic equation is written, multiplication may need to occur before a max/min value is determined.

Exponential expressions can also be rewritten, just as quadratic equations. Properties of exponents must be understood. Multiplying two exponential expressions with the same base involves adding the exponents:

$$a^m a^n = a^{m+n}$$

Dividing two exponential expressions with the same base involves subtracting the exponents:

$$\frac{a^m}{a^n} = a^{m-n}$$

Raising an exponential expression to another exponent includes multiplying the exponents:

$$(a^m)^n = a^{mn}$$

The zero power always gives a value of 1: $a^0 = 1$. Raising either a product or a fraction to a power involves distributing that power:

$$(ab)^m = a^m b^m \text{ and } \left(\frac{a}{b}\right)^m = \frac{a^m}{b^m}$$

Finally, raising a number to a negative exponent is equivalent to the reciprocal including the positive exponent:

$$a^{-m} = \frac{1}{a^m}$$

Solving Equations

Solving equations with one variable is the process of isolating a variable on one side of the equation. The letters in an equation are variables as they stand for unknown quantities that you are trying to solve for. The numbers attached to the variables by multiplication are called coefficients. X is commonly used as a variable, though any letter can be used. For example, in $3x - 7 = 20$, the variable is $3x$, and it needs to be isolated. The numbers (also called constants) are -7 and 20. That means $3x$ needs to be on one side of the equals sign (either side is fine), and all the numbers need to be on the other side of the equals sign.

Patterns and Algebra

To accomplish this, the equation must be manipulated by performing opposite operations of what already exists. Remember that addition and subtraction are opposites and that multiplication and division are opposites. Any action taken to one side of the equation must be taken on the other side to maintain equality.

So, since the 7 is being subtracted, it can be moved to the right side of the equation by adding seven to both sides:

$$3x - 7 = 20$$

$$3x - 7 + 7 = 20 + 7$$

$$3x = 27$$

Now that the variable $3x$ is on one side and the constants (now combined into one constant) are on the other side, the 3 needs to be moved to the right side. 3 and x are being multiplied together, so 3 then needs to be divided from each side.

$$\frac{3x}{3} = \frac{27}{3}$$

$$x = 9$$

Now that x has been completely isolated, we know its value.

The solution is found to be $x = 9$. This solution can be checked for accuracy by plugging $x = 9$ in the original equation. After simplifying the equation, $20 = 20$ is found, which is a true statement:

$$3 \times 9 - 7 = 20$$

$$27 - 7 = 20$$

$$20 = 20$$

Equations that require solving for a variable (*algebraic equations*) come in many forms. Here are some more examples:

No coefficient attached to the variable:

$$x + 8 = 20$$

$$x + 8 - 8 = 20 - 8$$

$$x = 12$$

A fractional coefficient:

$$\frac{1}{2}z + 24 = 36$$

$$\frac{1}{2}z + 24 - 24 = 36 - 24$$

$$\frac{1}{2}z = 12$$

Now we multiply the fraction by its inverse:

$$\frac{2}{1} \times \frac{1}{2}z = 12 \times \frac{2}{1}$$

$$z = 24$$

Multiple instances of x:

$$14x + x - 4 = 3x + 2$$

All instances of x can be combined.

$$15x - 4 = 3x + 2$$

$$15x - 4 + 4 = 3x + 2 + 4$$

$$15x = 3x + 6$$

$$15x - 3x = 3x + 6 - 3x$$

$$12x = 6$$

$$\frac{12x}{12} = \frac{6}{12}$$

$$x = \frac{1}{2}$$

When solving radical and rational equations, extraneous solutions must be accounted for when finding the answers. For example, the equation $\frac{x}{x-5} = \frac{3x}{x+3}$ has two values that create a 0 denominator: $x \neq 5, -3$. When solving for x, these values must be considered because they cannot be solutions. In the given equation, solving for x can be done using cross-multiplication, yielding the equation:

$$x(x + 3) = 3x(x - 5)$$

Distributing results in the quadratic equation $x^2 + 3x = 3x^2 - 15x$; therefore, all terms must be moved to one side of the equals sign. This results in $2x^2 - 18x = 0$, which in factored form is:

$$2x(x - 9) = 0$$

Patterns and Algebra

Setting each factor equal to zero, the apparent solutions are $x = 0$ and $x = 9$. These two solutions are neither 5 nor -3, so they are viable solutions. Neither 0 nor 9 create a 0 denominator in the original equation.

A similar process exists when solving radical equations. One must check to make sure the solutions are defined in the original equations. Solving an equation containing a square root involves isolating the root and then squaring both sides of the equals sign. Solving a cube root equation involves isolating the radical and then cubing both sides. In either case, the variable can then be solved for because there are no longer radicals in the equation.

Methods for Solving Equations

Equations with one variable can be solved using the addition principle and multiplication principle. If $a = b$, then $a + c = b + c$, and $ac = bc$. Given the equation $2x - 3 = 5x + 7$, the first step is to combine the variable terms and the constant terms. Using the principles, expressions can be added and subtracted onto and off both sides of the equals sign, so the equation turns into $-10 = 3x$. Dividing by 3 on both sides through the multiplication principle with $c = \frac{1}{3}$ results in the final answer of $x = \frac{-10}{3}$.

Some equations have a higher degree and are not solved by simply using opposite operations. When an equation has a degree of 2, completing the square is an option. For example, the quadratic equation $x^2 - 6x + 2 = 0$ can be rewritten by completing the square. The goal of completing the square is to get the equation into the form:

$$(x - p)^2 = q$$

Using the example, the constant term 2 first needs to be moved over to the opposite side by subtracting. Then, the square can be completed by adding 9 to both sides, which is the square of half of the coefficient of the middle term $-6x$. The current equation is:

$$x^2 - 6x + 9 = 7$$

The left side can be factored into a square of a binomial, resulting in:

$$(x - 3)^2 = 7$$

To solve for x, the square root of both sides should be taken, resulting in $(x - 3) = \pm\sqrt{7}$, and:

$$x = 3 \pm \sqrt{7}$$

Other ways of solving quadratic equations include graphing, factoring, and using the quadratic formula. The equation $y = x^2 - 4x + 3$ can be graphed on the coordinate plane, and the solutions can be observed where it crosses the x-axis. The graph will be a parabola that opens up with two solutions at 1 and 3.

The equation can also be factored to find the solutions. The original equation, $y = x^2 - 4x + 3$ can be factored into:

$$y = (x - 1)(x - 3)$$

Setting this equal to zero, the x-values are found to be 1 and 3, just as on the graph. Solving by factoring and graphing are not always possible. The quadratic formula is a method of solving quadratic equations that always results in exact solutions.

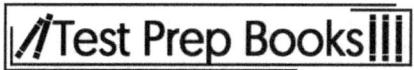

Patterns and Algebra

The formula is:

$$x = \frac{-b \pm \sqrt{b^2 - 4ac}}{2a}$$

$A, b,$ and c are the coefficients in the original equation in standard form:

$$y = ax^2 + bx + c$$

For this example:

$$x = \frac{4 \pm \sqrt{(-4)^2 - 4(1)(3)}}{2(1)} = \frac{4 \pm \sqrt{16 - 12}}{2} = \frac{4 \pm 2}{2} = 1, 3$$

The expression underneath the radical is called the *discriminant*. Without working out the entire formula, the value of the discriminant can reveal the nature of the solutions. If the value of the discriminant $b^2 - 4ac$ is positive, then there will be two real solutions. If the value is zero, there will be one real solution. If the value is negative, the two solutions will be imaginary or complex. If the solutions are complex, it means that the parabola never touches the x-axis. An example of a complex solution can be found by solving the following quadratic:

$$y = x^2 - 4x + 8$$

By using the quadratic formula, the solutions are found to be:

$$x = \frac{4 \pm \sqrt{(-4)^2 - 4(1)(8)}}{2(1)} = \frac{4 \pm \sqrt{16 - 32}}{2}$$

$$\frac{4 \pm \sqrt{-16}}{2} = 2 \pm 2i$$

The solutions both have a real part, 2, and an imaginary part, $2i$.

Systems of Equations

A *system of equations* is a group of equations that have the same variables or unknowns. These equations can be linear, but they are not always so. Finding a solution to a system of equations means finding the values of the variables that satisfy each equation. For a linear system of two equations and two variables, there could be a single solution, no solution, or infinitely many solutions.

A single solution occurs when there is one value for x and y that satisfies the system. This would be shown on the graph where the lines cross at exactly one point. When there is no solution, the lines are parallel and do not ever cross. With infinitely many solutions, the equations may look different, but they are the same line. One equation will be a multiple of the other, and on the graph, they lie on top of each other.

The process of elimination can be used to solve a system of equations. For example, the following equations make up a system: $x + 3y = 10$ and:

$$2x - 5y = 9$$

Patterns and Algebra

Immediately adding these equations does not eliminate a variable, but it is possible to change the first equation by multiplying the whole equation by -2.

This changes the first equation to:

$$-2x - 6y = -20$$

The equations can be then added to obtain $-11y = -11$. Solving for y yields $y = 1$. To find the rest of the solution, 1 can be substituted in for y in either original equation to find the value of $x = 7$. The solution to the system is (7, 1) because it makes both equations true, and it is the point in which the lines intersect. If the system is *dependent*—having infinitely many solutions—then both variables will cancel out when the elimination method is used, resulting in an equation that is true for many values of x and y. Since the system is dependent, both equations can be simplified to the same equation or line.

A system can also be solved using *substitution*. This involves solving one equation for a variable and then plugging that solved equation into the other equation in the system. For example, $x - y = -2$ and $3x + 2y = 9$ can be solved using substitution. The first equation can be solved for x, where:

$$x = -2 + y$$

Then it can be plugged into the other equation:

$$3(-2 + y) + 2y = 9$$

Solving for y yields $-6 + 3y + 2y = 9$, where $y = 3$. If $y = 3$, then $x = 1$. This solution can be checked by plugging in these values for the variables in each equation to see if it makes a true statement.

Finally, a solution to a system of equations can be found graphically. The solution to a linear system is the point or points where the lines cross. The values of x and y represent the coordinates (x, y) where the lines intersect. Using the same system of equations as above, they can be solved for y to put them in slope-intercept form, $y = mx + b$. These equations become $y = x + 2$ and:

$$y = -\frac{3}{2}x + 4.5$$

The slope is the coefficient of x, and the y-intercept is the constant value. This system with the solution is shown below:

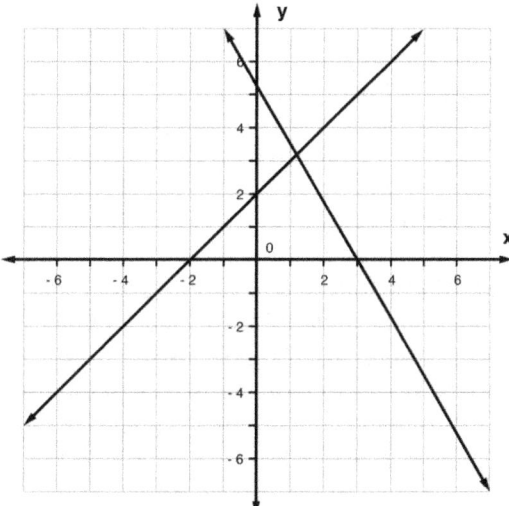

A system of equations may also be made up of a linear and a quadratic equation. These systems may have one solution, two solutions, or no solutions. The graph of these systems involves one straight line and one parabola. Algebraically, these systems can be solved by solving the linear equation for one variable and plugging that answer in to the quadratic equation. If possible, the equation can then be solved to find part of the answer. The graphing method is commonly used for these types of systems. On a graph, these two lines can be found to intersect at one point, at two points across the parabola, or at no points.

Matrices can also be used to solve systems of linear equations. Specifically, for systems, the coefficients of the linear equations in standard form are the entries in the matrix. Using the same system of linear equations as above, $x - y = -2$ and $3x + 2y = 9$, the matrix to represent the system is:

$$\begin{bmatrix} 1 & -1 \\ 3 & 2 \end{bmatrix} \begin{bmatrix} x \\ y \end{bmatrix} = \begin{bmatrix} -2 \\ 9 \end{bmatrix}$$

To solve this system using matrices, the inverse matrix must be found. For a general 2x2 matrix, $\begin{bmatrix} a & b \\ c & d \end{bmatrix}$, the inverse matrix is found by the expression:

$$\frac{1}{ad - bc} \begin{bmatrix} d & -b \\ -c & a \end{bmatrix}$$

The inverse matrix for the system given above is:

$$\frac{1}{2 - -3} \begin{bmatrix} 2 & 1 \\ -3 & 1 \end{bmatrix} = \frac{1}{5} \begin{bmatrix} 2 & 1 \\ -3 & 1 \end{bmatrix}$$

The next step in solving is to multiply this identity matrix by the system matrix above.

Patterns and Algebra

This is given by the following equation: $\frac{1}{5}\begin{bmatrix} 2 & 1 \\ -3 & 1 \end{bmatrix}\begin{bmatrix} 1 & -1 \\ 3 & 2 \end{bmatrix}\begin{bmatrix} x \\ y \end{bmatrix} = \begin{bmatrix} -2 \\ 9 \end{bmatrix}\begin{bmatrix} 2 & 1 \\ -3 & 1 \end{bmatrix}\frac{1}{5}$, which simplifies to:

$$\frac{1}{5}\begin{bmatrix} 5 & 0 \\ 0 & 5 \end{bmatrix}\begin{bmatrix} x \\ y \end{bmatrix} = \frac{1}{5}\begin{bmatrix} 5 \\ 15 \end{bmatrix}$$

Solving for the solution matrix, the answer is:

$$\begin{bmatrix} 1 & 0 \\ 0 & 1 \end{bmatrix}\begin{bmatrix} x \\ y \end{bmatrix} = \begin{bmatrix} 1 \\ 3 \end{bmatrix}$$

Since the first matrix is the identity matrix, the solution is $x = 1$ and $y = 3$.

Finding solutions to systems of equations is essentially finding what values of the variables make both equations true. It is finding the input value that yields the same output value in both equations. For functions $g(x)$ and $f(x)$, the equation $g(x) = f(x)$ means the output values are being set equal to each other. Solving for the value of x means finding the x-coordinate that gives the same output in both functions. For example, $f(x) = x + 2$ and $g(x) = -3x + 10$ is a system of equations. Setting $f(x) = g(x)$ yields the equation:

$$x + 2 = -3x + 10$$

Solving for x, gives the x-coordinate $x = 2$ where the two lines cross. This value can also be found by using a table or a graph. On a table, both equations can be given the same inputs, and the outputs can be recorded to find the point(s) where the lines cross. Any method of solving finds the same solution, but some methods are more appropriate for some systems of equations than others.

Systems of Linear Inequalities

Systems of *linear inequalities* are like systems of equations, but the solutions are different. Since inequalities have infinitely many solutions, their systems also have infinitely many solutions. Finding the solutions of inequalities involves graphs. A system of two equations and two inequalities is linear; thus, the lines can be graphed using slope-intercept form. If the inequality has an equals sign, the line is solid. If the inequality only has a greater than or less than symbol, the line on the graph is dotted. Dashed lines indicate that points lying on the line are not included in the solution. After the lines are graphed, a region is shaded on one side of the line. This side is found by determining if a point—known as a *test point*—lying on one side of the line produces a true inequality. If it does, that side of the graph is shaded. If the point produces a false inequality, the line is shaded on the opposite side from the point. The graph of a system of inequalities involves shading the intersection of the two shaded regions.

Translating Functions

A function can be translated in many ways. Typical translations involve shifting, reflecting, and scaling graphs. A shift is a translation that does not change the original shape of the function. A vertical shift adds or subtracts a constant from every y-coordinate, and is represented as:

$$y = f(x) \pm c$$

A horizontal shift adds or subtracts a constant from every x-coordinate, and is represented as:

$$y = f(x \pm c)$$

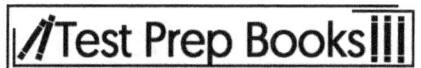

Patterns and Algebra

A reflection involves flipping a function over an axis. To reflect about the y-axis, every x-coordinate needs to be multiplied times -1. This reflection is represented as $y = f(-x)$. To reflect about the x-axis, every y-coordinate needs to be multiplied times -1. This reflection is represented as $y = -f(x)$.

Finally, a scale involves changing the shape of the graph through either a shrink or stretch. A scale either multiplies or divides each coordinate by a constant. A vertical scale involves multiplying or dividing every y-coordinate by a constant. This scaling is represented by $y = kf(x)$ and is a vertical stretch if $k > 1$ and vertical shrink if $0 < k < 1$. A horizontal scale involves multiplying or dividing every x-coordinate by a constant. This scaling is represented by $y = f(kx)$ and is a horizontal stretch if $0 < k < 1$ and horizontal shrink if $k > 1$.

Graphing Functions

Typically, a function can be graphed using a graphing calculator. However, some characteristics can be found that allow for enough information to be compounded to graph a very good sketch without technology. Such information includes significant points such as zeros, local extrema, and points where a function is not continuous and not differentiable. Zeros are points in which a function crosses the y-axis. These points are found by plugging 0 into the independent variable x and solving for the dependent variable y. Local extrema are points in which a function is either a local maxima or minima. These points occur where the derivative of the function is either equal to zero or undefined, and those points are known as critical values.

The first derivative test can be used to decide whether a critical value is a maximum or minimum. If a function increases to a point, showing that the first derivative is positive over that interval, and if a function decreases after that same point, showing that the derivative is negative over that interval, then the point is a local maximum. The opposite occurs at a local minimum. Finally, points in which a function is not continuous or not differentiable are also important points. A function is continuous over its domain. A function is not differentiable at a point if there exists a vertical tangent at that point, if there is a corner or a cusp at that point, or if the function is not defined at that point.

Asymptotes

An *asymptote* is a line that approaches the graph of a given function, but never meets it. Vertical asymptotes correspond to denominators of zero for a rational function. They also exist in logarithmic functions and trigonometric functions, such as tangent and cotangent. In rational functions and trigonometric functions, the asymptotes exist at x-values that cause a denominator equal to zero. For example, vertical asymptotes exist at $x = \pm 2$ for the function:

$$f(x) = \frac{x+1}{(x-2)(x+2)}$$

Horizontal and oblique asymptotes correspond to the behavior of a curve as the x-values approach either positive or negative infinity. For example, the graph of $f(x) = e^x$ has a horizontal asymptote of $y = 0$ as x approaches negative infinity. In regards to rational functions, there is a rule to follow. Consider the following rational function:

$$f(x) = \frac{ax^n + \cdots}{bx^m + \cdots}$$

The numerator is an nth degree polynomial and the denominator is an mth degree polynomial. If $m < n$, the line $y = 0$ is a horizontal asymptote. If $n = m$, the line $y = \frac{a}{b}$ is a horizontal asymptote. If $m >$

Patterns and Algebra

n, then there is an oblique asymptote. In order to find the equation of the oblique asymptote, the denominator is divided into the numerator using long division. The result, minus the remainder, gives the equation of the oblique asymptote.

Here is a graph that shows an example of both a slant and a vertical asymptote:

Graphed Asymptotes

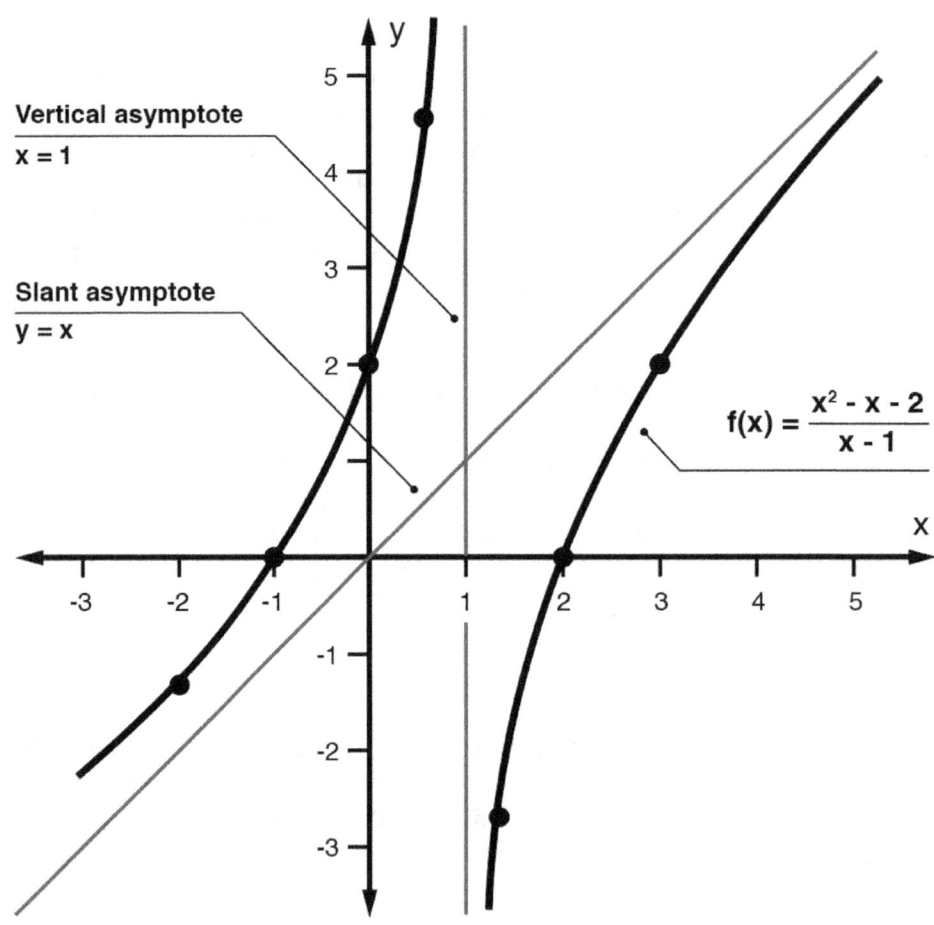

Inverse Variation and Rational Functions

The variable y varies inversely with respect to x if $y = \frac{k}{x}$, where k is the constant of variation. This means that as x decreases, y increases, and y is said to be inversely proportional to x. Also, this can be written as $k = xy$, and this specific example is known as inverse linear variation. The function $f(x) = \frac{k}{x}$ is a rational function because it is a rational fraction in which both the numerator and denominator are polynomials. Other types of inverse variation exist with nonlinear factors. The variable y can vary inversely with respect to x^2, and in this case: $y = \frac{k}{x^2}$. The exponent on the variable x can be any positive real number. In any case, the function will always be a rational function.

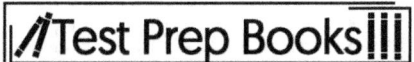

Operations with Polynomials

Addition and subtraction operations can be performed on polynomials with like terms. *Like terms refers to terms* that have the same variable and exponent. The two following polynomials can be added together by collecting like terms:

$$(x^2 + 3x - 4) + (4x^2 - 7x + 8)$$

The x^2 terms can be added as:
$$x^2 + 4x^2 = 5x^2$$

The x terms can be added as $3x + -7x = -4x$, and the constants can be added as $-4 + 8 = 4$. The following expression is the result of the addition:

$$5x^2 - 4x + 4$$

When subtracting polynomials, the same steps are followed, only subtracting like terms together.

Multiplication of polynomials can also be performed. Given the two polynomials, $(y^3 - 4)$ and $(x^2 + 8x - 7)$, each term in the first polynomial must be multiplied by each term in the second polynomial. The steps to multiply each term in the given example are as follows:

$$(y^3 * x^2) + (y^3 * 8x) + (y^3 * -7) + (-4 * x^2) + (-4 * 8x) + (-4 * -7)$$

Simplifying each multiplied part, yields:

$$x^2 y^3 + 8xy^3 - 7y^3 - 4x^2 - 32x + 28$$

None of the terms can be combined because there are no like terms in the final expression. Any polynomials can be multiplied by each other by following the same set of steps, then collecting like terms at the end.

Modeling Functions

Mathematical functions such as polynomials, rational functions, radical functions, absolute value functions, and piecewise-defined functions can be utilized to approximate, or model, real-life phenomena. For example, a function can be built that approximates the average amount of snowfall on a given day of the year in Chicago. This example could be as simple as a polynomial. Modeling situations using such functions has limitations; the most significant issue is the error that exists between the exact amount and the approximate amount. Typically, the model will not give exact values as outputs. However, choosing the type of function that provides the best fit of the data will reduce this error. Technology can be used to model situations. For example, given a set of data, the data can be inputted into tools such as graphing calculators or spreadsheet software that output a function with a good fit. Some examples of polynomial modeling are linear, quadratic, and cubic regression.

Representing Exponential and Logarithmic Functions

The logarithmic function with base b is denoted $y = \log_b x$. Its base must be greater than 0 and not equal to 1, and the domain is all $x > 0$. The exponential function with base b is denoted $y = b^x$. Exponential and logarithmic functions with base b are inverses. By definition, if $y = \log_b x$, $x = b^y$. Because exponential and logarithmic functions are inverses, the graph of one is obtained by reflecting the other over the line $y = x$. A common base used is e, and in this case $y = e^x$ and its inverse $y = \log_e x$ is commonly written as the natural logarithmic function $y = \ln x$.

Here is the graph of both functions:

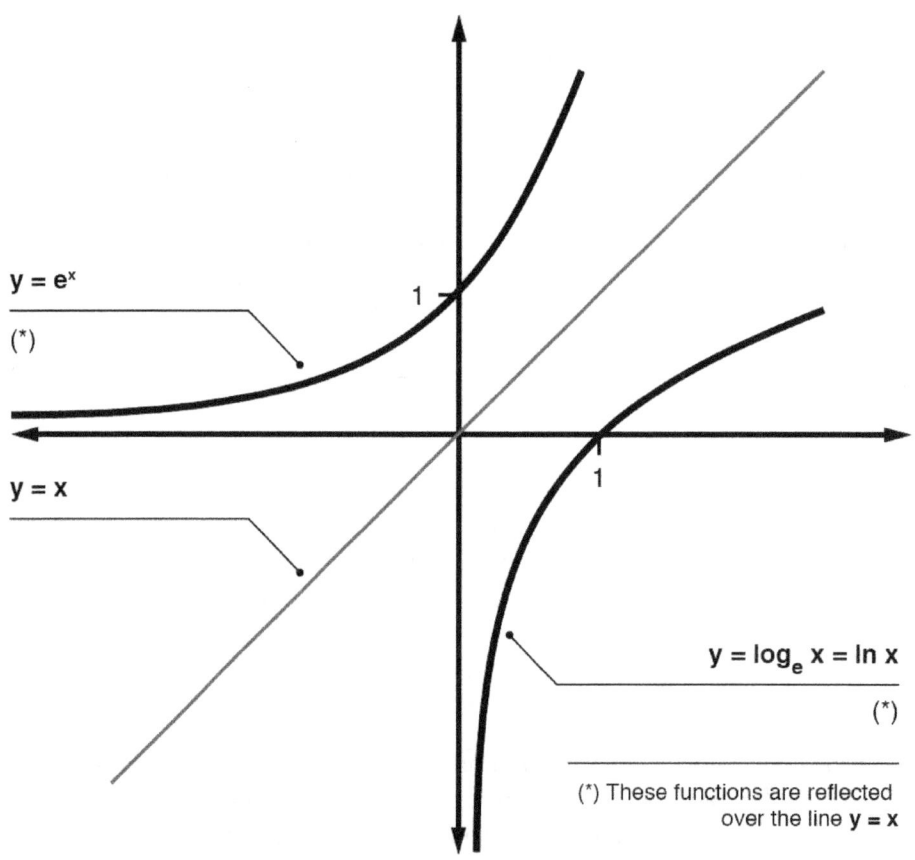

Graphing Functions

The x-intercept of the logarithmic function $y = \log_b x$ with any base is always the ordered pair $(1, 0)$. By the definition of inverse, the point $(0, 1)$ always lies on the exponential function $y = b^x$. This is true because any real number raised to the power of 0 equals 1. Therefore, the exponential function only has a y-intercept. The exponential function also has a horizontal asymptote of the x-axis as x approaches negative infinity. Because the graph is reflected over the line $y = x$, to obtain the graph of the logarithmic function, the asymptote is also reflected. Therefore, the logarithmic function has a one-sided vertical asymptote at $y = 0$. These asymptotes can be seen in the above graphs of $y = e^x$ and $y = \ln x$.

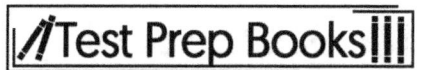

Solving Logarithmic and Exponential Functions

To solve an equation involving exponential expressions, the goal is to isolate the exponential expression. Once this process is completed, the logarithm—with the base equaling the base of the exponent of both sides—needs to be taken to get an expression for the variable. If the base is e, the natural log of both sides needs to be taken.

To solve an equation with logarithms, the given equation needs to be written in exponential form, using the fact that $\log_b y = x$ means $b^x = y$, and then solved for the given variable. Lastly, properties of logarithms can be used to simplify more than one logarithmic expression into one.

Some equations involving exponential and logarithmic functions can be solved algebraically, or analytically. To solve an equation involving exponential functions, the goal is to isolate the exponential expression. Then, the logarithm of both sides is found in order to yield an expression for the variable. Laws of Logarithms will be helpful at this point.

To solve an equation with logarithms, the equation needs to be rewritten in exponential form. The definition that $\log_b x = y$ means $b^y = x$ needs to be used. Then, one needs to solve for the given variable. Properties of logarithms can be used to simplify multiple logarithmic expressions into one.

Other methods can be used to solve equations containing logarithmic and exponential functions. Graphs and graphing calculators can be used to see points of intersection. In a similar manner, tables can be used to find points of intersection. Also, numerical methods can be utilized to find approximate solutions.

Exponential Growth and Decay

Exponential growth and decay are important concepts in modeling real-world phenomena. The growth and decay formula is $A(t) = Pe^{rt}$, where the independent variable t represents temperature, P represents an initial quantity, r represents the rate of increase or decrease, and $A(t)$ represents the amount of the quantity at time t. If $r > 0$, the equation models exponential growth and a common application is population growth. If $r < 0$, the equation models exponential decay and a common application is radioactive decay. Exponential and logarithmic solving techniques are necessary to work with the growth and decay formula.

Logarithmic Scales

A logarithmic scale is a scale of measurement that uses the logarithm of the given units instead of the actual given units. Each tick mark on such a scale is the product of the previous tick mark multiplied by a number. The advantage of using such a scale is that if one is working with large measurements, this technique reduces the scale into manageable quantities that are easier to read. The Richter magnitude scale is the famous logarithmic scale used to measure the intensity of earthquakes, and the decibel scale is commonly used to measure sound level in electronics.

Using Exponential and Logarithmic Functions in Finance Problems

Modeling within finance also involves exponential and logarithmic functions. Compound interest results when the bank pays interest on the original amount of money – the principal – and the interest that has accrued. The compound interest equation is $A(t) = P\left(1 + \frac{r}{n}\right)^{nt}$, where P is the principal, r is the interest rate, n is the number of times per year the interest is compounded, and t is the time in years. The result, $A(t)$, is the final amount after t years. Mathematical problems of this type that are frequently encountered involve receiving all but one of these quantities and solving for the missing

Patterns and Algebra

quantity. The solving process then involves employing properties of logarithmic and exponential functions. Interest can also be compounded continuously. This formula is given as $A(t) = Pe^{rt}$. If $1,000 was compounded continuously at a rate of 2% for 4 years, the result would be:

$$A(4) = 1,000e^{0.02 \cdot 4} = \$1,083$$

Rate of Change Proportional to the Current Quantity

Many quantities grow or decay as fast as exponential functions. Specifically, if such a quantity grows or decays at a rate proportional to the quantity itself, it shows exponential behavior. If a data set is given with such specific characteristics, the initial amount and an amount at a specific time, t, can be plugged into the exponential function $A(t) = Pe^{rt}$ for A and P. Using properties of exponents and logarithms, one can then solve for the rate, r. This solution yields enough information to have the entire model, which can allow for an estimation of the quantity at any time, t, and the ability to solve various problems using that model.

Trigonometric Functions

Trigonometric functions are also used to describe behavior in mathematics. *Trigonometry* is the relationship between the angles and sides of a triangle. *Trigonometric functions* include sine, cosine, tangent, secant, cosecant, and cotangent. The functions are defined through ratios in a right triangle. SOHCAHTOA is a common acronym used to remember these ratios, which are defined by the relationships of the sides and angles relative to the right angle. Sine is opposite over hypotenuse, cosine is adjacent over hypotenuse, and tangent is opposite over adjacent. These ratios are the reciprocals of secant, cosecant, and cotangent, respectively. Angles can be measured in degrees or radians. Here is a diagram of SOHCAHTOA:

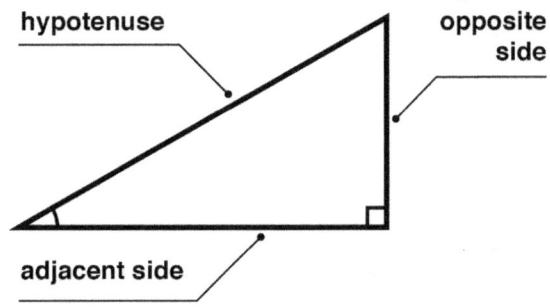

A *radian* is equal to the angle that subtends the arc with the same length as the radius of the circle. It is another unit for measuring angles, in addition to degrees. The unit circle is used to describe different radian measurements and the trigonometric ratios for special angles. The circle has a center at the origin, (0, 0), and a radius of 1, which can be seen below. The points where the circle crosses an axis are labeled.

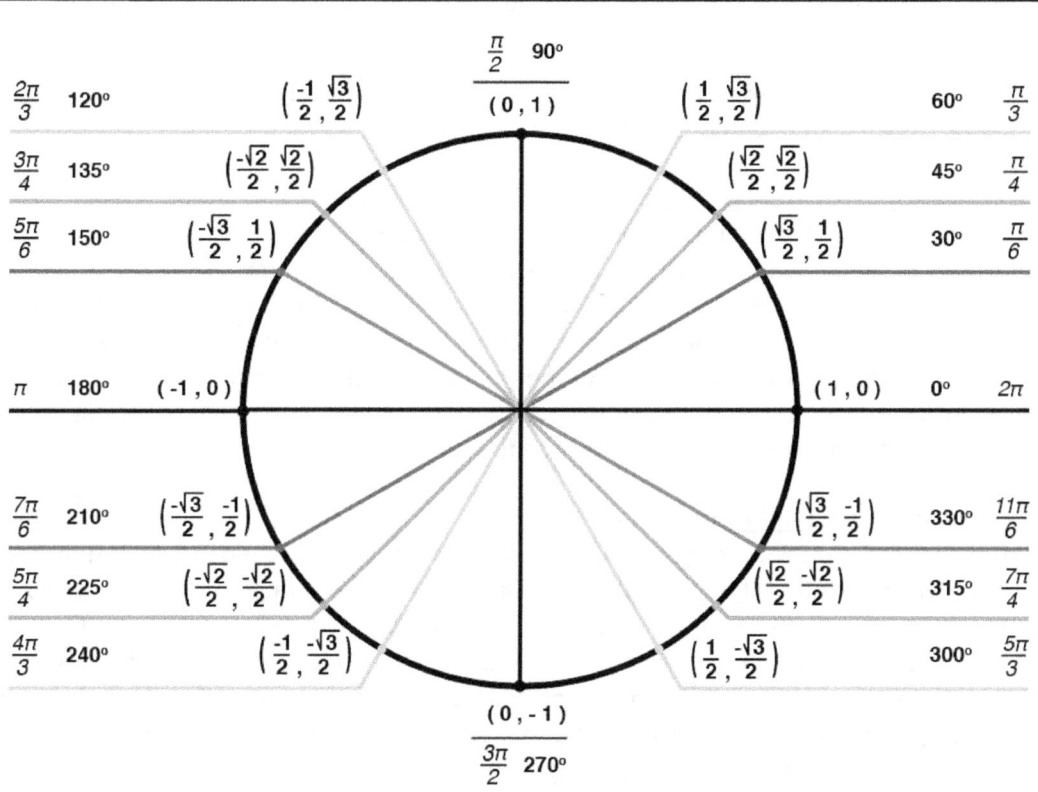

The circle begins on the right-hand side of the x-axis at 0 radians. Since the circumference of a circle is $2\pi r$ and the radius $r = 1$, the circumference is 2π. Zero and 2π are labeled as radian measurements at the point (1, 0) on the graph. The radian measures around the rest of the circle are labeled also in relation to π; π is at the point $(-1, 0)$, also known as 180 degrees. Since these two measurements are equal, $\pi = 180$ degrees written as a ratio can be used to convert degrees to radians or vice versa. For example, to convert 30 degrees to radians, 30 degrees $* \frac{\pi}{180 \text{ degrees}}$ can be used to obtain $\frac{1}{6}\pi$ or $\frac{\pi}{6}$. This radian measure is a point the unit circle

The coordinates labeled on the unit circle are found based on two common right triangles. The ratios formed in the coordinates can be found using these triangles. Each of these triangles can be inserted into the circle to correspond 30, 45, and 60 degrees or $\frac{\pi}{6}, \frac{\pi}{4}$, and $\frac{\pi}{3}$ radians.

Patterns and Algebra

By letting the hypotenuse length of these triangles equal 1, these triangles can be placed inside the unit circle. These coordinates can be used to find the trigonometric ratio for any of the radian measurements on the circle.

Given any (x, y) on the unit circle, $\sin(\theta) = y$, $\cos(\theta) = x$, and $\tan(\theta) = \frac{y}{x}$. The value θ is the angle that spans the arc around the unit circle. For example, finding $\sin\left(\frac{\pi}{4}\right)$ means finding the y-value corresponding to the angle $\theta = \frac{\pi}{4}$. The answer is $\frac{\sqrt{2}}{2}$. Finding $\cos\left(\frac{\pi}{3}\right)$ means finding the x-value corresponding to the angle $\theta = \frac{\pi}{3}$. The answer is $\frac{1}{2}$ or 0.5. Both angles lie in the first quadrant of the unit circle. Trigonometric ratios can also be calculated for radian measures past $\frac{\pi}{2}$, or 90 degrees. Since the same special angles can be moved around the circle, the results only differ with a change in sign. This can be seen at two points labeled in the second and third quadrant.

Representations of Trigonometric Functions

Besides their function form, trigonometric and inverse trigonometric functions can be represented in other various formats. Regardless of the form in which they are given – such as in a table, list of numbers, or graph – it is important to note their periodic tendencies. They all return to the same function values over regular intervals in the domain. Other important concepts to notice in the various formats are range and asymptotes. Many trigonometric functions have a minimum and maximum value, but some have vertical asymptotes at regular intervals, in which the function blows up. All of these properties can be seen in any representation of such functions.

Properties of Trigonometric Functions

Trigonometric functions are periodic. Both sine and cosine have period 2π. For each input angle value, the output value follows around the unit circle. Once it reaches the starting point, it continues around and around the circle. It is true that $\sin(0) = \sin(2\pi) = \sin(4\pi)$, etc., and $\cos(0) = \cos(2\pi) = \cos(4\pi)$. Tangent has period π, and its output values repeat themselves every half of the unit circle. The domain of sine and cosine are all real numbers, and the domain of tangent is all real numbers, except the points where cosine equals zero. It is also true that $\sin(-x) = -\sin x$, $\cos(-x) = \cos(x)$, and $\tan(-x) = -\tan(x)$, so sine and tangent are odd functions, while cosine is an even function. Sine and tangent are symmetric with respect the origin, and cosine is symmetric with respect to the y-axis.

The graph of trigonometric functions can be used to model different situations. General forms are $y = a \sin b(x - h) + k$, and:

$$y = a \cos b (x - h) + k$$

The variable a represents the amplitude, which shows the maximum and minimum value of the function. The b is used to find the period by using the ratio $\frac{2\pi}{b}$, h is the horizontal shift, and k is the vertical shift. The equation $y = \sin(x)$ is shown on the following graph with the thick black line. The stretched graph of $y = 2\sin(x)$ is shown in solid black, and the shrunken graph $y = \frac{1}{2}\sin(x)$ is shown with the dotted line.

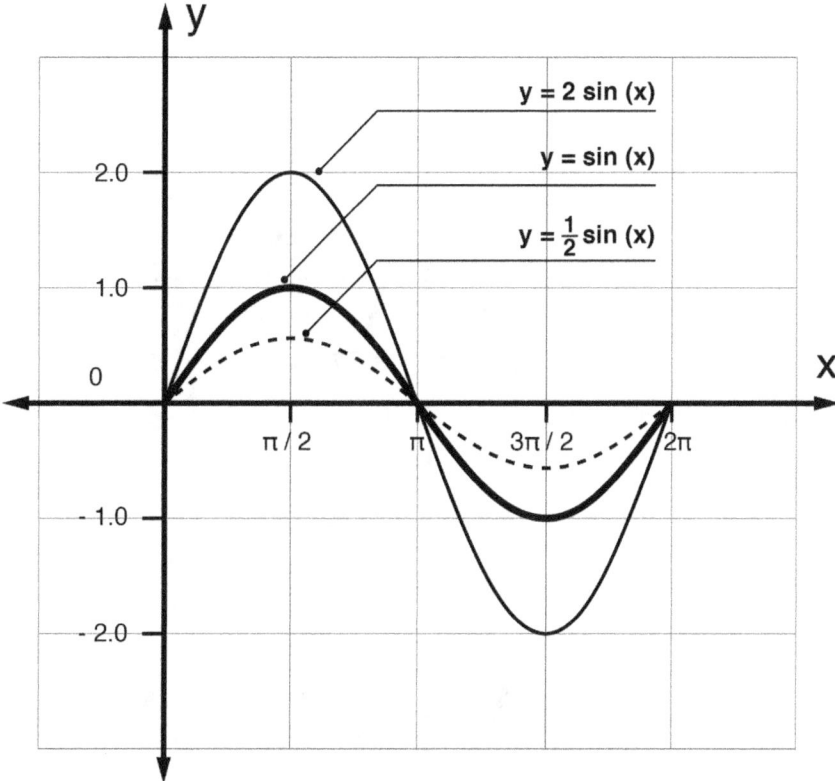

Trigonometric functions are used to find unknown ratios for a given angle measure. The inverse of these trig functions is used to find the unknown angle, given a ratio. For example, the expression $\arcsin\left(\frac{1}{2}\right)$ means finding the value of x for $\sin(x) = \frac{1}{2}$. Since $\sin(\theta) = \frac{y}{1}$ on the unit circle, the angle whose y-value is $\frac{1}{2}$ is $\frac{\pi}{6}$. The inverse of any of the trigonometric functions can be used to find a missing angle measurement. Values not found on the unit circle can be found using the trigonometric functions on the calculator, making sure its mode is set to degrees or radians.

Patterns and Algebra

In order for the inverse to exist, the function must be one-to-one over its domain. There cannot be two input values connected to the same output. For example, the following graphs show the functions $y = \cos(x)$ and $y = \arccos(x)$. In order to have an inverse, the domain of cosine is restricted from 0 to π. Therefore, the range of its inverse function is $[0, \pi]$.

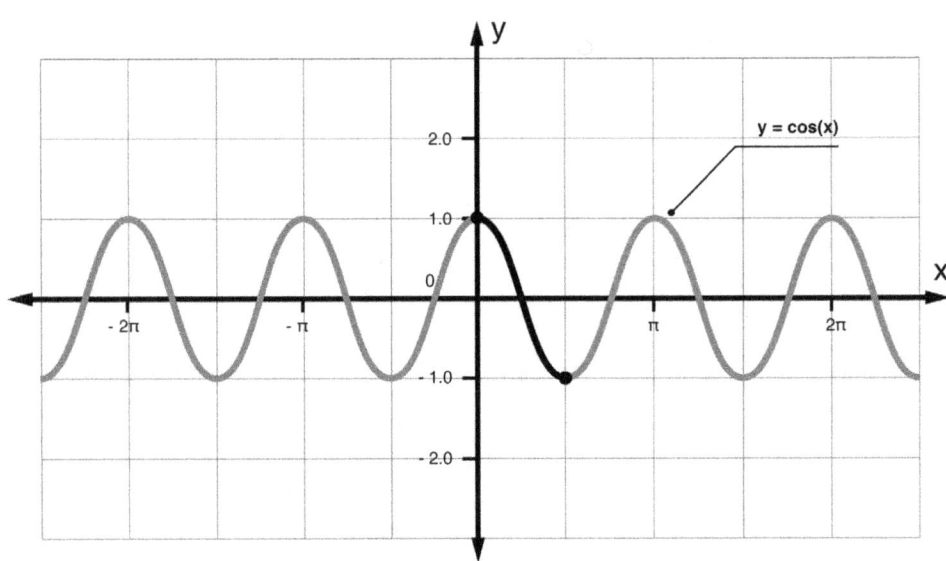

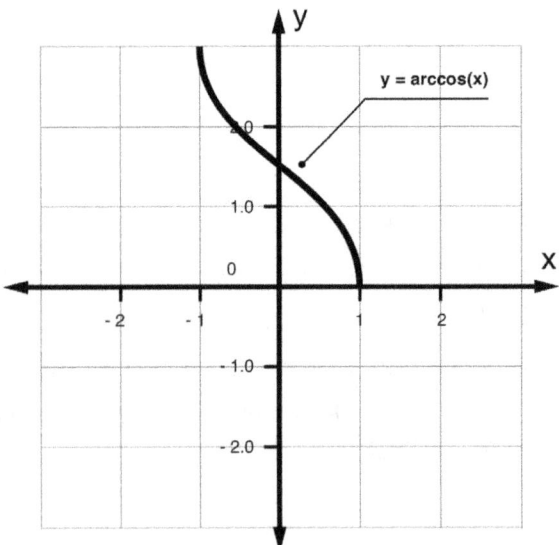

Inverses of trigonometric functions can be used to solve real-world problems. For example, there are many situations where the lengths of a perceived triangle can be found, but the angles are unknown. Consider a problem where the height of a flag (25 feet) and the distance on the ground to the flag is given (42 feet). The unknown, x, is the angle. To find this angle, the equation $\tan x = \frac{42}{25}$ is used. To solve for x, the inverse function can be used to turn the equation into $\tan^{-1}\frac{42}{25} = x$. Using the calculator, in degree mode, the answer is found to be $x = 59.2$ degrees

Trigonometric Identities

From the unit circle, the trigonometric ratios were found for the special right triangle with a hypotenuse of 1.

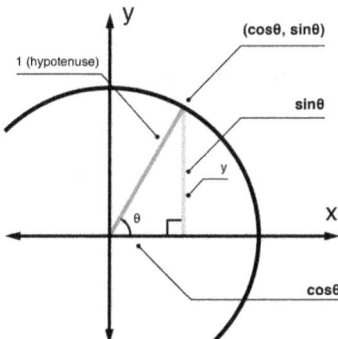

From this triangle, the following Pythagorean identities are formed: $\sin^2\theta + \cos^2\theta = 1$, $\tan^2\theta + 1 = \sec^2\theta$, and $1 + \cot^2\theta = \csc^2\theta$. The second two identities are formed by manipulating the first identity. Since identities are statements that are true for any value of the variable, then they may be used to manipulate equations. For example, a problem may ask for simplification of the expression $\cos^2 x + \cos^2 x \tan^2 x$. Using the fact that $\tan(x) = \frac{\sin x}{\cos x}$, $\frac{\sin^2 x}{\cos^2 x}$ can then be substituted in for $\tan^2 x$, making the expression:

$$\cos^2 x + \cos^2 x \frac{\sin^2 x}{\cos^2 x}$$

Then the two $\cos^2 x$ terms on top and bottom cancel each other out, simplifying the expression to $\cos^2 x + \sin^2 x$. By the first Pythagorean identity stated above, the expression can be turned into:

$$\cos^2 x + \sin^2 x = 1$$

Patterns and Algebra

Another set of trigonometric identities are the double-angle formulas:

$$\sin 2\alpha = 2 \sin \alpha \, \cos \alpha$$

$$\cos 2\alpha = \begin{cases} \cos^2\alpha - \sin^2\alpha \\ 2\cos^2\alpha - 1 \\ 1 - 2\sin^2\alpha \end{cases}$$

Using these formulas, the following identity can be proved:

$$\sin 2x = \frac{2 \tan x}{1 + \tan^2 x}$$

By using one of the Pythagorean identities, the denominator can be rewritten as:

$$1 + \tan^2 x = \sec^2 x$$

By knowing the reciprocals of the trigonometric identities, the secant term can be rewritten to form the equation:

$$\sin 2x = \frac{2 \tan x}{1} * \cos^2 x$$

Replacing $\tan(x)$, the equation becomes $\sin 2x = \frac{2 \sin x}{\cos x} * \cos^2 x$, where the $\cos x$ can cancel out. The new equation is:

$$\sin 2x = 2 \sin x * \cos x$$

This final equation is one of the double-angle formulas.

Other trigonometric identities such as half-angle formulas, sum and difference formulas, and difference of angles formulas can be used to prove and rewrite trigonometric equations. Depending on the given equation or expression, the correct identities need to be chosen to write equivalent statements.

The graph of sine is equal to the graph of cosine, shifted $\frac{\pi}{2}$ units. Therefore, the function $y = \sin x$ is equal to:

$$y = \cos\left(x - \frac{\pi}{2}\right)$$

Within functions, adding a constant to the independent variable shifts the graph either left or right. By shifting the cosine graph, the curve lies on top of the sine function. By transforming the function, the two equations give the same output for any given input.

Solving Trigonometric Functions

Solving trigonometric functions can be done with a knowledge of the unit circle and the trigonometric identities. It requires the use of opposite operations combined with trigonometric ratios for special triangles. For example, the problem may require solving the equation $2\cos^2 x - \sqrt{3}\cos x = 0$ for the values of x between 0 and 180 degrees. The first step is to factor out the $\cos x$ term, resulting in:

$$\cos x\,(2\cos x - \sqrt{3}) = 0$$

By the factoring method of solving, each factor can be set equal to zero: $\cos x = 0$ and:

$$(2\cos x - \sqrt{3}) = 0$$

The second equation can be solved to yield the following equation: $\cos x = \frac{\sqrt{3}}{2}$. Now that the value of x is found, the trigonometric ratios can be used to find the solutions of $x = 30$ and 90 degrees.

Solving trigonometric functions requires the use of algebra to isolate the variable and a knowledge of trigonometric ratios to find the value of the variable. The unit circle can be used to find answers for special triangles. Beyond those triangles, a calculator can be used to solve for variables within the trigonometric functions.

Using Graphing Calculators to Solve Trigonometric Problems

In addition to algebraic techniques, problems involving trigonometric functions can be solved using graphing calculators. For example, given an equation, both sides of the equals sign first need to be graphed as separate equations in the same window on the calculator. The point(s) of intersection are then found by zooming into an appropriate window. The points of intersection are the solutions. For example, consider $\cos x = \frac{1}{2}$. Solving this equation involves graphing both $y = \cos x$ and $y = \frac{1}{2}$ in the same window. If the calculator is set in Radians mode, the screen zoomed in from $[0, 2\pi]$ on the x-axis would look like:

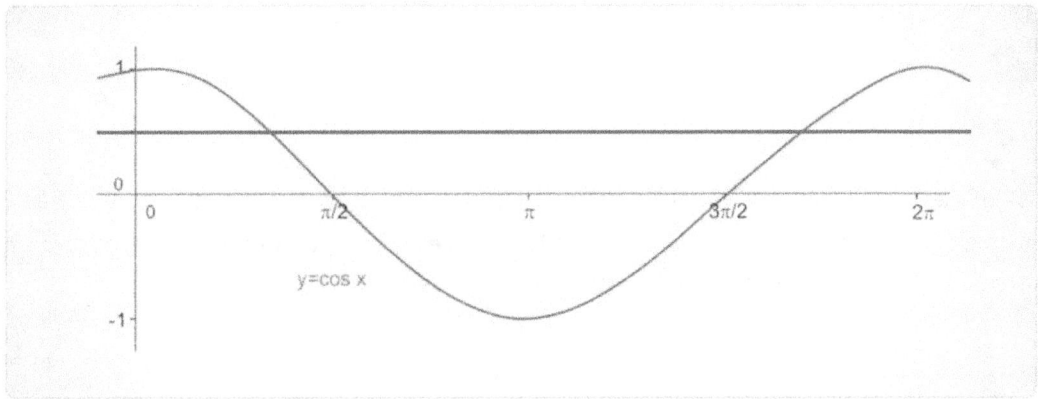

The trace function on the calculator allows the user to zoom into the point of intersection to obtain the two solutions from $[0, 2\pi]$. The periodic nature of the function must then be taken into consideration to obtain the entire solution set, which contains an infinite number of solutions.

Patterns and Algebra

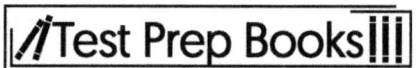

Using Integrals in Calculations

In calculus, the area problem involves finding the area under a positive function $y = f(x)$ from $x = a$ to $x = b$, above the x-axis. Such a region Ω is shown here:

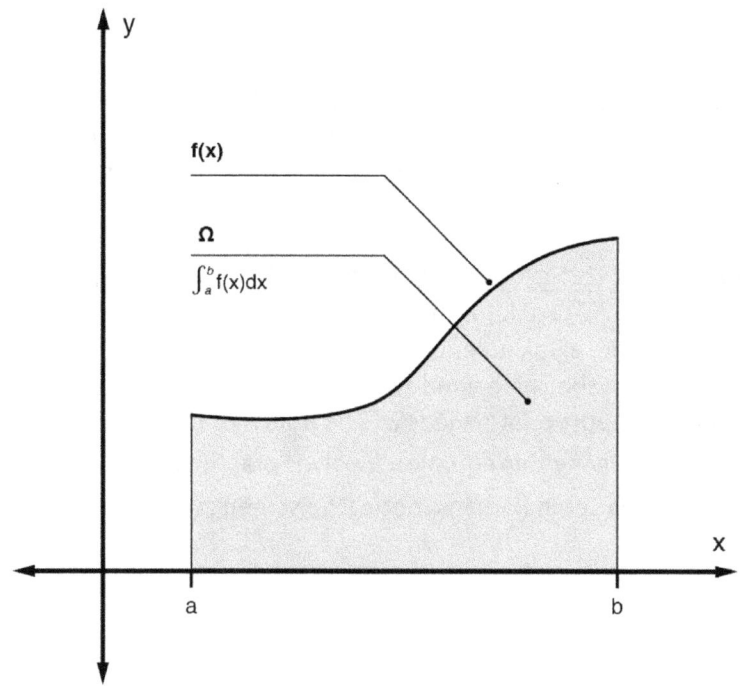

The Definite Integral

The area is defined as the definite integral of $y = f(x)$ from $x = a$ to $x = b$ and is denoted as $\int_a^b f(x)dx$. In a similar manner, the area between two curves $y = f(x)$ and $y = g(x)$ from $x = a$ to $x = b$ where $f(x) \geq g(x)$ over that same interval is given as:

$$\int_a^b (f(x) - g(x))dx.$$

Arc length can also be calculated using an integral. Consider the same function $y = f(x)$ from $x = a$ to $x = b$. The length of the curve over that interval, also known as arc length, is defined as:

$$L = \int_a^b \sqrt{1 + \left(\frac{dy}{dx}\right)^2}\, dx$$

All three of these integral definitions are based on proofs based on limits.

Limits of Functions

The *limit of a function* can be described as the output that is approached as the input approaches a certain value. Written in function notation, the limit of $f(x)$ as x approaches a is $\lim_{x \to a} f(x) = B$. As x draws near to some value a, represented by $x \to a$, then $f(x)$ approaches some number B. In the graph of the function $f(x) = \frac{x+2}{x+2}$, the line is continuous except where $x = -2$. Because $x = -2$ yields an undefined output and a hole in the graph, the function does not exist at this value. The limit, however, does exist. As the value $x = -2$ is approached from the left side, the output is getting very close to 1. From the right side, as the x-value approaches -2, the output gets close to 1 also. Since the function value from both sides approaches 1, then:

$$\lim_{x \to -2} \frac{x+2}{x+2} = 1$$

One special type of function, the *step function* $f(x) = [x]$, can be used to define right and left-hand limits. The graph is shown below. The left-hand limit as x approaches 1 is $\lim_{x \to 1^-} [x]$. From the graph, as x approaches 1 from the left side, the function approaches 0. For the right-hand limit, the expression is $\lim_{x \to 1^+} [x]$. The value for this limit is one. Since the function does not have the same limit for the left and right side, then the limit does not exist at $x = 1$. From that same reasoning, the limit does not exist for any integer for this function.

Below is an example:

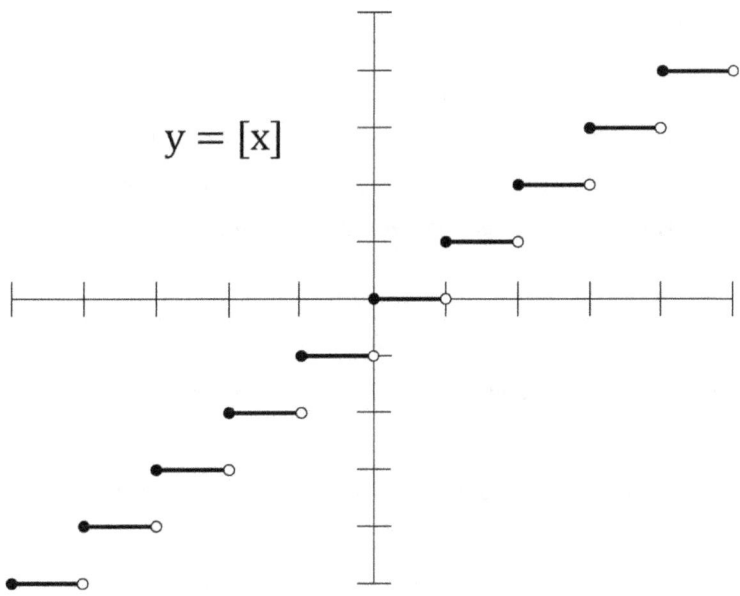

Sometimes a function approaches infinity as it draws near to a certain x-value. For example, the following graph shows the function:

$$f(x) = \frac{2x}{x-3}$$

There is an asymptote at $x = 3$. The limit as x approaches 3, $\lim_{x \to 3} \frac{2x}{x-3}$, does not exist. The right and left-hand side limits at 3 do not approach the same output value. One approaches positive infinity, and the

Patterns and Algebra

other approaches negative infinity. Infinite limits do not satisfy the definition of a limit. The limit of the function as x approaches a number must be equal to a finite value.

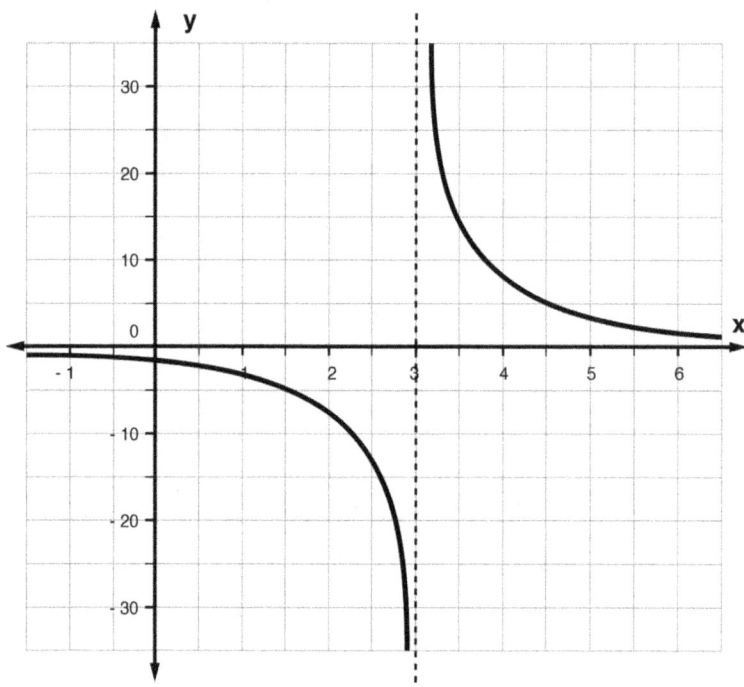

Horizontal asymptotes can be found using limits. Horizontal asymptotes are limits as x approaches either ∞ or $-\infty$. For example, to find $\lim_{x \to \infty} \frac{2x}{x-3}$, the graph can be used to see the value of the function as x grows larger and larger. For this example, the limit is 2, so it has a horizontal asymptote of $y = 2$. In considering $\lim_{x \to -\infty} \frac{2x}{x-3} = 2$, the limits can also be seen on a graphing calculator by plotting the equation:

$$y = \frac{2x}{x-3}$$

Then the table can be brought up. By scrolling up and down, the limit can be found as x approaches any value.

Limit laws exist that assist in finding limits of functions. These properties include multiplying by a constant, $\lim kf(x) = k \lim f(x)$, and the addition property,

$$\lim[f(x) + g(x)] = \lim f(x) + \lim g(x)$$

Two other properties are the multiplication property, $\lim f(x)g(x) = (\lim f(x))(\lim g(x))$, and the division property,

$$\lim \frac{f(x)}{g(x)} = \frac{\lim f(x)}{\lim g(x)} \ (if \lim g(x) \neq 0)$$

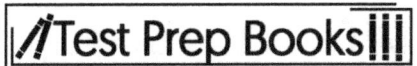

Patterns and Algebra

These properties are helpful in finding limits of polynomial functions algebraically. In $\lim_{x \to 2} 4x^2 - 3x + 8$, the constant and multiplication properties can be used together, and the problem can be rewritten as:

$$4\lim_{x \to 2} x^2 - \lim_{x \to 2} 3x + \lim_{x \to 2} 8$$

Since this is a continuous function, direct substitution can be used. The value of 2 is substituted in for x and evaluated as $4(2^2) - 3(2) + 8$, which yields a limit of 18. These properties allow functions to be rewritten so that limits can be calculated.

Continuity

To find if a function is continuous, the definition consists of three steps. These three steps include finding $f(a)$, finding $\lim_{x \to a} f(x)$, and finding $\lim_{x \to a} f(x) = f(a)$. If the limit of a function equals the function value at that point, then the function is continuous at $x = a$. For example, the function $f(x) = \frac{1}{x}$ is continuous everywhere except $x = 0$. $f(0) = \frac{1}{0}$ is undefined; therefore, the function is discontinuous at 0. Secondly, to determine if the function $f(x) = \frac{1}{x-1}$ is continuous at 2, its function value must equal its limit at 2. First,

$$f(2) = \frac{1}{2-1} = 1$$

Then the limit can be found by direct substitution:

$$\lim_{x \to 2} \frac{1}{x-1} = 1$$

Since these two values are equal, then the function is continuous at $x = 2$.

Differentiability and continuity are related in that if the derivative can be found at $x = c$, then the function is continuous at $x = c$. If the slope of the tangent line can be found at a certain point, then there is no hole or jump in the graph at that point. Some functions, however, can be continuous while not differentiable at a given point. An example is the graph of the function $f(x) = |x|$. At the origin, the derivative does not exist, but the function is still continuous. Points where a function is discontinuous are where a vertical tangent exists and where there is a cusp or corner at a given x-value.

Derivatives

The derivative of a function is found using the limit of the difference quotient:

$$\lim_{\Delta x \to 0} \frac{f(x + \Delta x) - f(x)}{\Delta x}$$

This finds the slope of the tangent line of the given function at a given point. It is the slope, $\frac{\Delta y}{\Delta x}$, as $\Delta x \to 0$. The derivative can be denoted in many ways, such as $f'(x)$, y', or $\frac{dy}{dx}$.

Patterns and Algebra

The following graph plots a function in black. The gray line represents a secant line, formed between two chosen points on the graph. The slope of this line can be found using rise over run. As these two points get closer to zero, meaning Δx approaches 0, the tangent line is found. The slope of the tangent line is equal to the limit of the slopes of the secant lines as $\Delta x \to 0$.

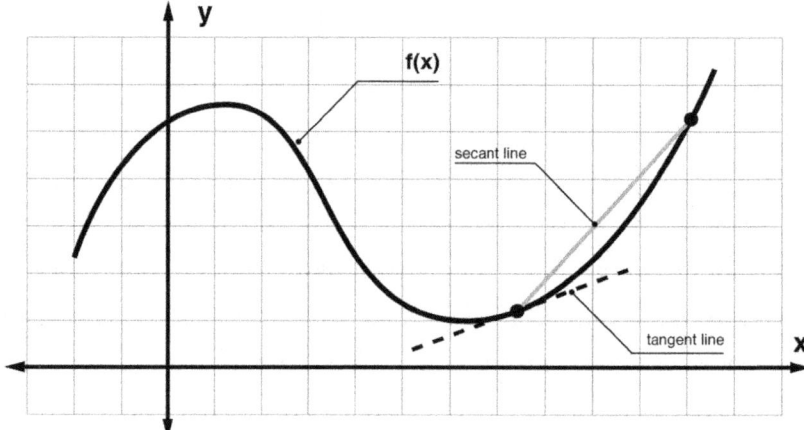

The derivative of a function can be found algebraically using the limit definition. Here is the process for finding the derivative of $f(x) = x^2 - 2$:

$$f'(x) = \lim_{h \to 0} \frac{f(x+h) - f(x)}{h}$$

$$= \lim_{h \to 0} \frac{(x+h)^2 - 2 - (x^2 - 2)}{h}$$

$$= \lim_{h \to 0} \frac{(x+h)(x+h) - 2 - x^2 + 2}{h}$$

$$= \lim_{h \to 0} \frac{x^2 + xh + xh + h^2 - 2 - x^2 + 2}{h}$$

$$= \lim_{h \to 0} \frac{x^2 + 2xh + h^2 - 2 - x^2 + 2}{h}$$

$$= \lim_{h \to 0} \frac{2xh + h^2}{h}$$

$$= \lim_{h \to 0} \frac{h(2x + h)}{h} = \lim_{h \to 0} 2x + h = 2x + 0 = 2x$$

Once the derivative function is found, it can be evaluated at any point by substituting that value in for x. Therefore, in this example, $f'(2)=4$.

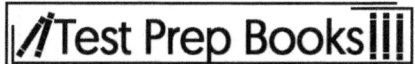

Behavior of a Function

Derivatives can be used to find the behavior of different functions such as the extrema, concavity, and symmetry. Given a function $f(x) = 3x^2$, the first derivative is $f'(x) = 6x$. This equation describes the slope of the line. Setting the derivative equal to zero means finding where the slope is zero, and these are potential points in which the function has extreme values. If the first derivative is positive over an interval, the function is increasing over that interval. If the first derivative is negative over an interval, the function is decreasing over that interval.

Therefore, if the derivative is equal to zero at a point and the function changes from increasing to decreasing, then the function has a minimum at that point. If the function changes from decreasing to increasing at that point, it is a maximum. The second derivative can be used to define concavity. If it is positive over an interval, the graph resembles a U and is concave up over that interval. If the second derivative is negative, the graph is concave down. For this equation, solving $f'(x) = 6x = 0$ gets $x = 0$, $f(0) = 0$. Also, the second derivative is 6, which is positive. The graph is concave up and, therefore, has a minimum value at (0,0).

Differentiation and Integration Techniques

Finding the derivative of a function can be done using the definition as described above, but rules proved via the different quotient can also be used. A few are listed below. These rules apply for functions that take the form inside the parentheses. For example, the function $f(x) = 3x^4$ would use the Power Rule and Constant Multiple Rule. To find the derivative, the exponent is brought down to be multiplied by the coefficient, and the new exponent is one less than the original. As an equation, the derivative is $f'(x) = 12x^3$:

$$\frac{d}{dx}(a^b) = 0$$

$$\frac{d}{dx}(x^n) = nx^{n-1}$$

$$\frac{d}{dx}(a^x) = a^x \ln a$$

$$\frac{d}{dx}(x^x) = x^x(1 = \ln x)$$

In relation to real-life problems, the position of a ball that is thrown into the area may be given by the equation:

$$p = 7 + 25t - 16t^2$$

The position, p, can be found for any time, t, after the ball is thrown. To find the initial position, $t = 0$ can be substituted into the equation to find p. That position would be 7ft above the ground, which is equal to the constant at the end of the equation.

Finding the derivative of the function would use the Power Rule. The derivative is:

$$p' = 25 - 32t$$

The derivative of a position function represents the velocity function. To find the initial velocity, the time $t = 0$ can be substituted into the equation. The initial velocity is found to be 25ft/s – the same as the coefficient of t in the position equation. Taking the derivative of the velocity equation yields the acceleration equation $p'' = -32$. This value is the acceleration at which a ball is pulled by gravity to the ground in feet per second squared.

Since integration is the inverse operation of finding the derivative, the integral is found by going backwards from the derivative. In relation to the ball problem, an acceleration function can be integrated to find the velocity function. That function can then be integrated to find the position function. From velocity, integration finds the position function $p = -16t^2 + 25t + c$, where c is an unknown constant. More information would need to be given in the original problem to integrate and find the value of c.

Foundational Theorems of Calculus

Per the fundamental theorem of calculus, on a closed interval [a, b], the following represents the definite integral: $f(x)$:

$$\int_a^b f(x)dx = F(b) - F(a)$$

$F(x)$ represents the antiderivative of the function $f(x)$. Other theorems allow constants to be moved to the front of the integral, negatives to be moved to the outside of the integral, and integrals to be split into two parts that make up a whole. An example of using these theorems can be seen in the following problem:

$$\int_{-1}^{3} (4x^3 - 2x)dx = (108 - 6) - (-4 + 2) = 104$$

The antiderivative of $4x^3 - 2x$ is $x^4 - x^2$.

Within the fundamental theorem of calculus, the antiderivative $F(x)$ exists. It is true that $F'(x) = f(x)$. Therefore, it is important to know how the graph of a function and a derivative relate. Because the derivative function represents the slope of the tangent of a function—where a function is horizontal—the derivative function has zeros. On intervals where the function is decreasing, the derivative function lies below the x-axis, and on intervals where the function is increasing, the derivative function lies above the y-axis.

Slope is defined in algebra to be a rate of change; therefore, the derivative function is a rate of change. The definite integral in the fundamental theorem of calculus can also be used to represent a rate of change. If one were to calculate the definite integral of a function $f(x)$ over the interval $[a, b]$ as $F(b) - F(a)$, where $F'(x) = f(x)$, the result is the net rate of change of $F(x)$ over the same interval.

The average value of a function can be found by the following integral:

$$\frac{1}{b-a} \int_a^b f(x)dx$$

The integral finds the area of the region bounded by the function and the x-axis, while the fraction divides the area to find the average value of the integral. An example of this is shown in the graph below. The function $f(x)$ is the black line. The light gray shading represents the area under the curve, while the rectangle drawn on top with added darker shading represents the same amount of area as the region under the graph of the given function over the interval of a to b. This rectangle has the base [a, b] and height f(c).

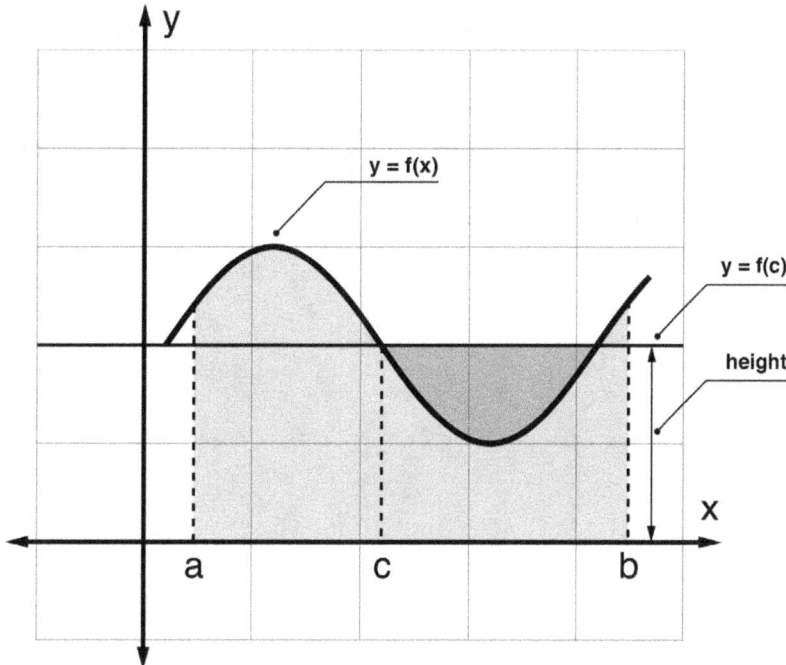

The *Mean Value Theorem* states that if f is a continuous function on interval [a, b], and f' is differentiable on (a, b), then there exists at least one number, c, in which the derivative at that point equals the slope of the secant line connecting the endpoints of the interval. This number can be found by the equation:

$$f'(c) = \frac{f(b) - f(a)}{b - a}$$

Differentiation and Integration in Real-World Problems

Integration can be described as an accumulation process because it takes many small areas and adds them up to find a total area over an interval. That process can be used in many real-world problems that deal with volume, area, and distance. Differentiation can also be used in real-world problems. For example, a company may want to maximize the size of the boxes it uses to ship its products. The boxes are to be cut out of a piece of cardboard that measures 8 inches long and 5 inches tall. Since squares must be cut out of the corners to make the boxes, the size of the square needs to be altered to maximize the box volume. The volume of a box can be found using the formula $V = l * w * h$. For length, the expression is $(8 - 2x)$ because the initial length is 8, and length x is taken from both sides of the original length to form the box. The width expression is $(5 - 2x)$. The height of the box is x. Therefore, the volume function is:

$$V = (8 - 2x)(5 - 2x)x = 40x - 26x^2 + 4x^3$$

Taking the derivative, $V' = 40 - 52x + 12x^2$, and setting it equal to zero will find the potential maximum and minimum points. If a maximum is found, the x-value represents the amount that needs to be cut from the corners of the box to maximize the volume. To find the volume at its max, the x-value can be substituted into the original equation.

Using Technology to Solve Calculus Problems

Technology can be of assistance in differential calculus. A graphing calculator or any other type of graphing software can be helpful when comparing a graph of a function versus its derivative or a graph of a function versus its antiderivative. Spreadsheet software, such as Microsoft Excel®, can also be of some help in problems involving numerical calculations and analysis. Finally, mathematical software, such as Mathematica or Wolfram Alpha, can actually perform symbolic calculations, such as finding derivatives and integrals based on explicit definitions of functions.

Practice Quiz

1. For which real numbers x is $-3x^2 + x - 8 > 0$?
   a. All real numbers x
   b. $-2\sqrt{\frac{2}{3}} < x < 2\sqrt{\frac{2}{3}}$
   c. $1 - 2\sqrt{\frac{2}{3}} < x < 1 + 2\sqrt{\frac{2}{3}}$
   d. For no real numbers x

2. The expression $\frac{x-4}{x^2-6x+8}$ is undefined for what value(s) of x?
   a. 4 and 2
   b. -4 and -2
   c. 2
   d. 4

3. If $3x = 6y = -2z = 24$, then what does $4xy + z$ equal?
   a. 116
   b. 130
   c. 84
   d. 108

4. What is the solution to the following system of equations?
$$\begin{cases} x^2 + y = 4 \\ 2x + y = 1 \end{cases}$$

   a. $(-1, 3)$
   b. $(-1, 3), (3, -5)$
   c. $(3, -5)$
   d. $(-1, -5)$

5. Which graph will be a line parallel to the graph of $y = 3x - 2$?
   a. $6x - 2y = -2$
   b. $4x - y = -4$
   c. $3y = x - 2$
   d. $2x - 2y = 2$

See answers on the next page.

Answer Explanations

1. D: Because the coefficient of x^2 is negative, this function has a graph that is a parabola that opens downward. Therefore, it will be greater than 0 between its real roots, if it has any. Checking the discriminant, the result is:

$$1^2 - 4(-3)(-8) = 1 - 96 = -95$$

Since the discriminant is negative, this equation has no real solutions. Since this has no real roots, it must be always positive or always negative. Its graph opens downward, so it has at least some negative values. That means it is always negative. Thus, it is greater than zero for no real numbers.

2. A: The expression in the denominator can be factored into the two binomials $(x-4)(x-2)$. Once the expression is rewritten as $\frac{x-4}{(x-4)(x-2)}$, we can see that the values of $x = 4$ and $x = 2$ result in a denominator with a value of 0. Since 0 cannot be in the denominator of a fraction, the expression is undefined at the values of $x = 2, 4$.

3. A: First solve for x, y, and z. So, $3x = 24$, $x = 8$, $6y = 24$, $y = 4$, and $-2z = 24$, $z = -12$. This means the expression $4xy + z$ would be $4(8)(4) + (-12)$, which equals 116.

4. B: The system can be solved using substitution. Solve the second equation for y, resulting in $y = 1 - 2x$. Plugging this into the first equation results in the quadratic equation:

$$x^2 - 2x + 1 = 4$$

In standard form, this equation is equivalent to $x^2 - 2x - 3 = 0$ and in factored form is $(x-3)(x+1) = 0$. Its solutions are $x = 3$ and $x = -1$. Plugging these values into the second equation results in $y = -5$ and $y = 3$, respectively. Therefore, the solutions are the ordered pairs $(-1, 3)$ and $(3, -5)$.

5. A: Parallel lines have the same slope. The slope of the given equation is 3. The slope of Choice C can be seen to be $\frac{1}{3}$ by dividing both sides by 3. The other choices are in standard form $Ax + By = C$, for which the slope is given by $\frac{-A}{B}$. For Choice A, the equation can be written as $6x - 2y = -2$. Therefore, the slope is:

$$\frac{-A}{B} = \frac{-6}{-2} = 3$$

This is the same as the given equation. The slope of Choice B is:

$$\frac{-A}{B} = \frac{-4}{-1} = 4$$

The slope of Choice B is 4. The slope of Choice D is:

$$\frac{-A}{B} = \frac{-2}{-2} = 1$$

Geometry and Measurement

Solving Problems by Quantitative Reasoning

Dimensional analysis is the process of converting between different units using equivalent measurement statements. For instance, running 5 kilometers is approximately the same as running 3.1 miles. This conversion can be found by knowing that 1 kilometer is equal to approximately 0.62 miles.

When setting up the dimensional analysis calculations, the original units need to be opposite one another in each of the two fractions: one in the original amount (essentially in the numerator) and one in the denominator of the conversion factor. This enables them to cancel after multiplying, leaving the converted result.

Calculations involving formulas, such as determining volume and area, are a common situation in which units need to be interpreted and used. However, graphs can also carry meaning through units. The graph below is an example. It represents a graph of the position of an object over time. The y-axis represents the position or the number of meters the object is from the starting point at time s, in seconds. Interpreting this graph, the origin shows that at time zero seconds, the object is zero meters away from the starting point. As the time increases to one second, the position increases to five meters away. This trend continues until 6 seconds, where the object is 30 meters away from the starting position. After this point in time—since the graph remains horizontal from 6 to 10 seconds—the object must have stopped moving.

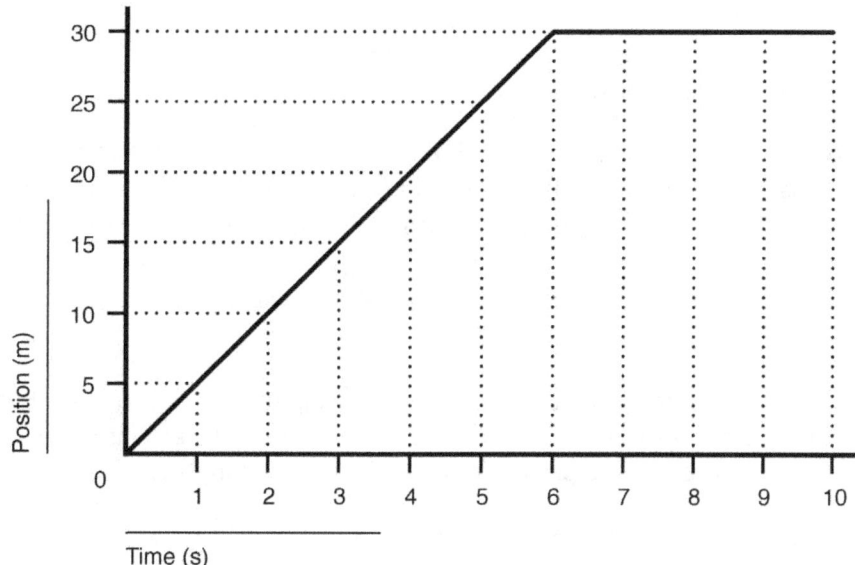

When solving problems with units, it's important to consider the reasonableness of the answer. If conversions are used, it's helpful to have an estimated value to compare the final answer to. This way, if the final answer is too distant from the estimate, it will be obvious that a mistake was made.

Geometry and Measurement

Perimeter and Area

Perimeter is the measurement of a distance around something or the sum of all sides of a polygon. Think of perimeter as the length of the boundary, like a fence. In contrast, *area* is the space occupied by a defined enclosure, like a field enclosed by a fence.

When thinking about perimeter, think about walking around the outside of something. When thinking about area, think about the amount of space or *surface area* something takes up.

Squares

The perimeter of a square is measured by adding together all of the sides. Since a square has four equal sides, its perimeter can be calculated by multiplying the length of one side by 4. Thus, the formula is $P = 4 \times s$, where s equals one side. For example, the following square has side lengths of 5 meters:

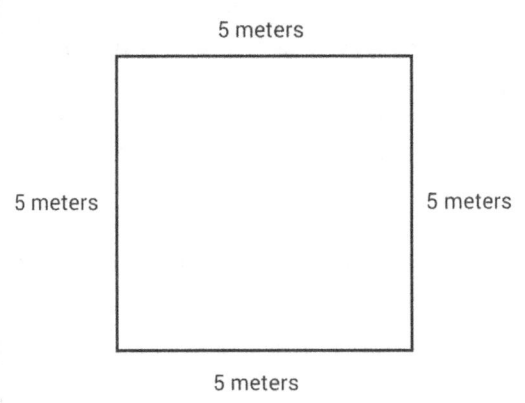

The perimeter is 20 meters because 4 times 5 is 20.

The area of a square is the length of a side squared. For example, if a side of a square is 7 centimeters, then the area is 49 square centimeters. The formula for this example is $A = s^2 = 7^2 = 49$ square centimeters. An example is if the rectangle has a length of 6 inches and a width of 7 inches, then the area is 42 square inches:

$$A = lw = 6(7) = 42 \text{ square inches}$$

Rectangles

Like a square, a rectangle's perimeter is measured by adding together all of the sides. But as the sides are unequal, the formula is different. A rectangle has equal values for its lengths (long sides) and equal values for its widths (short sides), so the perimeter formula for a rectangle is:

$$P = l + l + w + w = 2l + 2w$$

l equals length
w equals width

The area is found by multiplying the length by the width, so the formula is $A = l \times w$.

For example, if the length of a rectangle is 10 inches and the width 8 inches, then the perimeter is 36 inches because:

$$P = 2l + 2w = 2(10) + 2(8) = 20 + 16 = 36 \text{ inches}$$

Triangles

A triangle's perimeter is measured by adding together the three sides, so the formula is $P = a + b + c$, where $a, b,$ and c are the values of the three sides. The area is the product of one-half the base and height so the formula is:

$$A = \frac{1}{2} \times b \times h$$

It can be simplified to:

$$A = \frac{bh}{2}$$

The base is the bottom of the triangle, and the height is the distance from the base to the peak. If a problem asks to calculate the area of a triangle, it will provide the base and height.

For example, if the base of the triangle is 2 feet and the height 4 feet, then the area is 4 square feet. The following equation shows the formula used to calculate the area of the triangle:

$$A = \frac{1}{2}bh = \frac{1}{2}(2)(4) = 4 \text{ square feet}$$

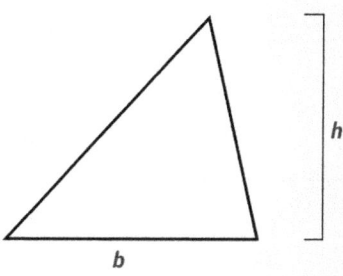

Circles

A circle's perimeter—also known as its circumference—is measured by multiplying the diameter by π.

Diameter is the straight line measured from a point on one side of the circle to a point directly across on the opposite side of the circle.

π is referred to as pi and is equal to 3.14 (with rounding).

So the formula is $\pi \times d$.

Geometry and Measurement

This is sometimes expressed by the formula $C = 2 \times \pi \times r$, where r is the radius of the circle. These formulas are equivalent, as the radius equals half of the diameter.

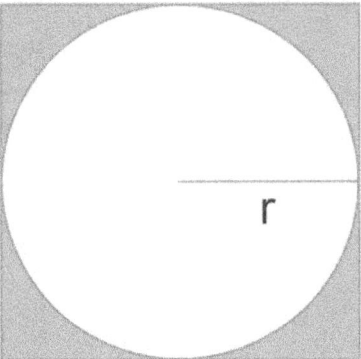

The area of a circle is calculated through the formula $A = \pi \times r^2$. The test will indicate either to leave the answer with π attached or to calculate to the nearest decimal place, which means multiplying by 3.14 for π.

Parallelograms
Similar to triangles, the height of the parallelogram is measured from one base to the other at a 90° angle (or perpendicular).

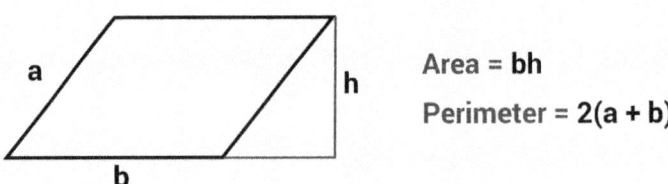

Trapezoid
The area of a trapezoid can be calculated using the formula: $A = \frac{1}{2} \times h(b_1 + b_2)$, where h is the height and b_1 and b_2 are the parallel bases of the trapezoid.

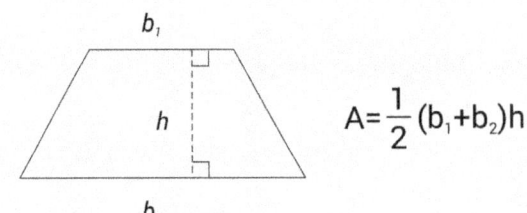

Regular Polygon
The area of a regular polygon can be determined by using its perimeter and the length of the apothem. The apothem is a line from the center of the regular polygon to any of its sides at a right angle. (Note

that the perimeter of a regular polygon can be determined given the length of only one side.) The formula for the area (A) of a regular polygon is $A = \frac{1}{2} \times a \times P$, where a is the length of the apothem, and P is the perimeter of the figure. Consider the following regular pentagon:

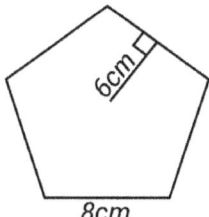

To find the area, the perimeter (P) is calculated first:

$$8cm \times 5 \rightarrow P = 40cm$$

Then the perimeter and the apothem are used to find the area (A):

$$A = \frac{1}{2} \times a \times P \rightarrow A = \frac{1}{2} \times (6cm) \times (40cm) \rightarrow A = 120cm^2$$

Note that the unit is $cm^2 \rightarrow cm \times cm = cm^2$.

Irregular Shapes

The perimeter of an irregular polygon is found by adding the lengths of all of the sides. In cases where all of the sides are given, this will be very straightforward, as it will simply involve finding the sum of the provided lengths. Other times, a side length may be missing and must be determined before the perimeter can be calculated. Consider the example below:

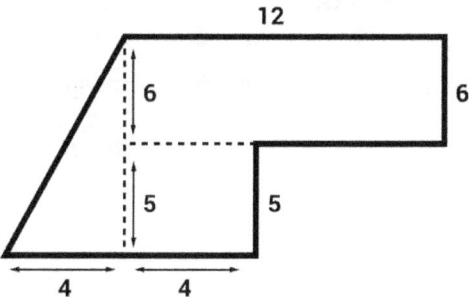

All of the side lengths are provided except for the angled side on the left. Test takers should notice that this is the hypotenuse of a right triangle. The other two sides of the triangle are provided (the base is 4 and the height is 6 + 5 = 11). The Pythagorean Theorem can be used to find the length of the hypotenuse, remembering that $a^2 + b^2 = c^2$.

Geometry and Measurement

Substituting the side values provided yields:

$$(4)^2 + (11)^2 = c^2$$

Therefore, c = $\sqrt{16 + 121}$ = 11.7

Finally, the perimeter can be found by adding this new side length with the other provided lengths to get the total length around the figure:

$$4 + 4 + 5 + 8 + 6 + 12 + 11.7 = 50.7$$

Although units are not provided in this figure, remember that reporting units with a measurement is important.

The area of irregular polygons is found by decomposing, or breaking apart, the figure into smaller shapes. When the area of the smaller shapes is determined, the area of the smaller shapes will produce the area of the original figure when added together. Consider the earlier example:

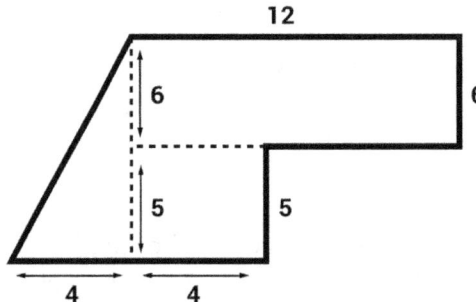

The irregular polygon is decomposed into two rectangles and a triangle. The area of the large rectangle ($A = l \times w \rightarrow A = 12 \times 6$) is 72 square units. The area of the small rectangle is 20 square units ($A = 4 \times 5$). The area of the triangle ($A = \frac{1}{2} \times b \times h \rightarrow A = \frac{1}{2} \times 4 \times 11$) is 22 square units. The sum of the areas of these figures produces the total area of the original polygon:

$$A = 72 + 20 + 22 \rightarrow A = 114 \text{ square units}$$

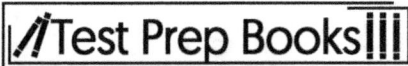

Geometry and Measurement

Here's another example:

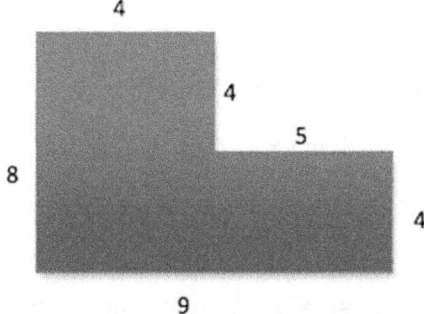

This irregular polygon is decomposed into two rectangles. The area of the large rectangle ($A = l \times w \rightarrow A = 8 \times 4$) is 32 square units. The area of the small rectangle is 20 square units ($A = 4 \times 5$). The sum of the areas of these figures produces the total area of the original polygon: $A = 32 + 20 \rightarrow A$ = 52 square units.

Surface Area of Three-Dimensional Figures

The area of a two-dimensional figure refers to the number of square units needed to cover the interior region of the figure. This concept is similar to wallpaper covering the flat surface of a wall. For example, if a rectangle has an area of 21 square centimeters (written $21 cm^2$), it will take 21 squares, each with sides one centimeter in length, to cover the interior region of the rectangle. Note that area is measured in square units such as: square feet or ft^2; square yards or yd^2; square miles or mi^2.

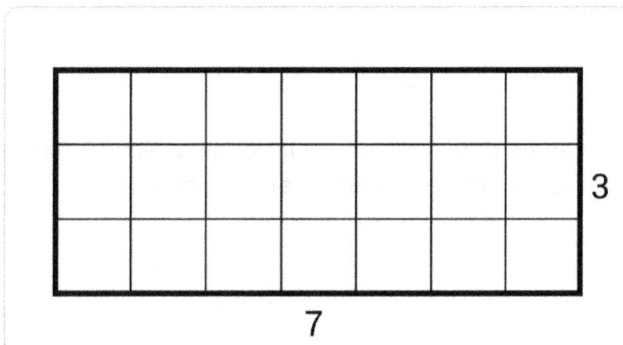

The surface area of a three-dimensional figure refers to the number of square units needed to cover the entire surface of the figure. This concept is similar to using wrapping paper to completely cover the outside of a box. For example, if a triangular pyramid has a surface area of 17 square inches (written $17 in^2$), it will take 17 squares, each with sides one inch in length, to cover the entire surface of the pyramid. Surface area is also measured in square units.

Many three-dimensional figures (solid figures) can be represented by nets consisting of rectangles and triangles. The surface area of such solids can be determined by adding the areas of each of its faces and

Geometry and Measurement

bases. Finding the surface area using this method requires calculating the areas of rectangles and triangles. To find the area (A) of a rectangle, the length (l) is multiplied by the width:

$$(w) \rightarrow A = l \times w$$

The area of a rectangle with a length of 8cm and a width of 4cm is calculated:

$$A = (8cm) \times (4cm) \rightarrow A = 32cm^2$$

To calculate the area (A) of a triangle, the product of $\frac{1}{2}$, the base (b), and the height (h) is found $\rightarrow A = \frac{1}{2} \times b \times h$. Note that the height of a triangle is measured from the base to the vertex opposite of it forming a right angle with the base. The area of a triangle with a base of 11cm and a height of 6cm is calculated:

$$A = \frac{1}{2} \times (11cm) \times (6cm) \rightarrow A = 33cm^2$$

Consider the following triangular prism, which is represented by a net consisting of two triangles and three rectangles.

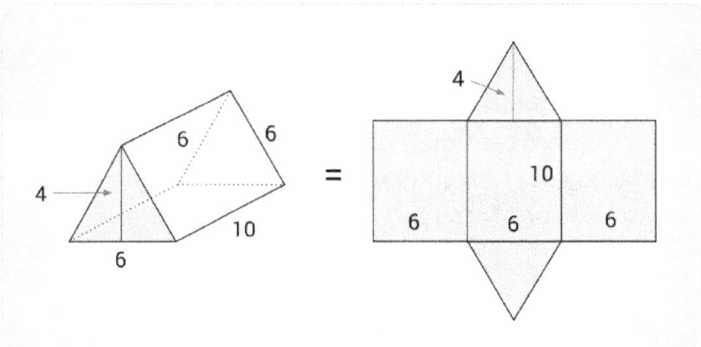

The surface area of the prism can be determined by adding the areas of each of its faces and bases. The surface area (SA) = area of triangle + area of triangle + area of rectangle + area of rectangle + area of rectangle.

$$SA = \left(\frac{1}{2} \times b \times h\right) + \left(\frac{1}{2} \times b \times h\right) + (l \times w) + (l \times w) + (l \times w)$$

$$SA = \left(\frac{1}{2} \times 6 \times 4\right) + \left(\frac{1}{2} \times 6 \times 4\right) + (6 \times 10) + (6 \times 10) + (6 \times 10)$$

$$SA = (12) + (12) + (60) + (60) + (60)$$

$$SA = 204 \text{ square units}$$

Effects of Changes to Dimensions on Area and Volume

Similar polygons are figures that are the same shape but different sizes. Likewise, similar solids are different sizes but are the same shape. In both cases, corresponding angles in the same positions for both figures are congruent (equal), and corresponding sides are proportional in length. For example, the triangles below are similar. The following pairs of corresponding angles are congruent: ∠A and ∠D; ∠B and ∠E; ∠C and ∠F. The corresponding sides are proportional:

$$\frac{AB}{DE} = \frac{6}{3} = 2$$

$$\frac{BC}{EF} = \frac{9}{4.5} = 2$$

$$\frac{CA}{FD} = \frac{10}{5} = 2$$

In other words, triangle ABC is the same shape but twice as large as triangle DEF.

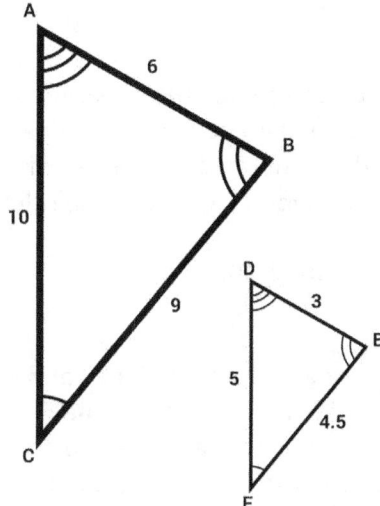

An example of similar triangular pyramids is shown below.

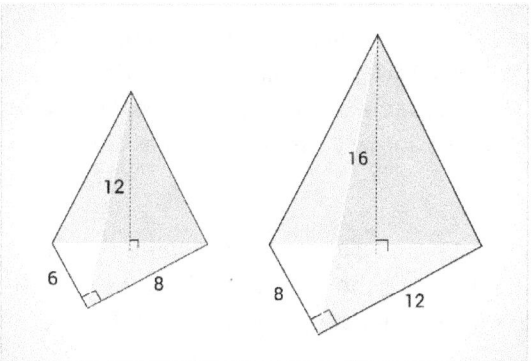

Given the nature of two- and three-dimensional measurements, changing dimensions by a given scale (multiplier) does not change the area of volume by the same scale. Consider a rectangle with a length of 5 centimeters and a width of 4 centimeters. The area of the rectangle is $20 cm^2$. Doubling the dimensions of the rectangle (multiplying by a scale factor of 2) to 10 centimeters and 8 centimeters *does*

not double the area to $40cm^2$. Area is a two-dimensional measurement (measured in square units). Therefore, the dimensions are multiplied by a scale that is squared (raised to the second power) to determine the scale of the corresponding areas. For the previous example, the length and width are multiplied by 2. Therefore, the area is multiplied by 2^2, or 4. The area of a 5cm × 4cm rectangle is $20cm^2$. The area of a 10cm × 8cm rectangle is $80cm^2$.

Volume is a three-dimensional measurement, which is measured in cubic units. Therefore, the scale between dimensions of similar solids is cubed (raised to the third power) to determine the scale between their volumes. Consider similar right rectangular prisms: one with a length of 8 inches, a width of 24 inches, and a height of 16 inches; the second with a length of 4 inches, a width of 12 inches, and a height of 8 inches. The first prism, multiplied by a scalar of $\frac{1}{2}$, produces the measurement of the second prism. The volume of the first prism, multiplied by $(\frac{1}{2})^3$, which equals $\frac{1}{8}$, produces the volume of the second prism. The volume of the first prism is 8in × 24in × 16in which equals $3,072in^3$. The volume of the second prism is 4in × 12in × 8in which equals $384in^3$ ($3,072in^3 \times \frac{1}{8} = 384in^3$).

The rules for squaring the scalar for area and cubing the scalar for volume only hold true for similar figures. In other words, if only one dimension is changed (changing the width of a rectangle but not the length) or dimensions are changed at different rates (the length of a prism is doubled and its height is tripled) the figures are not similar (same shape). Therefore, the rules above do not apply.

Trigonometric Ratios in Right Triangles

Trigonometric Functions

Within similar triangles, corresponding sides are proportional, and angles are congruent. In addition, within similar triangles, the ratio of the side lengths is the same. This property is true even if side lengths are different. Within right triangles, trigonometric ratios can be defined for the acute angles within the triangle. The functions are defined through ratios in a right triangle. Sine of acute angle, A, is opposite over hypotenuse, cosine is adjacent over hypotenuse, and tangent is opposite over adjacent. Note that expanding or shrinking the triangle won't change the ratios. However, changing the angle measurements will alter the calculations.

Complementary Angles

Angles that add up to 90 degrees are *complementary*. Within a right triangle, two complementary angles exist because the third angle is always 90 degrees. In this scenario, the *sine* of one of the complementary angles is equal to the *cosine* of the other angle. The opposite is also true. This relationship exists because sine and cosine will be calculated as the ratios of the same side lengths.

The Pythagorean Theorem

The *Pythagorean theorem* is an important relationship between the three sides of a right triangle. It states that the square of the side opposite the right triangle, known as the *hypotenuse* (denoted as c^2), is equal to the sum of the squares of the other two sides ($a^2 + b^2$). Thus, $a^2 + b^2 = c^2$.

Both the trigonometric functions and the Pythagorean theorem can be used in problems that involve finding either a missing side or a missing angle of a right triangle. To do so, one must look to see what sides and angles are given and select the correct relationship that will help find the missing value. These relationships can also be used to solve application problems involving right triangles. Often, it's helpful to draw a figure to represent the problem to see what's missing.

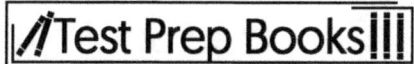

Geometry and Measurement

Estimating Derivatives and Integrals

Since the derivative is a slope, a table of values can be used to approximate the derivative. The change in y divided by the change in x gives the slope at a point. Using the points in the table, slopes of secant lines can be calculated. Based on the limit of those slopes, the derivative at that point can be approximated. Take the following table for example:

x	$f(x)$
0	0
1	1
4	2
9	3
16	4

To find $f'(4)$ using the table, the slope between $f(4)$ and each of the other points needs to be calculated. The following table shows the slopes between different points. Based on the slopes found from the table, the value of $f'(4)$ is between 0.2 and 0.5.

Given Point	Point to find Secant Line	Slope
(4, 2)	(0, 0)	0.5
(4, 2)	(1, 1)	0.333333
(4, 2)	(9, 3)	0.2
(4, 2)	(16, 4)	0.16667

An integral is the antiderivative, and the integral of $f(x)$ is denoted as $\int f(x)dx$. An integral can be explained through the following equation:

$$\frac{dy}{dx}\int_a^x f(t)dt = f(x)$$

Taking the derivative of the integral of a function yields the original function. On a graph, integrals find the area under a curve.

One way to estimate integrals is by the *trapezoid rule*. Over a defined integral, the area under the curve can be split up into trapezoids. These shapes come close to covering the area under the curve. Once split into trapezoids, the area of each shape is found, and then all areas are added together. The following graph offers an example of how to use the trapezoid rule. The defined integral of the function from 1 to 5 is split into four trapezoids. For each trapezoid, the width is 1. The two lengths can then be averaged.

Geometry and Measurement

These two numbers are multiplied together to find the area. Once all four areas are calculated, the approximate integral can be found.

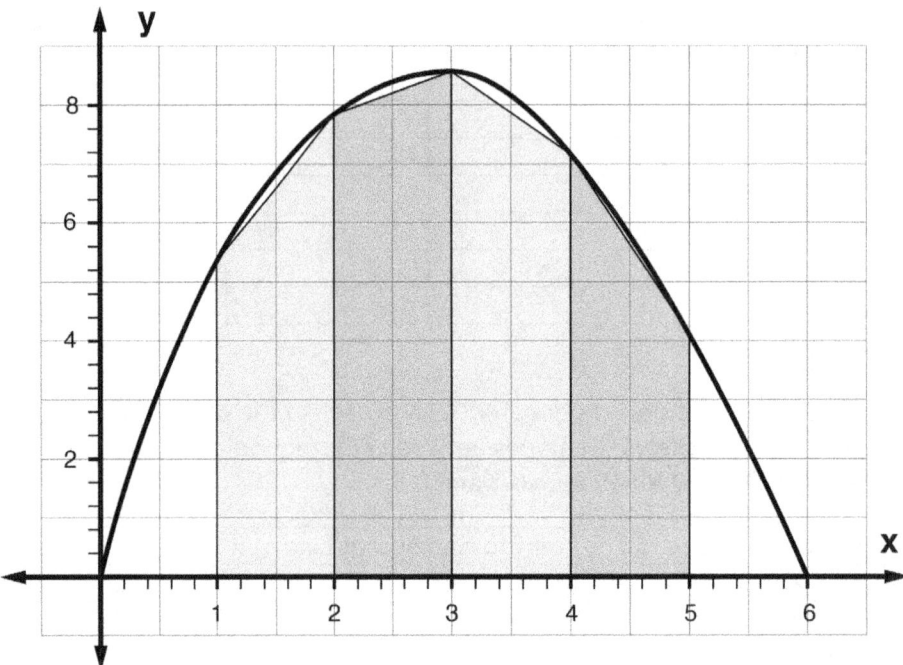

The *midpoint rule* uses rectangles instead of trapezoids to calculate area, and the height of each rectangle equals the function evaluated at the midpoint of each subinterval.

Riemann Sums

Riemann sums can be used to calculate the area under a curve $y = f(x)$ from $x = a$ to $x = b$. In other words, Riemann sums can be used to find $\int_a^b f(x)dx$. The interval from a to b is divided into n subintervals of equal length Δx, and the function is evaluated at a point x_i^* in each interval. This creates a rectangle over each subinterval, and the area of each rectangle can be found and summed. The area of each rectangle is $f(x_i^*)\Delta x$, and the total area is:

$$\sum_{i=1}^{n} f(x_i^*)\Delta x.$$

If there are infinitely many subintervals, the limit of this expression can be taken as $n \to \infty$ to represent the definite integral.

Axiomatic Systems and Their Components

An axiomatic system is a set of axioms that are used to prove theorems. Theorems are mathematical statements that have been proved based on other established statements, such as other theorems and axioms. Geometries are based on axiomatic systems. In geometry, formal definitions are formed using defined words. Three undefined terms exist, which are not formally defined. Those three terms are *point, line*, and *plane*. In geometry, these three terms are used to define everything else. Examples are scenarios that support a statement, and counterexamples are scenarios that disprove propositions. For example, if the claim was made that all even numbers are positive, the number -2 would be a counterexample.

Points, Lines, Planes, and Angles

A point is a place, not a thing, and therefore has no dimensions or size. A set of points that lies on the same line is called collinear. A set of points that lies on the same plane is called coplanar.

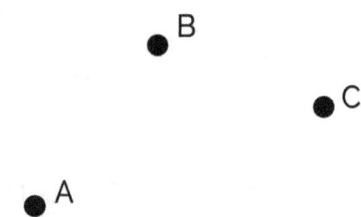

The image above displays point *A*, point *B*, and point *C*.

A line is as series of points that extends in both directions without ending. It consists of an infinite number of points and is drawn with arrows on both ends to indicate it extends infinitely. Lines can be named by two points on the line or with a single, cursive, lower case letter. The lines below are named: line *AB* or line *BA* or $\overleftrightarrow{AB}$ or $\overleftrightarrow{BA}$; and line *m*.

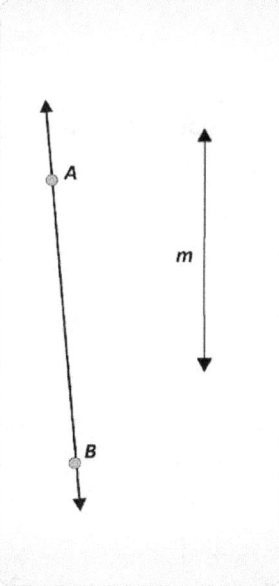

Two lines are considered parallel to each other if, while extending infinitely, they will never intersect (or meet). Parallel lines point in the same direction and are always the same distance apart. Two lines are

Geometry and Measurement

considered perpendicular if they intersect to form right angles. Right angles are 90°. Typically, a small box is drawn at the intersection point to indicate the right angle.

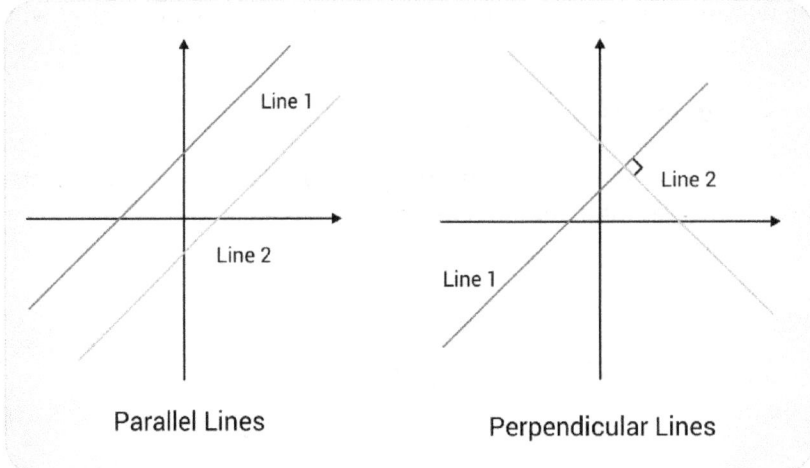

Parallel Lines   Perpendicular Lines

Line 1 is parallel to line 2 in the left image and is written as line 1 || line 2. Line 1 is perpendicular to line 2 in the right image and is written as line 1 ⊥ line 2.

A ray has a specific starting point and extends in one direction without ending. The endpoint of a ray is its starting point. Rays are named using the endpoint first, and any other point on the ray. The following ray can be named ray AB and written $\overrightarrow{AB}$.

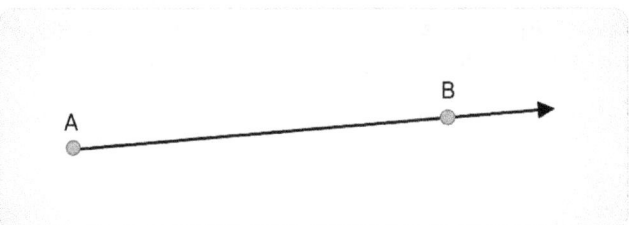

A line segment has specific starting and ending points. A line segment consists of two endpoints and all the points in between. Line segments are named by the two endpoints. The example below is named segment KL or segment LK, written $\overline{KL}$ or $\overline{LK}$.

Classification of Angles

An angle consists of two rays that have a common endpoint. This common endpoint is called the vertex of the angle. The two rays can be called sides of the angle. The angle below has a vertex at point B and the sides consist of ray BA and ray BC. An angle can be named in three ways:

1. Using the vertex and a point from each side, with the vertex letter in the middle.
2. Using only the vertex. This can only be used if it is the only angle with that vertex.
3. Using a number that is written inside the angle.

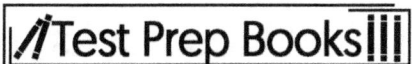
Geometry and Measurement

The angle below can be written ∠ABC (read angle ABC), ∠CBA, ∠B, or ∠1.

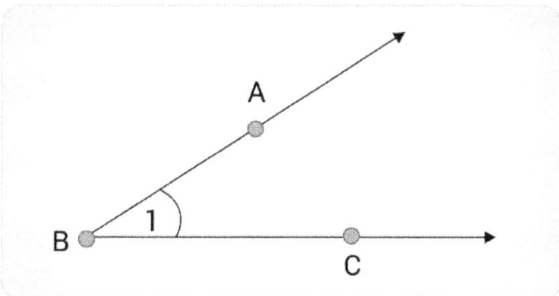

An angle divides a plane, or flat surface, into three parts: the angle itself, the interior (inside) of the angle, and the exterior (outside) of the angle. The figure below shows point M on the interior of the angle and point N on the exterior of the angle.

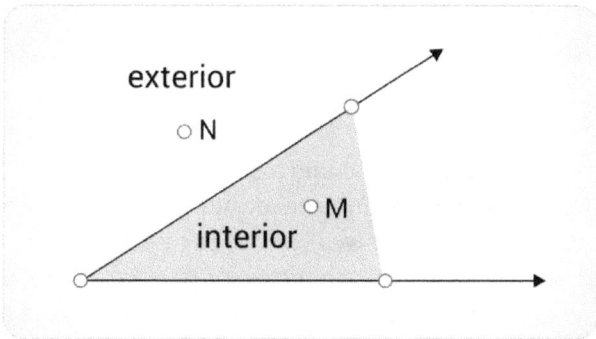

Angles can be measured in units called degrees, with the symbol °. The degree measure of an angle is between 0° and 180° and can be obtained by using a protractor.

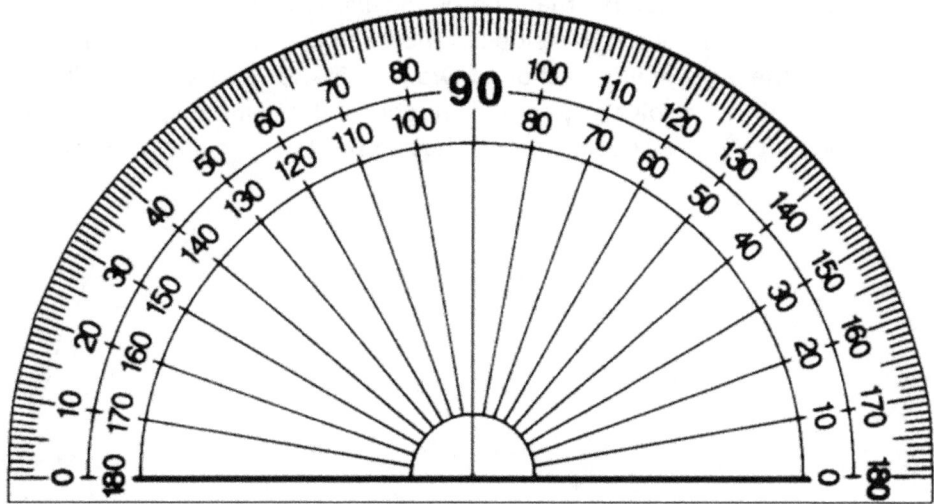

A straight angle (or simply a line) measures exactly 180°. A right angle's sides meet at the vertex to create a square corner. A right-angle measures exactly 90° and is typically indicated by a box drawn in the interior of the angle. An acute angle has an interior that is narrower than a right angle. The measure of an acute angle is any value less than 90° and greater than 0°. For example, 89.9°, 47°, 12°, and 1°. An obtuse angle has an interior that is wider than a right angle. The measure of an obtuse angle is any value greater than 90° but less than 180°. For example, 90.1°, 110°, 150°, and 179.9°.

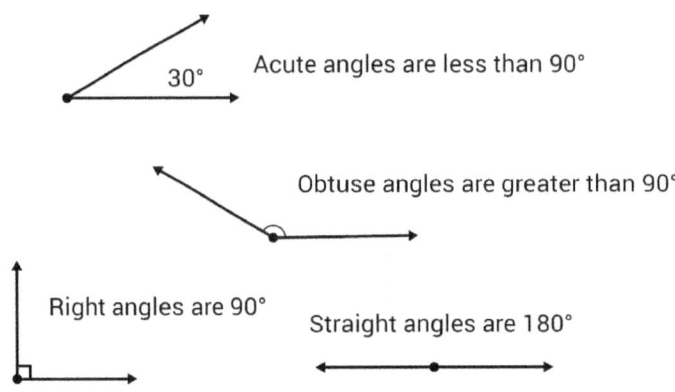

Solving Line Problems

Two lines are parallel if they have the same slope and a different intercept. Two lines are perpendicular if the product of their slope equals -1. Parallel lines never intersect unless they are the same line, and perpendicular lines intersect at a right angle. If two lines aren't parallel, they must intersect at one point. Determining equations of lines based on properties of parallel and perpendicular lines appears in word problems. To find an equation of a line, both the slope and a point the line goes through are necessary. Therefore, if an equation of a line is needed that's parallel to a given line and runs through a specified point, the slope of the given line and the point are plugged into the point-slope form of an equation of a line.

Secondly, if an equation of a line is needed that's perpendicular to a given line running through a specified point, the negative reciprocal of the slope of the given line and the point are plugged into the point-slope form. Also, if the point of intersection of two lines is known, that point will be used to solve the set of equations. Therefore, to solve a system of equations, the point of intersection must be found. If a set of two equations with two unknown variables has no solution, the lines are parallel.

Solving Problems with Parallel and Perpendicular Lines

Two lines can be parallel, perpendicular, or neither. If two lines are parallel, they have the same slope. This is proven using the idea of similar triangles. Consider the following diagram with two parallel lines, L1 and L2:

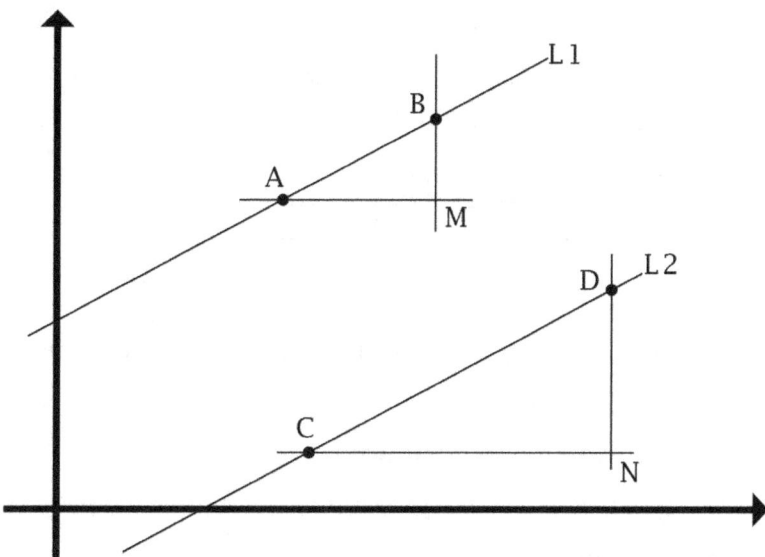

A and B are points on L1, and C and D are points on L2. Right triangles are formed with vertex M and N where lines BM and DN are parallel to the y-axis and AM and CN are parallel to the x-axis. Because all three sets of lines are parallel, the triangles are similar. Therefore, $\frac{BM}{DN} = \frac{MA}{NC}$. This shows that the rise/run is equal for lines L1 and L2. Hence, their slopes are equal.

Secondly, if two lines are perpendicular, the product of their slopes equals -1. This means that their slopes are negative reciprocals of each other. Consider two perpendicular lines, *l* and *n*:

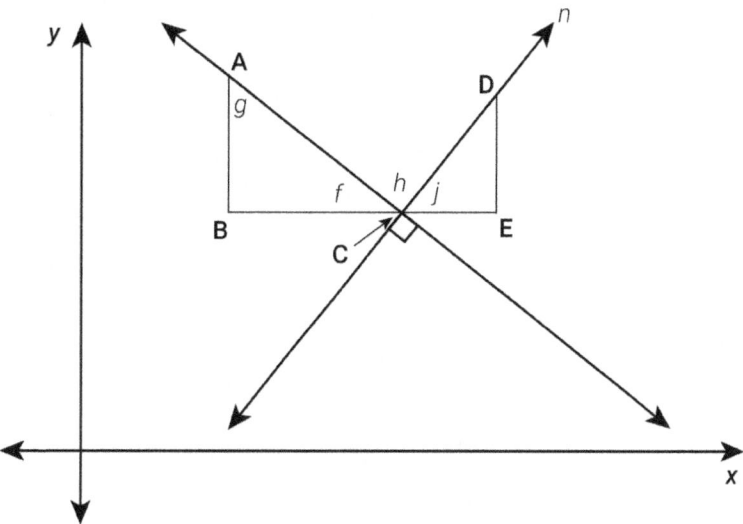

Right triangles ABC and CDE are formed so that lines BC and CE are parallel to the x-axis, and AB and DE are parallel to the y-axis. Because line BE is a straight line, angles:

$$f + h + i = 180 \text{ degrees}$$

However, angle h is a right angle, so:

$$f + j = 90 \text{ degrees}$$

By construction, $f + g = 90$, which means that $g = j$. Therefore, because angles $B = E$ and $g = j$, the triangles are similar and $\frac{AB}{BC} = \frac{CE}{DE}$. Because slope is equal to rise/run, the slope of line l is $-\frac{AB}{BC}$ and the slope of line n is $\frac{DE}{CE}$. Multiplying the slopes together gives:

$$-\frac{AB}{BC} \cdot \frac{DE}{CE} = -\frac{CE}{DE} \cdot \frac{DE}{CE} = -1$$

This proves that the product of the slopes of two perpendicular lines equals -1. Both parallel and perpendicular lines can be integral in many geometric proofs, so knowing and understanding their properties is crucial for problem-solving.

Congruence and Similarity in Terms of Transformations

Rigid Motion

A *rigid motion* is a transformation that preserves distance and length. Every line segment in the resulting image is congruent to the corresponding line segment in the pre-image. Congruence between two figures means a series of transformations (or a rigid motion) can be defined that maps one of the figures onto the other. Basically, two figures are congruent if they have the same shape and size.

Dilation

A shape is dilated, or a *dilation* occurs, when each side of the original image is multiplied by a given scale factor. If the scale factor is less than 1 and greater than 0, the dilation contracts the shape, and the resulting shape is smaller. If the scale factor equals 1, the resulting shape is the same size, and the dilation is a rigid motion. Finally, if the scale factor is greater than 1, the resulting shape is larger and the dilation expands the shape. The *center of dilation* is the point where the distance from it to any point on the new shape equals the scale factor times the distance from the center to the corresponding point in the pre-image. Dilation isn't an isometric transformation because distance isn't preserved. However, angle measure, parallel lines, and points on a line all remain unchanged. The following figure is an example of translation, rotation, dilation, and reflection:

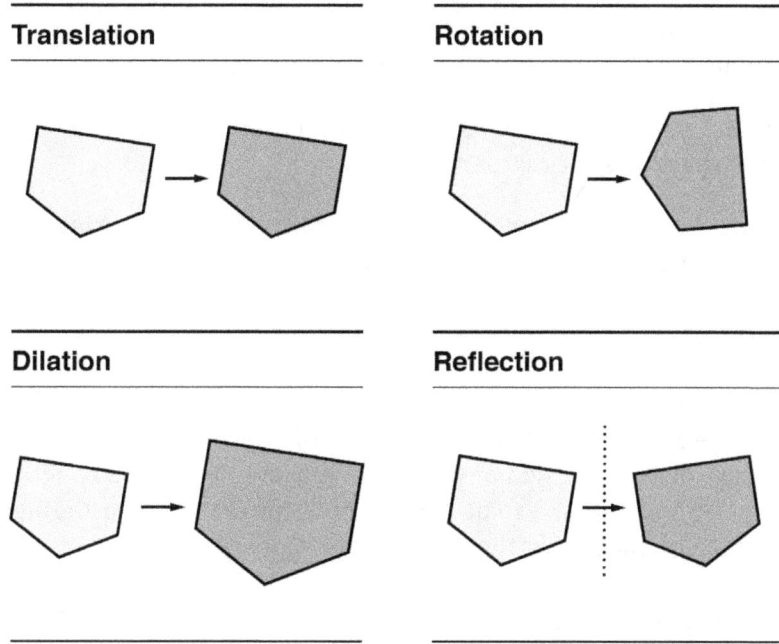

Determining Congruence

Two figures are congruent if there is a rigid motion that can map one figure onto the other. Therefore, all pairs of sides and angles within the image and pre-image must be congruent. For example, in triangles, each pair of the three sides and three angles must be congruent. Similarly, in two four-sided figures, each pair of the four sides and four angles must be congruent.

Similarity

Two figures are *similar* if there is a combination of translations, reflections, rotations, and dilations, which maps one figure onto the other. The difference between congruence and similarity is that dilation can be used in similarity. Therefore, side lengths between each shape can differ. However, angle measure must be preserved within this definition. If two polygons differ in size so that the lengths of corresponding line segments differ by the same factor, but corresponding angles have the same measurement, they are similar.

Triangle Congruence

There are five theorems to show that triangles are congruent when it's unknown whether each pair of angles and sides are congruent. Each theorem is a shortcut that involves different combinations of sides and angles that must be true for the two triangles to be congruent.

Side-side-side (SSS) states that if all sides are equal, the triangles are congruent.

Side-angle-side (SAS) states that if two pairs of sides are equal and the included angles are congruent, then the triangles are congruent.

Similarly, *angle-side-angle (ASA)* states that if two pairs of angles are congruent and the included side lengths are equal, the triangles are congruent.

Angle-angle-side (AAS) states that two triangles are congruent if they have two pairs of congruent angles and a pair of corresponding equal side lengths that aren't included.

Finally, *hypotenuse-leg (HL)* states that if two right triangles have equal hypotenuses and an equal pair of shorter sides, then the triangles are congruent.

An important item to note is that angle-angle-angle *(AAA)* is not enough information to have congruence. It's important to understand why these rules work by using rigid motions to show congruence between the triangles with the given properties. For example, three reflections are needed to show why *SAS* follows from the definition of congruence.

Similarity for Two Triangles

If two angles of one triangle are congruent with two angles of a second triangle, the triangles are similar. This is because, within any triangle, the sum of the angle measurements is 180 degrees. Therefore, if two are congruent, the third angle must also be congruent because their measurements are equal. Three congruent pairs of angles mean that the triangles are similar.

Proving Congruence and Similarity

The criteria needed to prove triangles are congruent involves both angle and side congruence. Both pairs of related angles and sides need to be of the same measurement to use congruence in a proof. The criteria to prove similarity in triangles involves proportionality of side lengths. Angles must be congruent in similar triangles; however, corresponding side lengths only need to be a constant multiple of each other. Once similarity is established, it can be used in proofs as well. Relationships in geometric figures other than triangles can be proven using triangle congruence and similarity. If a similar or congruent triangle can be found within another type of geometric figure, their criteria can be used to prove a relationship about a given formula. For instance, a rectangle can be broken up into two congruent triangles.

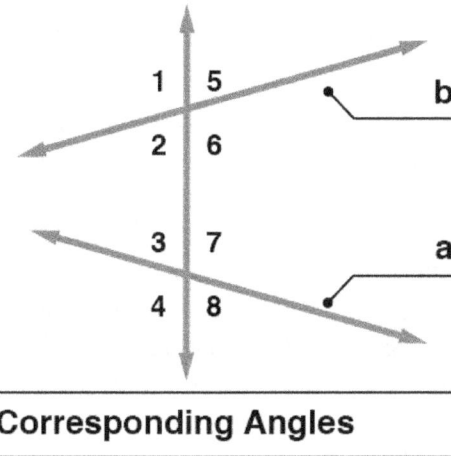

Corresponding Angles

Relationships between Angles
Supplementary angles add up to 180 degrees. *Vertical angles* are two nonadjacent angles formed by two intersecting lines. *Corresponding angles* are two angles in the same position whenever a straight line (known as a *transversal*) crosses two others. If the two lines are parallel, the corresponding angles are equal. *Alternate interior angles* are also a pair of angles formed when two lines are crossed by a transversal. They are opposite angles that exist inside of the two lines.

In the corresponding angles diagram above, angles 2 and 7 are alternate interior angles, as well as angles 6 and 3. *Alternate exterior angles* are opposite angles formed by a transversal but, in contrast to interior angles, exterior angles exist outside the two original lines. Therefore, angles 1 and 8 are alternate exterior angles and so are angles 5 and 4. Finally, *consecutive interior angles* are pairs of angles formed by a transversal. These angles are located on the same side of the transversal and inside the two original lines. Therefore, angles 2 and 3 are a pair of consecutive interior angles, and so are angles 6 and 7. These definitions are instrumental in solving many problems that involve determining relationships between angles.

Medians, Midpoints, and Altitudes
A *median* of a triangle is a line segment that connects a vertex to the midpoint on the other side of the triangle. A triangle has three medians, and their point of intersection is known as the *centroid*. An *altitude* is a line drawn from a vertex perpendicular to the opposite side. A triangle has three altitudes, and their point of intersection is known as the *orthocenter*. An altitude can actually exist outside, inside, or on the triangle depending on the placement of the vertex. Many problems involve these definitions. For example, given one endpoint of a line segment and the midpoint, the other endpoint can be determined by using the midpoint formula. In addition, area problems heavily depend on these definitions. For example, it can be proven that the median of a triangle divides it into two regions of equal areas. The actual formula for the area of a triangle depends on its altitude.

Special Triangles
An *isosceles triangle* contains at least two equal sides. Therefore, it must also contain two equal angles and, subsequently, contain two medians of the same length. An isosceles triangle can also be labelled as an *equilateral triangle* (which contains three equal sides and three equal angles) when it meets these

conditions. In an equilateral triangle, the measure of each angle is always 60 degrees. Also within an equilateral triangle, the medians are of the same length. A *scalene triangle* can never be an equilateral or an isosceles triangle because it contains no equal sides and no equal angles. Also, medians in a scalene triangle can't have the same length. However, a *right triangle*, which is a triangle containing a 90-degree angle, can be a scalene triangle.

There are two types of special right triangles. The *30-60-90 right triangle* has angle measurements of 30 degrees, 60 degrees, and 90 degrees. Because of the nature of this triangle, and through the use of the Pythagorean theorem, the side lengths have a special relationship. If x is the length opposite the 30-degree angle, the length opposite the 60-degree angle is $\sqrt{3}x$, and the hypotenuse has length $2x$. The *45-45-90 right triangle* is also special as it contains two angle measurements of 45 degrees. It can be proven that, if x is the length of the two equal sides, the hypotenuse is $x\sqrt{2}$. The properties of all of these special triangles are extremely useful in determining both side lengths and angle measurements in problems where some of these quantities are given and some are not.

Special Quadrilaterals

A special quadrilateral is one in which both pairs of opposite sides are parallel. This type of quadrilateral is known as a *parallelogram*. A parallelogram has six important properties:

- Opposite sides are congruent.
- Opposite angles are congruent.
- Within a parallelogram, consecutive angles are supplementary, so their measurements total 180 degrees.
- If one angle is a right angle, all of them have to be right angles.
- The diagonals of the angles bisect each other.
- These diagonals form two congruent triangles.

A parallelogram with four congruent sides is a *rhombus*. A quadrilateral containing only one set of parallel sides is known as a *trapezoid*. The parallel sides are known as bases, and the other two sides are known as legs. If the legs are congruent, the trapezoid can be labelled an *isosceles trapezoid*. An important property of an isosceles trapezoid is that its diagonals are congruent. Also, the median of a trapezoid is parallel to the bases, and its length is equal to half of the sum of the base lengths.

Quadrilateral Relationships

Rectangles, squares, and rhombuses are *polygons* with four sides. By definition, all rectangles are parallelograms, but only some rectangles are squares. However, some parallelograms are rectangles. Also, it's true that all squares are rectangles, and some rhombuses are squares. There are no rectangles, squares, or rhombuses that are trapezoids though, because they have more than one set of parallel sides.

Diagonals and Angles

Diagonals are lines (excluding sides) that connect two vertices within a polygon. *Mutually bisecting diagonals* intersect at their midpoints. Parallelograms, rectangles, squares, and rhombuses have mutually bisecting diagonals. However, trapezoids don't have such lines. *Perpendicular diagonals* occur when they form four right triangles at their point of intersection. Squares and rhombuses have perpendicular diagonals, but trapezoids, rectangles, and parallelograms do not. Finally, *perpendicular bisecting* diagonals (also known as *perpendicular bisectors*) form four right triangles at their point of intersection, but this intersection is also the midpoint of the two lines. Both rhombuses and squares

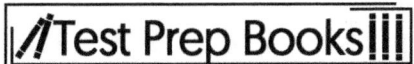

have perpendicular bisecting angles, but trapezoids, rectangles, and parallelograms do not. Knowing these definitions can help tremendously in problems that involve both angles and diagonals.

Polygons with More Than Four Sides

A *pentagon* is a five-sided figure. A six-sided shape is a *hexagon*. A seven-sided figure is classified as a *heptagon*, and an eight-sided figure is called an *octagon*. An important characteristic is whether a polygon is regular or irregular. If it's *regular*, the side lengths and angle measurements are all equal. An *irregular* polygon has unequal side lengths and angle measurements. Mathematical problems involving polygons with more than four sides usually involve side length and angle measurements. The sum of all internal angles in a polygon equals $180(n - 2)$ degrees, where n is the number of sides. Therefore, the total of all internal angles in a pentagon is 540 degrees because there are five sides so $180(5 - 2)$ = 540 degrees. Unfortunately, area formulas don't exist for polygons with more than four sides. However, their shapes can be split up into triangles, and the formula for area of a triangle can be applied and totaled to obtain the area for the entire figure.

Congruency

Two figures are congruent if they have the same shape and same size. The two figures could have been rotated, reflected, or translated. Two figures are similar if they have been rotated, reflected, translated, and resized. Angle measure is preserved in similar figures. Both angle and side length are preserved in congruent figures.

Geometric Constructions Made with a Variety of Tools and Methods

Geometric Construction Tools

The tools needed to make formal geometric constructions are a compass, a ruler, paper folding, or geometry software. These tools can be used to copy or bisect (split into two equal halves) a line segment or angle. They can also replicate a specific shape and construct perpendicular lines, a perpendicular and construct a line parallel to a given line through a specified point.

Formal Geometric Constructions

Beginning with formal geometric constructions, various geometric figures and shapes can be built. Definitions and theorems for lines and angles can be used in parallel with geometric constructions to build shapes such as equilateral triangles, squares, and rectangular hexagons inscribed in a circle. Definitions of shapes involving congruence of sides and angles within each type of figure must be understood and used in parallel with constructing congruent line segments, parallel and perpendicular lines, and congruent angles.

Using Geometry Software

Many tools allow geometric figures to be explored so that their properties can be seen. One such tool is Geometry Explorer, which is a specific type of interactive geometry software. With such tools, figures can be constructed by first inserting points and lines, and then using them to build either two- or three-dimensional figures that can be analyzed. Once the figures are built, properties can be seen and points can be moved to examine how the figure changes.

Geometry and Measurement

Euclidean Geometry Versus Non-Euclidean Geometry

The main difference between Euclidean geometry and non-Euclidean geometry is the definition of parallel lines. In Euclidean geometry, given a point and a line that does not contain the given point, there is only one line running through the point that exists in the same plane as the given line but never intersects it. Hyperbolic and elliptic geometry (non-Euclidean) are curved spaces, and in both geometries, there is more than one line that would pass through the given point that are parallel to the given line.

Two- and Three-Dimensional Shapes

A polygon is a closed geometric figure in a plane (flat surface) consisting of at least 3 sides formed by line segments. These are often defined as two-dimensional shapes. Common two-dimensional shapes include circles, triangles, squares, rectangles, pentagons, and hexagons. Note that a circle is a two-dimensional shape without sides.

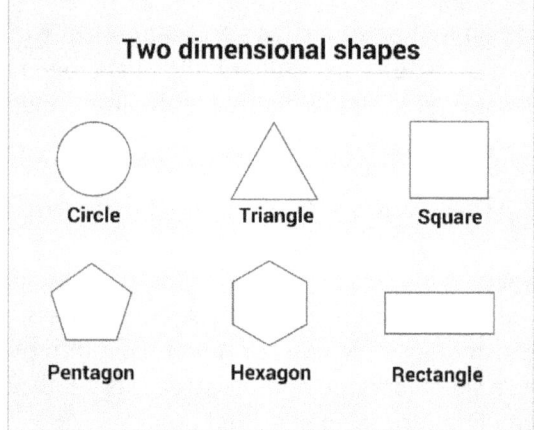

A solid figure, or simple solid, is a figure that encloses a part of space. Some solids consist of flat surfaces only while others include curved surfaces. Solid figures are often defined as three-dimensional shapes. Common three-dimensional shapes include spheres, prisms, cubes, pyramids, cylinders, and cones.

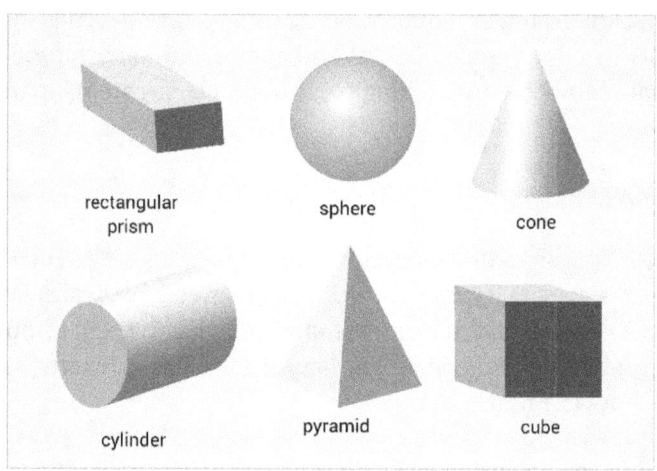

Composing two- or three-dimensional shapes involves putting together two or more shapes to create a new larger figure. For example, a semi-circle (half circle), rectangle, and two triangles can be used to compose the figure of the sailboat shown below.

Similarly, solid figures can be placed together to compose an endless number of three-dimensional objects.

Decomposing two- and three-dimensional figures involves breaking the shapes apart into smaller, simpler shapes. Consider the following two-dimensional representations of a house:

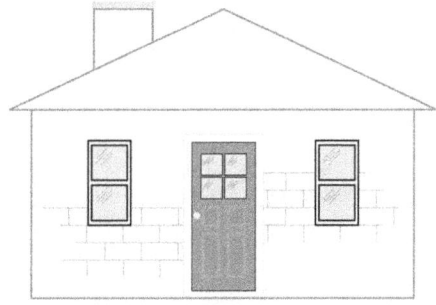

This complex figure can be decomposed into the following basic two-dimensional shapes: large rectangle (body of house); large triangle (roof); small rectangle and small triangle (chimney). Decomposing figures is often done more than one way. To illustrate, the figure of the house could also be decomposed into: two large triangles (body); two medium triangles (roof); two smaller triangles of unequal size (chimney).

Polygons and Solids

A polygon is a closed two-dimensional figure consisting of three or more sides. Polygons can be either convex or concave. A polygon that has interior angles all measuring less than 180° is convex. A concave polygon has one or more interior angles measuring greater than 180°. Examples are shown below.

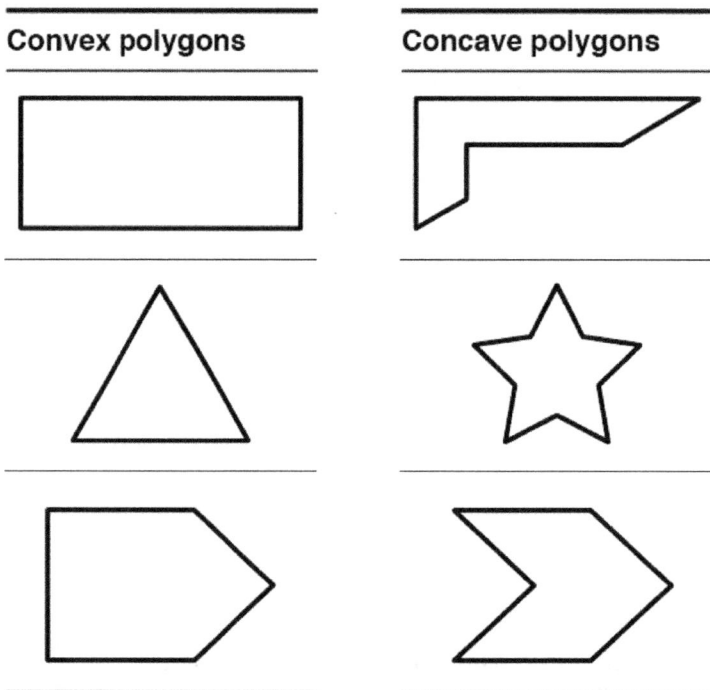

Polygons can be classified by the number of sides (also equal to the number of angles) they have. The following are the names of polygons with a given number of sides or angles:

# of Sides	Name of Polygon
3	Triangle
4	Quadrilateral
5	Pentagon
6	Hexagon
7	Septagon (or heptagon)
8	Octagon
9	Nonagon
10	Decagon

Equiangular polygons are polygons in which the measure of every interior angle is the same. The sides of equilateral polygons are always the same length. If a polygon is both equiangular and equilateral, the polygon is defined as a regular polygon. Examples are shown below.

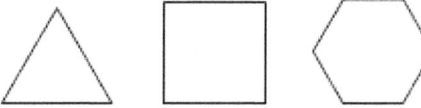

Triangles can be further classified by their sides and angles. A triangle with its largest angle measuring 90° is a right triangle. A triangle with the largest angle less than 90° is an acute triangle. A triangle with the largest angle greater than 90° is an obtuse triangle.

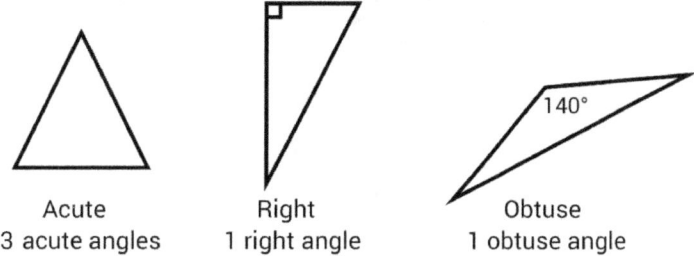

Acute
3 acute angles

Right
1 right angle

Obtuse
1 obtuse angle

Geometry and Measurement

A triangle consisting of two equal sides and two equal angles is an isosceles triangle. A triangle with three equal sides and three equal angles is an equilateral triangle. A triangle with no equal sides or angles is a scalene triangle.

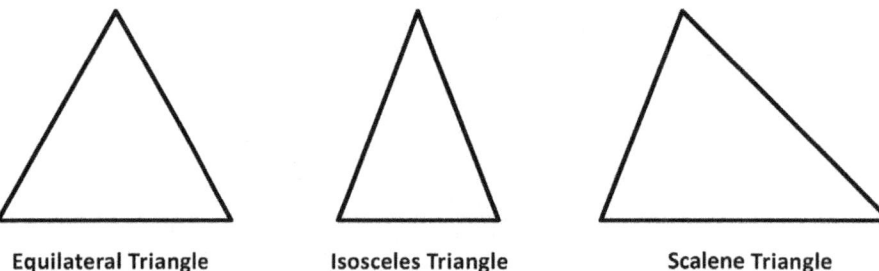

Equilateral Triangle   Isosceles Triangle   Scalene Triangle

Quadrilaterals can be further classified according to their sides and angles. A quadrilateral with exactly one pair of parallel sides is called a trapezoid. A quadrilateral that shows both pairs of opposite sides parallel is a parallelogram. Parallelograms include rhombuses, rectangles, and squares. A rhombus has four equal sides. A rectangle has four equal angles (90° each). A square has four 90° angles and four equal sides. Therefore, a square is both a rhombus and a rectangle.

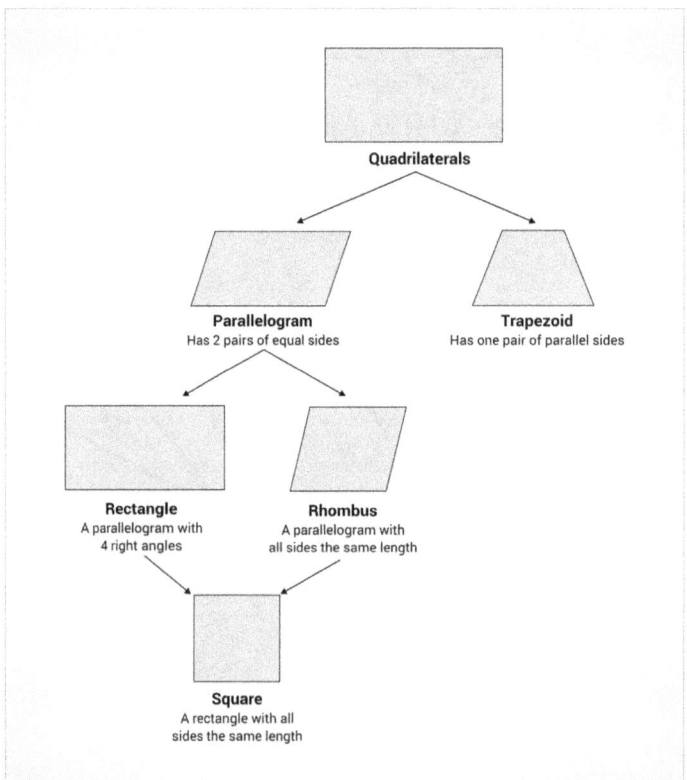

A solid is a three-dimensional figure that encloses a part of space. Solids consisting of all flat surfaces that are polygons are called polyhedrons. The two-dimensional surfaces that make up a polyhedron are called faces. Types of polyhedrons include prisms and pyramids. A prism consists of two parallel faces that are congruent (or the same shape and same size), and lateral faces going around (which are parallelograms).

A prism is further classified by the shape of its base, as shown below:

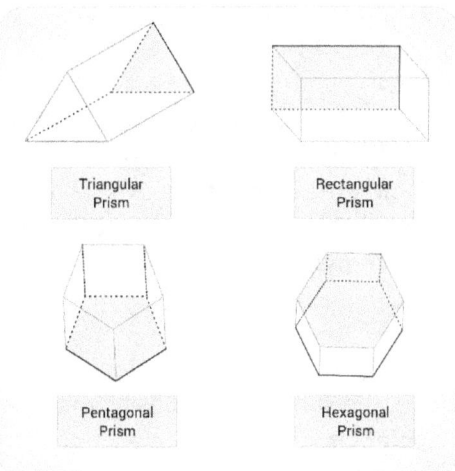

A pyramid consists of lateral faces (triangles) that meet at a common point called the vertex and one other face that is a polygon, called the base. A pyramid can be further classified by the shape of its base, as shown below.

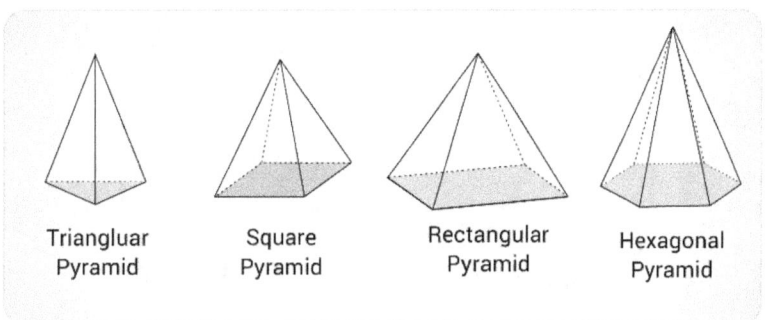

A tetrahedron is another name for a triangular pyramid. All the faces of a tetrahedron are triangles.

Solids that are not polyhedrons include spheres, cylinders, and cones. A sphere is the set of all points a given distance from a given center point. A sphere is commonly thought of as a three-dimensional circle. A cylinder consists of two parallel, congruent (same size) circles and a lateral curved surface. A cone consists of a circle as its base and a lateral curved surface that narrows to a point called the vertex.

Similar polygons are the same shape but different sizes. More specifically, their corresponding angle measures are congruent (or equal) and the length of their sides is proportional. For example, all sides of one polygon may be double the length of the sides of another. Likewise, similar solids are the same shape but different sizes. Any corresponding faces or bases of similar solids are the same polygons that are proportional by a consistent value.

Circle Theorems

Circle Angles
The distance from the middle of a circle to any other point on the circle is known as the *radius*. A *chord* of a circle is a straight line formed when its endpoints are allowed to be any two points on the circle.

Many angles exist within a circle. A *central angle* is formed by using two radii as its rays and the center of the circle as its vertex. An inscribed angle is formed by using two chords as its rays, and its vertex is a point on the circle itself. Finally, a *circumscribed angle* has a vertex that is a point outside the circle and rays that are tangent to circle.

Some relationships exist between these types of angles, and, in order to define these relationships, arc measure must be understood. An *arc* of a circle is a portion of the circumference. Finding the *arc measure* is the same as finding the degree measure of the central angle that intersects the circle to form the arc. The measure of an inscribed angle is half the measure of its intercepted arc. It's also true that the measure of a circumscribed angle is equal to 180 degrees minus the measure of the central angle that forms the arc in the angle.

Quadrilateral Angles

If a quadrilateral is inscribed in a circle, the sum of its opposite angles is 180 degrees. Consider the quadrilateral ABCD centered at the point O:

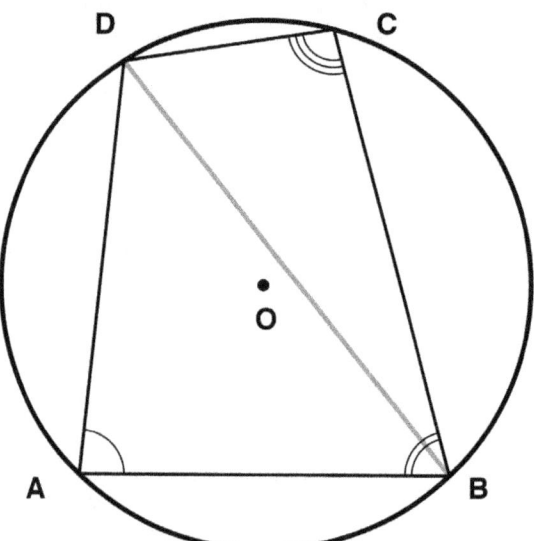

Each of the four line segments within the quadrilateral is a chord of the circle. Consider the diagonal DB. Angle DAB is an inscribed angle leaning on the arc DCB. Therefore, angle DAB is half the measure of the arc DCB. Conversely, angle DCB is an inscribed angle leaning on the arc DAB. Therefore, angle DCB is half the measure of the arc DAB. The sum of arcs DCB and DAB is 360 degrees because they make up the entire circle. Therefore, the sum of angles DAB and DCB equals half of 360 degrees, which is 180 degrees.

Circle Lines

A *tangent line* is a line that touches a curve at a single point without going through it. A *compass* and a *straight edge* are the tools necessary to construct a tangent line from a point *P* outside the circle to the circle. A tangent line is constructed by drawing a line segment from the center of the circle *O* to the point *P*, and then finding its midpoint *M* by bisecting the line segment. By using *M* as the center, a compass is used to draw a circle through points *O* and *P*. *N* is defined as the intersection of the two circles. Finally, a line segment is drawn through P and N. This is the tangent line. Each point on a circle has only one tangent line, which is perpendicular to the radius at that point. A line similar to a tangent line is a *secant line*. Instead of intersecting the circle at one point, a secant line intersects the circle at two points. A *chord* is a smaller portion of a secant line.

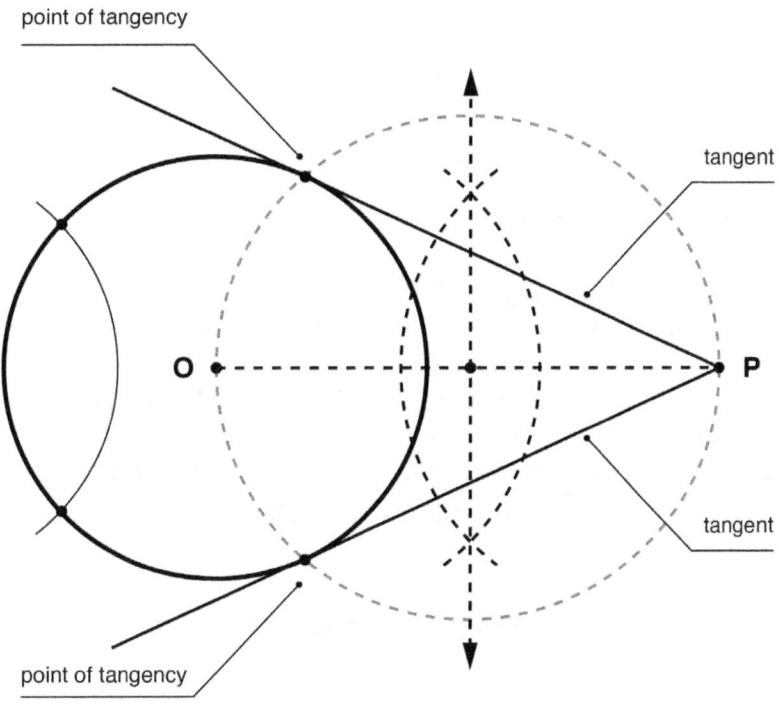

Arc Length and Area Measurements of Sectors of Circles

Arc Length

As previously mentioned, angles can be measured in radians, and 180 degrees equals π radians. Therefore, the measure of a complete circle is 2π radians. In addition to arc measure, arc length can also be found because the length of an arc is a portion of the circle's circumference. The following proportion is true:

$$\frac{\text{arc measure}}{360 \text{ degrees}} = \frac{\text{arc length}}{\text{circle circumference}}$$

Arc measure is the same as the measure of the central angle, and this proportion can be rewritten as:

$$\text{arc length} = \frac{\text{central angle}}{360 \text{ degrees}} \times \text{circumference}$$

In addition, the degree measure can be replaced with radians to allow the use of both units. Note that arc length is a fractional part of circumference because:

$$\frac{\text{central angle}}{360 \text{ degrees}} < 1$$

Geometry and Measurement

Area of a Sector

A *sector* of a circle is a portion of the circle that's enclosed by two radii and an arc. It resembles a piece of a pie, and the area of a sector can be derived using known definitions. The area of a circle can be calculated using the formula $A = \pi r^2$, where r is the radius of the circle. The area of a sector of a circle is a fraction of that calculation. For example, if the central angle θ is known in radians, the area of a sector is defined as:

$$A_s = \pi r^2 \frac{\theta}{2\pi} = \frac{\theta r^2}{2}$$

If the angle θ in degrees is known, the area of the sector is $A_s = \frac{\theta \pi r^2}{360}$. Finally, if the arc length L is known, the area of the sector can be reduced to $A_s = \frac{rL}{2}$.

Perimeter, Area and Volume of Irregular Figures

Any shape that does not have a designated formula for calculating perimeter, area, and volume, can be broken up into shapes that have known formulas. Once those are calculated, the values are summed together to obtain the desired quantity. For example, irregular polygons can be split up into triangles, and total area can be found by adding up the area of each individual triangle. Another technique involves using area of sectors of circles. If the arc length of a sector, L, and the radius of the circle, R, are known, the area of the sector is $\frac{RL}{2}$. This formula can be utilized to find the area of a portion of a circular region.

Visualizing Relationships Between Two-Dimensional and Three-Dimensional Objects

Cross-Sections and Nets of Three-Dimensional Shapes

One way to analyze a three-dimensional shape is to view its cross-sections in a two-dimensional plane. A cross-section is an intersection of the shape with a plane. Also, a three-dimensional shape can be represented in a two-dimensional plane by its net, which is an unfolded, flat representation of the all sides of the shape. For example, a rectangular prism has cross sections that are squares and rectangles and the following figure shows its net:

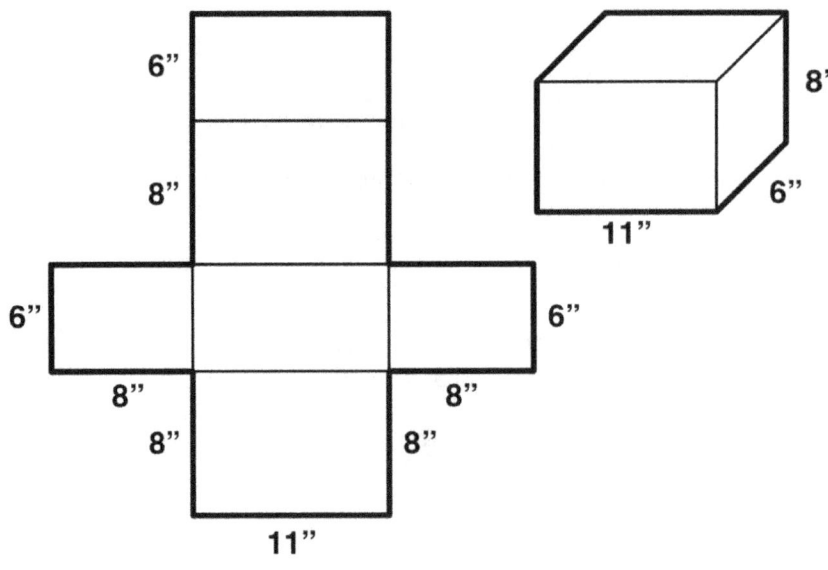

Cross Sections and Rotations

Two-dimensional objects are formed when three-dimensional objects are "sliced" in various ways. For example, any cross section of a sphere is a circle. Some three-dimensional objects have different cross sections depending on how the object is sliced. For example, the cross section of a cylinder can be a circle or a rectangle, and the cross section of a pyramid can be a square or a triangle. In addition, three-dimensional objects can be formed by rotating two-dimensional objects. Certain rotations can relate the two-dimensional cross sections back to the original three-dimensional objects. The objects must be rotated around an imaginary line known as the *rotation axis*. For example, a right triangle can be rotated around one of its legs to form a cone. A sphere can be formed by rotating a semicircle around a line segment formed from its diameter. Finally, rotating a square around one of its sides forms a cylinder.

Three-Dimensional Figures with Nets

A net is a construction of two-dimensional figures that can be folded to form a given three-dimensional figure. More than one net may exist to fold and produce the same solid, or three-dimensional figure. The bases and faces of the solid figure are analyzed to determine the polygons (two-dimensional figures) needed to form the net.

Consider the following triangular prism:

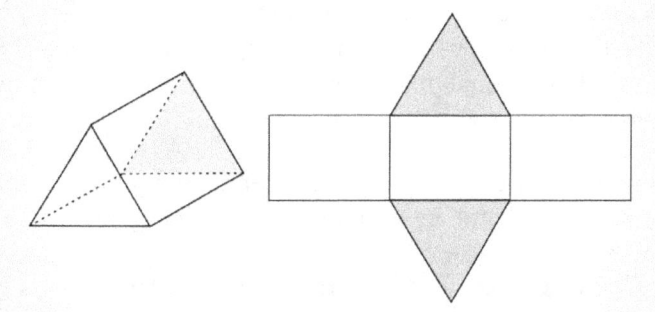

The surface of the prism consists of two triangular bases and three rectangular faces. The net beside it can be used to construct the triangular prism by first folding the triangles up to be parallel to each other, and then folding the two outside rectangles up and to the center with the outer edges touching.

Consider the following cylinder:

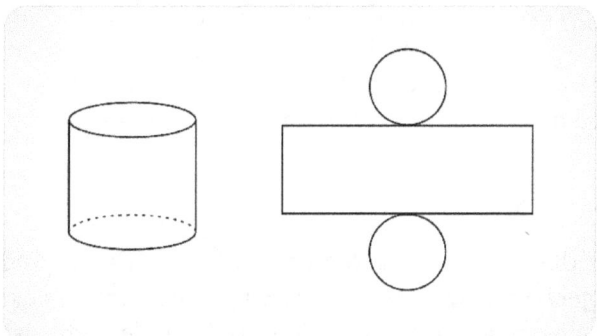

The surface consists of two circular bases and a curved lateral surface that can be opened and flattened into a rectangle. The net beside it can be used to construct the cylinder by first folding the circles up to be parallel to each other, and then curving the sides of the rectangle up to touch each other. The top and bottom of the folded rectangle should be touching the outside of both circles.

Consider the following square pyramid below on the left. The surface consists of one square base and four triangular faces. The net below on the right can be used to construct the square pyramid by folding each triangle towards the center of the square. The top points of the triangle meet at the vertex.

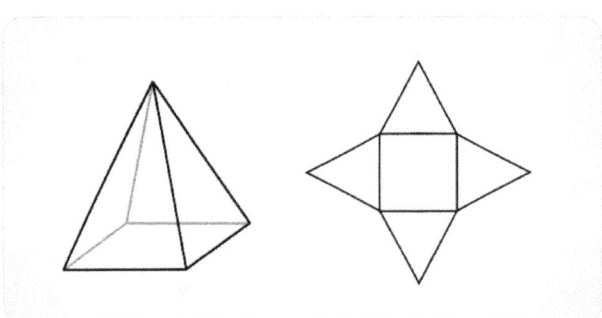

Simplifying Three-Dimensional Objects

Three-dimensional objects can be simplified into related two-dimensional shapes to solve problems. This simplification can make problem-solving a much easier experience. An isometric representation of a three-dimensional object can be completed so that important properties (e.g., shape, relationships of faces and surfaces) are noted. Edges and vertices can be translated into two-dimensional objects as well. For example, below is a three-dimensional object that's been partitioned into two-dimensional representations of its faces.

The net represents the sum of the three different faces. Depending on the problem, using a smaller portion of the given shape may be helpful, by simplifying the steps necessary to solve.

Applying Geometric Concepts to Real-World Situations

Real-World Geometry

Many real-world objects can be compared to geometric shapes. Describing certain objects using the measurements and properties of two- and three-dimensional shapes is an important part of geometry. For example, basic ideas such as angles and line segments can be seen in real-world objects. The corner of any room is an angle, and the intersection of a wall with the floor is like a line segment. Building upon this idea, entire objects can be related to both two- and three-dimensional shapes. An entire room can be thought of as square, rectangle, or a sum of a few three-dimensional shapes. Knowing what properties and measures are needed to make decisions in real life is why geometry is such a useful branch of mathematics. One obvious relationship between a real-life situation and geometry exists in construction. For example, to build an addition onto a house, several geometric measurements will be used.

Density

The *density* of a substance is the ratio of mass to area or volume. It's a relationship between the mass and how much space the object actually takes up. Knowing which units to use in each situation is crucial. Population density is an example of a real-life situation that's modeled by using density concepts. It involves calculating the ratio of the number of people to the number of square miles. The amount of material needed per a specific unit of area or volume is another application. For example, estimating the number of BTUs per cubic foot of a home is a measurement that relates to heating or cooling the house based on the desired temperature and the house's size.

Solving Design Problem
Design problems are an important application of geometry (e.g., building structures that satisfy physical constraints and/or minimize costs). These problems involve optimizing a situation based on what's given and required. For example, determining what size barn to build, given certain dimensions and a specific budget, uses both geometric properties and other mathematical concepts. Equations are formed using geometric definitions and the given constraints. In the end, such problems involve solving a system of equations and rely heavily on a strong background in algebra. *Typographic grid systems* also help with such design problems. A grid made up of intersecting straight or curved lines can be used as a visual representation of the structure being designed. This concept is seen in the blueprints used throughout the graphic design process.

Application of Trigonometry to General Triangles

The Area Formula
A triangle that isn't a right triangle is known as an *oblique triangle*. It should be noted that even if the triangle consists of three acute angles, it is still referred to as an oblique triangle. *Oblique*, in this case, does not refer to an angle measurement. Consider the following oblique triangle:

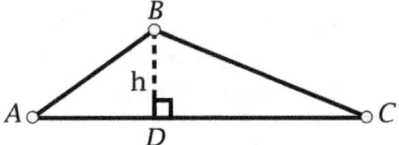

For this triangle, $Area = 1/2 \cdot base \cdot height = 1/2 \cdot AC \cdot BD$. The auxiliary line drawn from the vertex B perpendicular to the opposite side AC represents the height of the triangle. This line splits the larger triangle into two smaller right triangles, which allows for the use of the trigonometric functions (specifically that $\sin A = h/AB$). Therefore,

$$Area = 1/2 \cdot AC \cdot AB \cdot \sin A$$

Typically, the sides are labelled as the lowercase letter of the vertex that's opposite. Therefore, the formula can be written as $Area = \frac{1}{2} bc \sin A$. This area formula can be used to find areas of triangles when given side lengths and angle measurements, or it can be used to find side lengths or angle measurements based on a specific area and other characteristics of the triangle.

Laws of Sines and Cosines
The *law of sines* and *law of cosines* are two more relationships that exist within oblique triangles. Consider a triangle with sides *a*, *b*, and *c*, and angles *A*, *B*, and *C* opposite the corresponding sides.

The law of cosines states that:

$$c^2 = a^2 + b^2 - 2ab \cos C$$

Geometry and Measurement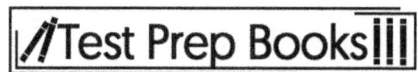

The law of sines states that:

$$\frac{\sin A}{a} = \frac{\sin B}{b} = \frac{\sin C}{c}$$

In addition to the area formula, these two relationships can help find unknown angle and side measurements in oblique triangles.

Transformations in a Plane

Transformations in the Plane
A *transformation* occurs when a shape is altered in the plane where it exists. There are three major types of transformation: translations, reflections, and rotations. A *translation* consists of shifting a shape in one direction. A *reflection* results when a shape is transformed over a line to its mirror image. Finally, a *rotation* occurs when a shape moves in a circular motion around a specified point. The object can be turned clockwise or counterclockwise and, if rotated 360 degrees, returns to its original location.

Distance and Angle Measure
The three major types of transformations preserve distance and angle measurement. The shapes stay the same, but they are moved to another place in the plane. Therefore, the distance between any two points on the shape doesn't change. Also, any original angle measure between two line segments doesn't change. However, there are transformations that don't preserve distance and angle measurements, including those that don't preserve the original shape. For example, transformations that involve stretching and shrinking shapes don't preserve distance and angle measures. In these cases, the input variables are multiplied by either a number greater than one (*stretch*) or less than one (*shrink*).

Solving Problems Using Transformations
Most problems in geometry consist of using either congruent or similar shapes and the proofs that follow. The criteria needed to prove triangles are congruent involve both angle and side congruence, which can be proven through properties of transformations. Both pairs of related angles and sides need to be of the same measurement to prove congruence, meaning one triangle can be obtained from the other via reflections, translations, and rotations. The criteria for triangles to be similar involve proportionality of side lengths. Angles are congruent in similar triangles; however, corresponding side lengths only need to be a constant multiple of each other. Relationships in geometric figures other than triangles can be proven using triangle congruence and similarity. If a similar or congruent triangle can be found within another type of geometric figure, their criteria can be utilized to prove a relationship about a given formula. For instance, a rectangle can be broken up into two congruent triangles.

Rotations and Reflections
A *point of symmetry* is used to determine translations that map a shape onto itself. When a line is drawn through a point of symmetry, it crosses the shape on one side of the point while crossing the shape on the other side at the exact same distance. A shape can be rotated 180 degrees around a point of symmetry to get back to its original shape. Simple examples are the center of a circle and a square. A *line of symmetry* is a line that a shape is folded over to have its sides align, and it goes through the point of symmetry. A combination of reflecting an original shape around a line of symmetry and rotating it can map the original image onto itself. A shape has *rotational symmetry* if it can be rotated to get back to its original shape, and it has *reflection symmetry* if it can be reflected onto itself over some line. Shapes such as rectangles, parallelograms, trapezoids, and regular polygons can be mapped onto themselves through such rotations and reflections.

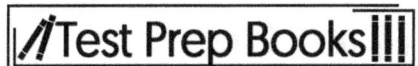

Isometric Transformations

Rotations, reflections, and translations are isometric transformations, because throughout each transformation the distance of line segments is maintained, the angle measure is maintained, parallel lines in the original shape remain parallel, and points on lines remain on those lines.

A rotation turns a shape around a specific point (*O*) known as the *center of rotation*. An *angle of rotation* is formed by drawing a ray from the center of rotation to a point (*P*) on the original shape and to the point's image (*P'*) on the reflected shape. Thus, it's true that *OP=OP'*.

A reflection over a line (*l*), known as the *line of reflection*, takes an original point P and maps it to its image P' on the opposite side of *l*. The line of reflection is the perpendicular bisector of every line formed by an original point and its image.

A translation maps each point P in the original shape to a new point P'. The line segment formed between each point and its image consists of the same length, and the line segment formed by two original points is parallel to the line segment formed from their two images.

Transformation Figures

Once the major transformations are defined, a shape can be altered by performing given transformations. An image is determined from a pre-image by carrying out a series of rotations, reflections, and translations. Once transformations are understood completely, moving and manipulating figures can be related to real-word situations. The transformed figure can then be drawn using either a pencil and paper or geometry software.

Transformation Mapping

Given a pre-image and an image, transformations can be determined that turn one shape into the other. A sequence of rotations, reflections, and translations can be defined that map the pre-image onto the other shape.

Solving Problems in the Coordinate Plane

The location of a point on a coordinate grid is identified by writing it as an ordered pair. An ordered pair is a set of numbers indicating the *x*-and *y*-coordinates of the point. Ordered pairs are written in the form (*x, y*) where *x* and *y* are values which indicate their respective coordinates. For example, the point (3, -2) has an *x*-coordinate of 3 and a *y*-coordinate of -2.

Plotting a point on the coordinate plane with a given coordinate means starting from the origin (0, 0). To determine the value of the *x*-coordinate, move right (positive number) or left (negative number) along the *x*-axis. Next, move up (positive number) or down (negative number) to the value of the *y*-coordinate. Finally, plot and label the point. For example, plotting the point (1, -2) requires starting from the origin and moving right along the *x*-axis to positive one, then moving down until straight across from negative 2 on the *y*-axis. The point is plotted and labeled.

Geometry and Measurement

This point, along with three other points, are plotted and labeled on the graph below.

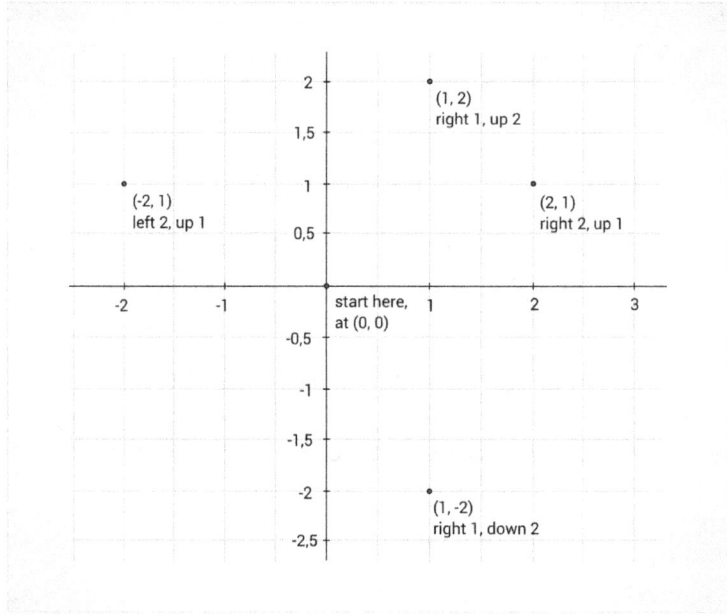

To write the coordinates of a point on the coordinate grid, a line should be traced directly above or below the point until reaching the x-axis (noting the value on the x-axis). Then, returning to the point, a line should be traced directly to the right or left of the point until reaching the y-axis (noting the value on the y-axis). The ordered pair (x, y) should be written with the values determined for the x- and y-coordinates.

Polygons can be drawn in the coordinate plane given the coordinates of their vertices. These coordinates can be used to determine the perimeter and area of the figure. Suppose triangle *RQP* has vertices located at the points: *R*(-4, 2), *Q*(1, 6), and *P*(1, 2). By plotting the points for the three vertices, the triangle can be constructed as follows:

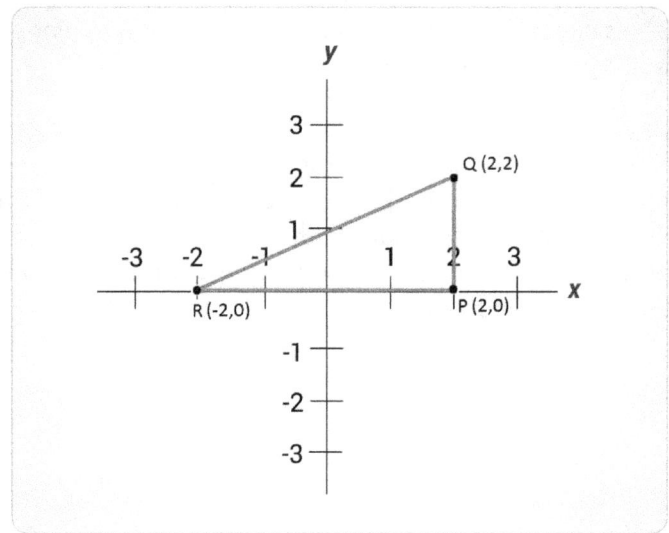

Because points R and P have the same y-coordinates (they are directly across from each other), the distance between them is determined by subtracting their x-coordinates (or simply counting units from one point to the other): 2 − (-2) = 4. Therefore, the length of side RP is 4 units. Because points Q and P have the same x-coordinate (they are directly above and below each other), the distance between them is determined by subtracting their y-coordinates (or counting units between them): 2 − 0 = 2. Therefore, the length of side PQ is 2 units. Knowing the length of side RP, which is the base of the triangle, and the length of side PQ, which is the height of the triangle, the area of the figure can be determined by using the formula $A = \frac{1}{2}bh$.

To determine the perimeter of the triangle, the lengths of all three sides are needed. Points R and Q are neither directly across nor directly above and below each other. Therefore, the distance formula must be used to find the length of side RQ. The distance formula is as follows:

$$d = \sqrt{(x_2 - x_1)^2 + (y_2 - y_1)^2}$$

$$d = \sqrt{(2 - (-2))^2 + (2 - 0)^2}$$

$$d = \sqrt{(4)^2 + (2)^2}$$

$$d = \sqrt{16 + 4} \rightarrow d = \sqrt{20}$$

The perimeter is determined by adding the lengths of the three sides of the triangle.

Using Coordinate Geometry to Algebraically Prove Simple Geometric Theorems

Proving Theorems with Coordinates

Many important formulas and equations exist in geometry that use coordinates. The distance between two points (x_1, y_1) and (x_2, y_2) is:

$$d = \sqrt{(x_2 - x_1)^2 + (y_2 - y_1)^2}$$

The slope of the line containing the same two points is $m = \frac{y_2 - y_1}{x_2 - x_1}$. Also, the midpoint of the line segment with endpoints (x_1, y_1) and (x_2, y_2) is:

$$M = \left(\frac{x_1 + x_2}{2}, \frac{y_1 + y_2}{2}\right)$$

The equations of a circle, parabola, ellipse, and hyperbola can also be used to prove theorems algebraically. Knowing when to use which formula or equation is extremely important, and knowing which formula applies to which property of a given geometric shape is an integral part of the process. In some cases, there are a number of ways to prove a theorem; however, only one way is required.

Formulas for Ratios

If a line segment with endpoints (x_1, y_1) and (x_2, y_2) is partitioned into two equal parts, the formula for midpoint is used. Recall this formula is $M = \left(\frac{x_1 + x_2}{2}, \frac{y_1 + y_2}{2}\right)$ and the ratio of line segments is 1:1. However, if the ratio needs to be anything other than 1:1, a different formula must be used. Consider a

Geometry and Measurement

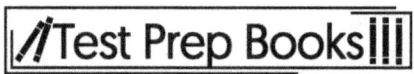

ratio that is $a:b$. This means the desired point that partitions the line segment is $\frac{a}{a+b}$ of the way from (x_1, y_1) to (x_2, y_2). The actual formula for the coordinate is:

$$\left(\frac{bx_1 + ax_2}{a+b}, \frac{by_1 + ay_2}{a+b}\right)$$

Computing Side Length, Perimeter, and Area

The side lengths of each shape can be found by plugging the endpoints into the distance formula:

$$d = \sqrt{(x_2 - x_1)^2 + (y_2 - y_1)^2}$$

between two ordered pairs (x_1, y_1) and (x_2, y_2). The distance formula is derived from the Pythagorean theorem. Once the side lengths are found, they can be added together to obtain the perimeter of the given polygon. Simplifications can be made for specific shapes such as squares and equilateral triangles.

For example, one side length can be multiplied by 4 to obtain the perimeter of a square. Also, one side length can be multiplied by 3 to obtain the perimeter of an equilateral triangle. A similar technique can be used to calculate areas. For polygons, both side length and height can be found by using the same distance formula. Areas of triangles and quadrilaterals are straightforward through the use of $A = \frac{1}{2}bh$ or $A = bh$, depending on the shape. To find the area of other polygons, their shapes can be partitioned into rectangles and triangles. The areas of these simpler shapes can be calculated and then added together to find the total area of the polygon.

Proving Geometric Theorems

Proving Theorems About Lines and Angles

To prove any geometric theorem, the proven theorems must be linked in a logical order that flows from an original point to the desired result. Proving theorems about lines and angles is the basis of proving theorems that involve other shapes. A *transversal* is a line that passes through two lines at two points. Common theorems that need to be proved are: vertical angles are congruent; a transversal passing through two parallel lines forms two alternate interior angles that are congruent and two corresponding angles that are congruent; and points on a perpendicular bisector of a line segment are equidistant from the endpoints of the line segment.

Triangle Theorems

To prove theorems about triangles, basic definitions involving triangles (e.g., equilateral, isosceles, etc.) need to be realized. Proven theorems concerning lines and angles can be applied to prove theorems about triangles. Common theorems to be proved include: the sum of all angles in a triangle equals 180 degrees; the sum of the lengths of two sides of a triangle is greater than the length of the third side; the base angles of an isosceles triangle are congruent; the line segment connecting the midpoint of two sides of a triangle is parallel to the third side and its length is half the length of the third side; and the medians of a triangle all meet at a single point.

Parallelogram Theorems

A *parallelogram* is a quadrilateral with parallel opposing sides. Within parallelograms, opposite sides and angles are congruent and the diagonals bisect each other. Known theorems about parallel lines, transversals, complementary angles, and congruent triangles can be used to prove theorems about parallelograms. Theorems that need to be proved include: opposite sides of a parallelogram are congruent; opposite angles are congruent; the diagonals bisect each other; and rectangles are parallelograms with congruent diagonals.

Translating Between a Geometric Description and an Equation for a Conic Section

Equation of a Circle

A *circle* can be defined as the set of all points that are the same distance (known as the radius, *r*) from a single point *C* (known as the center of the circle). The center has coordinates (h, k), and any point on the circle can be labelled with coordinates (x, y). As shown below, a *right triangle* is formed with these two points:

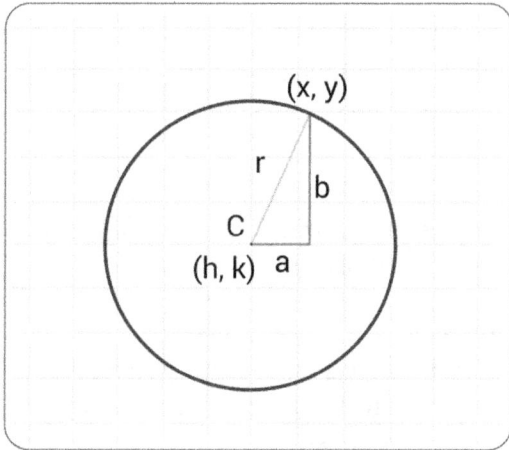

The Pythagorean theorem states that:
$$a^2 + b^2 = r^2$$

However, *a* can be replaced by $|x - h|$ and *b* can be replaced by $|y - k|$ by using the *distance formula*. That substitution results in $(x - h)^2 + (y - k)^2 = r^2$, which is the formula for finding the equation of any circle with a center (h, k) and a radius *r*. Note that sometimes *c* is used instead of *r*.

Finding the Center and Radius

Circles aren't always given in the form of the circle equation where the center and radius can be seen so easily. Oftentimes, they're given in the more general format of:

$$ax^2 + by^2 + cx + dy + e = 0$$

This can be converted to the center-radius form using the algebra technique of completing the square in both variables. First, the constant term is moved over to the other side of the equals sign, and then the *x* and *y* variable terms are grouped together. Then the equation is divided through by *a* and, because this is the equation of a circle, $a = b$. At this point, the *x*-term coefficient is divided by 2, squared, and then added to both sides of the equation. This value is grouped with the *x* terms. The same steps then need to be completed with the *y*-term coefficient. The trinomial in both *x* and *y* can now be factored into a square of a binomial, which gives both $(x - h)^2$ and $(y - k)^2$.

Parabola Equations

A *parabola* is defined as a specific type of curve such that any point on it is the same distance from a fixed point (called the *focus*) and a fixed straight line (called the *directrix*). A parabola is the shape formed from the intersection of a cone with a plane that's parallel to its side. Every parabola has an *axis of symmetry*, and its vertex (h, k) is the point at which the axis of symmetry intersects the curve. If the parabola has an axis of symmetry parallel to the y-axis, the focus is the point $(h, k + f)$ and the directrix is the line $y = k - f$. For example, a parabola may have a vertex at the origin, focus $(0, f)$, and directrix $y = -f$. The equation of this parabola can be derived by using both the focus and the directrix. The distance from any coordinate on the curve to the focus is the same as the distance to the directrix, and the Pythagorean theorem can be used to find the length of d. The triangle has sides with length $|x|$ and $|y - f|$ and therefore,

$$d = \sqrt{x^2 + (y - f)^2}$$

By definition, the vertex is halfway between the focus and the directrix and $d = y + f$. Setting these two equations equal to one another, squaring each side, simplifying, and solving for y gives the equation of a parabola with the focus f and the vertex being the origin:

$$y = \frac{1}{4f} x^2$$

If the vertex (h, k) is not the origin, a similar process can be completed to derive the equation $(x - h)^2 = 4f(y - k)$ for a parabola with focus f.

Ellipse and Hyperbola Equations

An *ellipse* is the set of all points for which the sum of the distances from two fixed points (known as the *foci*) is constant. A *hyperbola* is the set of all points for which the difference between the distances from two fixed points (also known as the *foci*) is constant. The *distance formula* can be used to derive the formulas of both an ellipse and a hyperbola, given the coordinates of the foci. Consider an ellipse where its major axis is horizontal (i.e., it's longer along the x-axis) and its foci are the coordinates $(-c, 0)$ and $(c, 0)$. The distance from any point (x, y) to $(-c, 0)$ is $d_1 = \sqrt{(x + c)^2 + y^2}$, and the distance from the same point (x, y) to $(c, 0)$ is:

$$d_1 = \sqrt{(x - c)^2 + y^2}$$

Using the definition of an ellipse, it's true that the sum of the distances from the vertex a to each foci is equal to $d_1 + d_2$. Therefore:

$$d_1 + d_2$$

$$(a + c) + (a - c)$$

$$2a \quad \sqrt{(x + c)^2 + y^2} + \sqrt{(x - c)^2 + y^2}$$

$$2a$$

After a series of algebraic steps, this equation can be simplified to $\frac{x^2}{a^2} + \frac{y^2}{b^2} = 1$, which is the equation of an ellipse with a horizontal major axis. In this case, $a > b$. When the ellipse has a vertical major axis, similar techniques result in $\frac{x^2}{b^2} + \frac{y^2}{a^2} = 1$, and $a > b$.

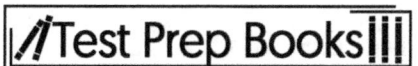

Geometry and Measurement

The equation of a hyperbola can be derived in a similar fashion. Consider a hyperbola with a horizontal major axis and its foci are also the coordinates $(-c, 0)$ and $(c, 0)$. Again, the distance from any point (x, y) to $(-c, 0)$ is $d_1 = \sqrt{(x+c)^2 + y^2}$ and the distance from the same point (x, y) to $(c, 0)$ is:

$$d_1 = \sqrt{(x-c)^2 + y^2}$$

Using the definition of a hyperbola, it's true that the difference of the distances from the vertex a to each foci is equal to $d_1 - d_2$. Therefore:

$$d_1 - d_2 = (c + a) - (c - a) = 2a$$

This means that:

$$\sqrt{(x+c)^2 + y^2} - \sqrt{(x-c)^2 + y^2} = 2a$$

After a series of algebraic steps, this equation can be simplified to $\frac{x^2}{a^2} - \frac{y^2}{b^2} = 1$, which is the equation of a hyperbola with a horizontal major axis. In this case, $a > b$. Similar techniques result in the equation $\frac{x^2}{b} - \frac{y^2}{a^2} = 1$, where $a > b$, when the hyperbola has a vertical major axis.

Vectors

A vector can be thought of as a list of numbers. These can be thought of as an abstract list of numbers, or else as giving a location in a space. For example, the coordinates (x, y) for points in the Cartesian plane are vectors. Each entry in a vector can be referred to by its location in the list: first, second, and so on. The total length of the list is the *dimension* of the vector. A vector is often denoted as such by putting an arrow on top of it, e.g. $\vec{v} = (v_1, v_2, v_3)$

Add Vectors Graphically and Algebraically

There are two basic operations for vectors. First, two vectors can be added together. Let:

$$\vec{v} = (v_1, v_2, v_3), \vec{w} = (w_1, w_2, w_3)$$

The sum of the two vectors is defined to be:

$$\vec{v} + \vec{w} = (v_1 + w_1, v_2 + w_2, v_3 + w_3)$$

Subtraction of vectors can be defined similarly.

Vector addition can be visualized in the following manner. First, visualize each vector as an arrow. Then place the base of one arrow at the tip of the other arrow. The tip of this first arrow now hits some point in the space, and there will be an arrow from the origin to this point. This new arrow corresponds to the new vector. In subtraction, we reverse the direction of the arrow being subtracted.

For example, consider adding together the vectors (-2, 3) and (4, 1). The new vector will be (-2+4, 3+1), or (2, 4). Graphically, this may be pictured in the following manner.

Geometry and Measurement

Perform Scalar Multiplication

The second basic operation for vectors is called *scalar multiplication*. Scalar multiplication allows us to multiply any vector by any real number, which is denoted here as a scalar. Let $\vec{v} = (v_1, v_2, v_3)$, and let a be an arbitrary real number. Then the scalar multiple:

$$a\vec{v} = (av_1, av_2, av_3)$$

Graphically, this corresponds to changing the length of the arrow corresponding to the vector by a factor, or scale, of a. That is why the real number is called a scalar in this instance.

As an example, let $\vec{v} = \left(2, -1, \frac{1}{3}\right)$. Then:

$$3\vec{v} = \left(3 \cdot 2, 3(-1), 3 \cdot \frac{1}{3}\right) = (6, -3, 1)$$

Note that scalar multiplication is *distributive* over vector addition, meaning that:

$$a(\vec{v} + \vec{w}) = a\vec{v} + a\vec{w}$$

Represent Vector Equations of Lines and Planes

Since vectors can be thought of as giving directions, and since lines continue on in a single direction, it is possible to represent any line by using vectors. To do so requires two things: a vector $\vec{p}$ that goes to a point on the line, and a vector $\vec{r}$ which gives the direction of a line. The equation for the line will then be all vectors of the form $\vec{v} = \vec{p} + s\vec{r}$, where s can take the value of any real number.

Suppose we know two points on the line, A and B. Then we can take $\vec{p}$ to be the vector pointing to A, and take $\vec{r}$ to be the vector that goes from A to B. This will be the vector going to B minus the vector going to A. Of course, there will be many different vector equations corresponding to the same line, since any two points on the line may be used.

Consider a line in the Cartesian plane which passes through the points (1, -2) and (2, 3). Call the first point A and the second point B. Then we can take $\vec{p} = (-1, 2)$, and:

$$\vec{r} = (2, 3) - (-1, 2) = (3, 1)$$

Then the vector equation for the line will be:

$$\vec{v} = (-1, 2) + s(3, 1)$$

A plane in three dimensions can similarly be represented by using vectors. In this case, three vectors are needed: first, a vector $\vec{p}$ pointing to some point on the plane, and then two vectors $\vec{q}$ and $\vec{r}$ corresponding to the two directions in which the plane goes. If three points on the plane are given, A, B, and C, then one can take $\vec{p}$ to be the vector pointing to A, $\vec{q}$ to be the vector from A to B, and $\vec{r}$ to be the vector from A to C. The vector equation for the plane is then:

$$\vec{v} = \vec{p} + s\vec{q} + t\vec{r}$$

Note, however, that this requires the three given points to not all lie on the same line. If they all lie upon a single line, then they do not define a unique plane.

Suppose, then, that the points $(0, 3, 3), (-2, 2, 2), (-1, 1, 0)$ lie on a plane. We can take $\vec{p} = (0, 3, 3)$, $\vec{q} = (-2, 2, 2) - (0, 3, 3) = (-2, -1, -1)$, and $\vec{r} = (-1, 1, 0) - (0, 3, 3) = (-1, -2, -3)$. The vector equation for the plane will now be:

$$\vec{v} = (0, 3, 3) + s(-2, -1, -1) + t(-1, -2, -3)$$

Practice Quiz

1. In the xy-plane, the graph of $y = x^2 + 2$ and the circle with center $(0,1)$ and radius 1 have how many points of intersection?
    a. 0
    b. 1
    c. 2
    d. 3

2.

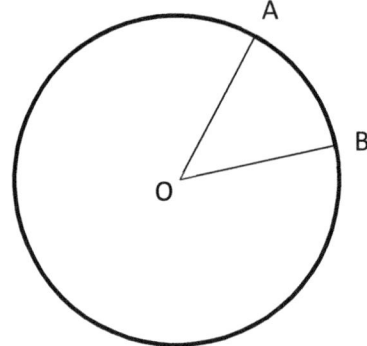

The length of arc $AB = 3\pi$ cm. The length of $\overline{OA} = 12$ cm. What is the degree measure of $\angle AOB$?
    a. 30 degrees
    b. 40 degrees
    c. 45 degrees
    d. 55 degrees

3. A pyramid has a square base with a side length of 6 inches, and the pyramid's height is 9 inches. What is the pyramid's volume?
    a. 324 in^3
    b. 72 in^3
    c. 108 in^3
    d. 18 in^3

4.

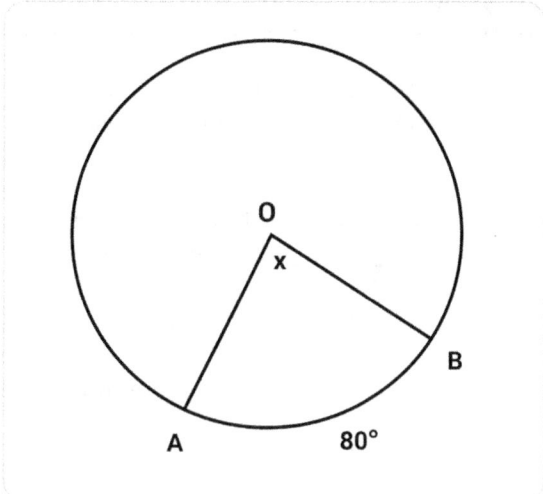

The area of circle O is $49\pi\ m$. What is the area of the sector formed by $\angle AOB$?
- a. $80\pi\ m$
- b. $10.9\pi\ m$
- c. $4.9\pi\ m$
- d. $10\pi\ m$

5. What is the measurement of angle f in the following picture? Assume the lines are parallel.

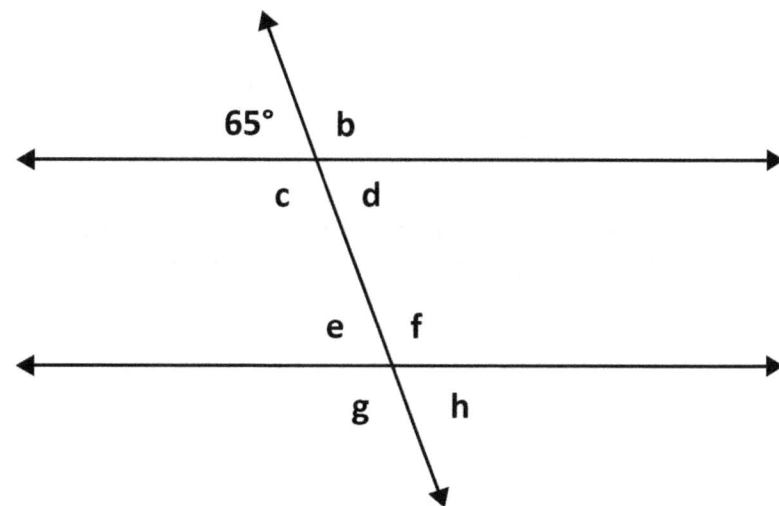

- a. 68 degrees
- b. 112 degrees
- c. 128 degrees
- d. 52 degrees

See answers on the next page.

Answer Explanations

1. B: The graph of $y = x^2 + 2$ has a vertex at $(0, 2)$ on the y-axis. The circle with a center at $(0, 1)$ also lies on the y-axis. With a radius of 1, the circle touches the parabola at one point: the vertex of the parabola, $(0, 2)$.

2. C: The formula to find arc length is $s = \theta r$, where s is the arc length, θ is the radian measure of the central angle, and r is the radius of the circle. Substituting the given information produces:

$$3\pi \text{ cm} = \theta \times 12 \text{ cm}$$

Solving for θ yields $\theta = \frac{\pi}{4}$. To convert from radian to degrees, multiply the radian measure by $\frac{180}{\pi}$:

$$\frac{\pi}{4} \times \frac{180}{\pi} = 45°$$

3. C: The formula for the volume of a pyramid is $V = \frac{lwh}{3}$. Here, the length and width are each 6 in, and the height is 9 in, so we calculate $V = \frac{6 \times 6 \times 9}{3} = 108 \text{ in}^3$.

4. B: Given the area of the circle, the radius can be found using the formula $A = \pi r^2$. In this case, $49\pi = \pi r^2$, which yields $r = 7$ m. A central angle is equal to the degree measure of the arc it inscribes; therefore, $\angle x = 80°$. The area of a sector can be found using the formula:

$$A = \frac{\theta}{360°} \times \pi r^2$$

In this case,

$$A = \frac{80°}{360°} \times \pi(7)r^2 = 10.9\pi \text{ m}$$

5. B: Because the 68-degree angle and angle b sum to 180 degrees, the measurement of angle b is 112 degrees. Because of corresponding angles, angle b is equal to angle f. Therefore, angle f measures 112 degrees.

Probability and Statistics

Measurement Scales

There are four types of scales used in mathematics and statistics to standardize measurements: nominal, ordinal, interval, and ratio. A nominal scale is not a measurement; rather, it replaces labels or categories with numbers. To track people's political affiliations, a researcher might assign Republicans the number one, Democrats the number two, Libertarians the number three, and so on. This is an example of a nominal scale. An ordinal scale places items in order from least to greatest or greatest to least, but the distance or interval between each item is unknown. Contests use the ordinal scale. In a science fair, students might be ranked in first, second, or third place, but they wouldn't know how much *better* first was from second and so forth.

An interval includes the order and the distance between each item. It lacks an absolute zero; in other words, a complete absence of whatever it is you're measuring. The Fahrenheit Scale is an excellent example. Someone might understand that forty degrees Fahrenheit is twice as hot as twenty, but, at the same, there's no true zero, where it can't get any colder. Lastly, is the ratio scale. Ratio scales can be ranked from least to greatest or greatest to least, the order and the distance between each item is known, and ratio scales include an absolute zero, or the absence of whatever is being measured. Body weight is a common example of something measured on a ratio scale. When someone steps on a scale, he or she knows that one hundred pounds is exactly twice as much as fifty, and when that person steps off the scale, the needle jumps back to zero, indicating a complete absence of weight.

Interpreting Displays of Data

A set of data can be visually displayed in various forms allowing for quick identification of characteristics of the set. Histograms, such as the one shown below, display the number of data points (vertical axis) that fall into given intervals (horizontal axis) across the range of the set. The histogram below displays the heights of black cherry trees in a certain city park. Each rectangle represents the number of trees with heights between a given five-point span. For example, the furthest bar to the right indicates that two trees are between 85 and 90 feet. Histograms can describe the center, spread, shape, and any unusual characteristics of a data set.

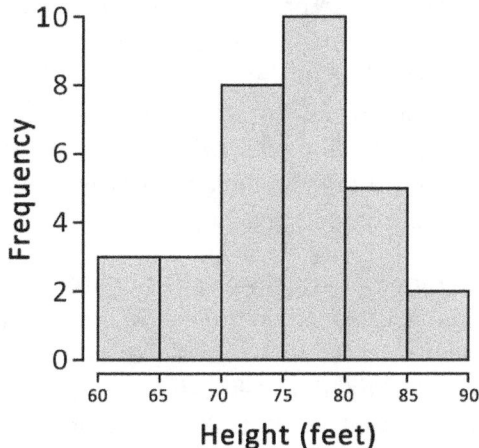

Probability and Statistics

A box plot, also called a box-and-whisker plot, divides the data points into four groups and displays the five-number summary for the set as well as any outliers. The five-number summary consists of:

- The lower extreme: the lowest value that is not an outlier
- The higher extreme: the highest value that is not an outlier
- The median of the set: also referred to as the second quartile or Q_2
- The first quartile or Q_1: the median of values below Q_2
- The third quartile or Q_3: the median of values above Q_2

To construct a box (or box-and-whisker) plot, the five-number summary for the data set is calculated as follows: the second quartile (Q_2) is the median of the set. The first quartile (Q_1) is the median of the values below Q_2. The third quartile (Q_3) is the median of the values above Q_2. The upper extreme is the highest value in the data set if it is not an outlier (greater than 1.5 times the interquartile range $Q_3 - Q_1$). The lower extreme is the least value in the data set if it is not an outlier (more than 1.5 times lower than the interquartile range). To construct the box-and-whisker plot, each value is plotted on a number line, along with any outliers. The box consists of Q_1 and Q_3 as its top and bottom and Q_2 as the dividing line inside the box. The whiskers extend from the lower extreme to Q_1 and from Q_3 to the upper extreme.

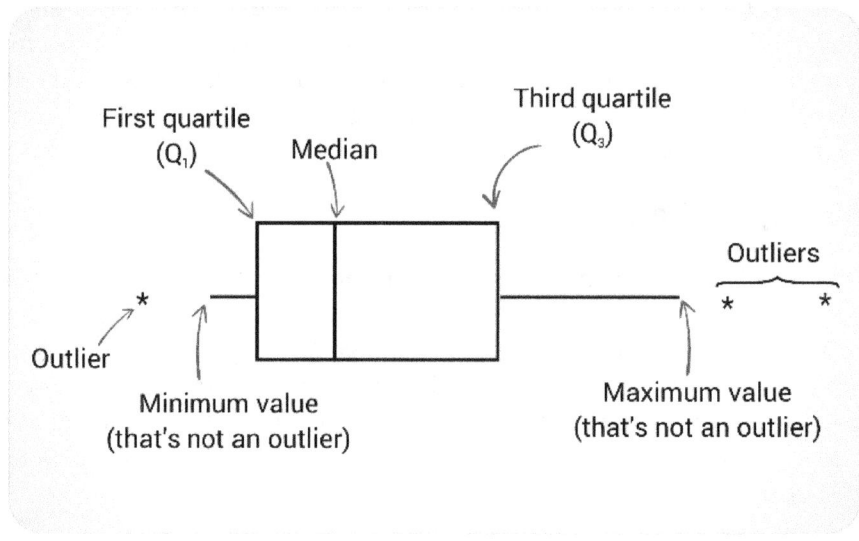

Suppose the box plot displays IQ scores for 12th grade students at a given school. The five-number summary of the data consists of: lower extreme (67); upper extreme (127); Q_2 or median (100); Q_1 (91); Q_3 (108); and outliers (135 and 140). Although all data points are not known from the plot, the points are divided into four quartiles each, including 25% of the data points. Therefore, 25% of students scored between 67 and 91, 25% scored between 91 and 100, 25% scored between 100 and 108, and 25% scored between 108 and 127. These percentages include the normal values for the set and exclude the outliers. This information is useful when comparing a given score with the rest of the scores in the set.

A scatter plot is a mathematical diagram that visually displays the relationship or connection between two variables. The independent variable is placed on the *x*-axis, or horizontal axis, and the dependent variable is placed on the *y*-axis, or vertical axis. When visually examining the points on the graph, if the points model a linear relationship, or if a line of best-fit can be drawn through the points with the points relatively close on either side, then a correlation exists. If the line of best-fit has a positive slope (rises from left to right), then the variables have a positive correlation. If the line of best-fit has a negative slope (falls from left to right), then the variables have a negative correlation. If a line of best-fit cannot be drawn, then no correlation exists. A positive or negative correlation can be categorized as strong or weak, depending on how closely the points are graphed around the line of best-fit.

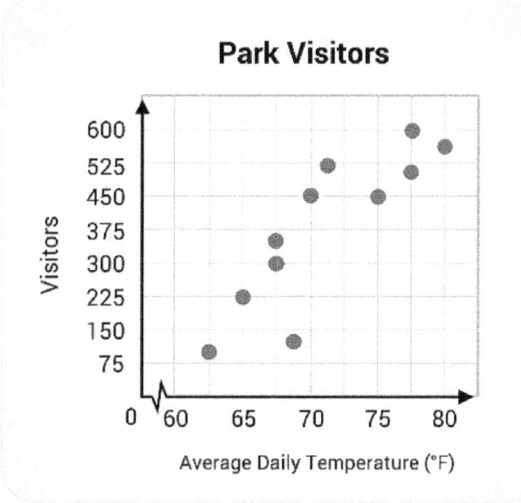

Graphical Representation of Data

Like a scatter plot, a line graph compares variables that change continuously, typically over time. Paired data values (ordered pairs) are plotted on a coordinate grid with the x- and y-axis representing the variables. A line is drawn from each point to the next, going from left to right. The line graph below displays cell phone use for given years (two variables) for men, women, and both sexes (three data sets).

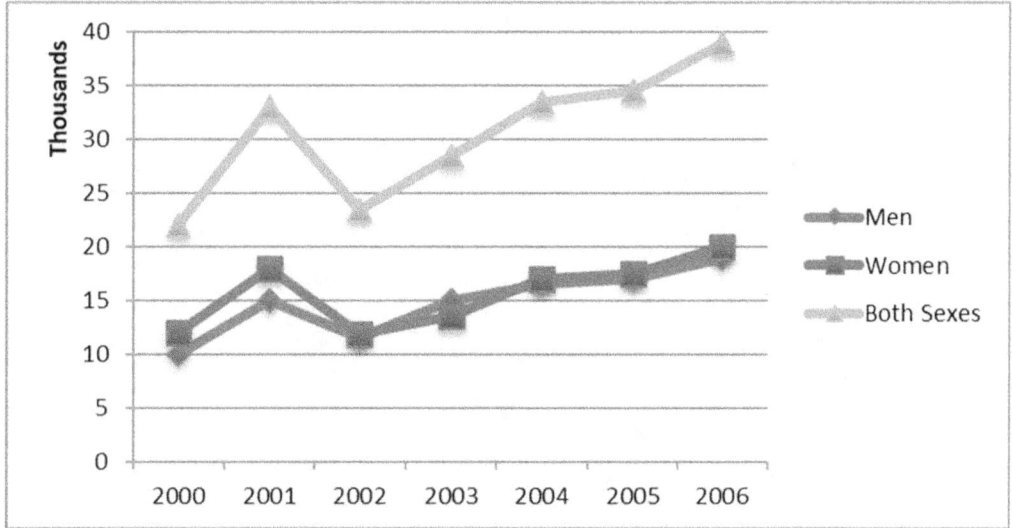

A line plot, also called dot plot, displays the frequency of data (numerical values) on a number line. To construct a line plot, a number line is used that includes all unique data values. It is marked with x's or dots above the value the number of times that the value occurs in the data set. The line plot shown below indicates the number of hours spent playing video games for each day of the week. The first day there were zero hours, the second day there were 2 hours, and so on.

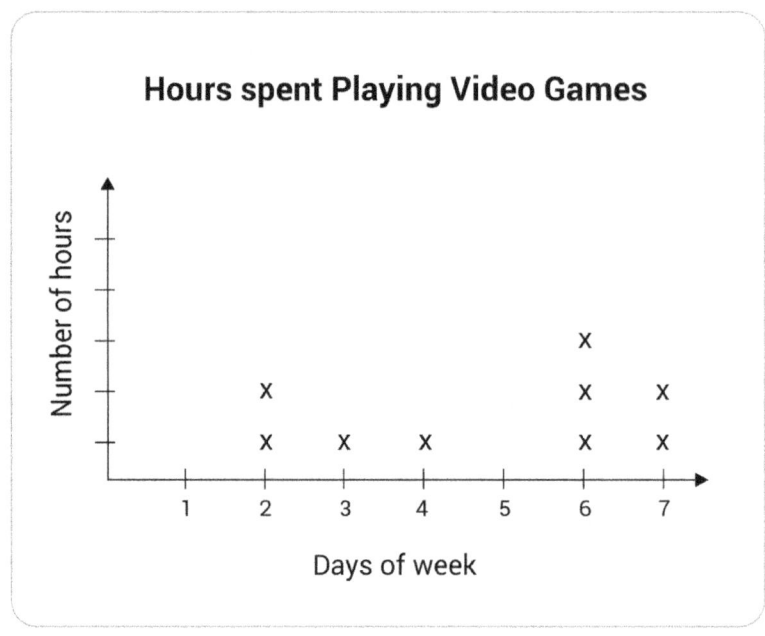

A bar graph looks similar to a histogram but displays categorical data. The horizontal axis represents each category and the vertical axis represents the frequency for the category. A bar is drawn for each category (often different colors) with a height extending to the frequency for that category within the data set. A double bar graph displays two sets of data that contain data points consisting of the same categories. The double bar graph below indicates that two girls and four boys like Pad Thai the most out of all the foods, two boys and five girls like pizza, and so on.

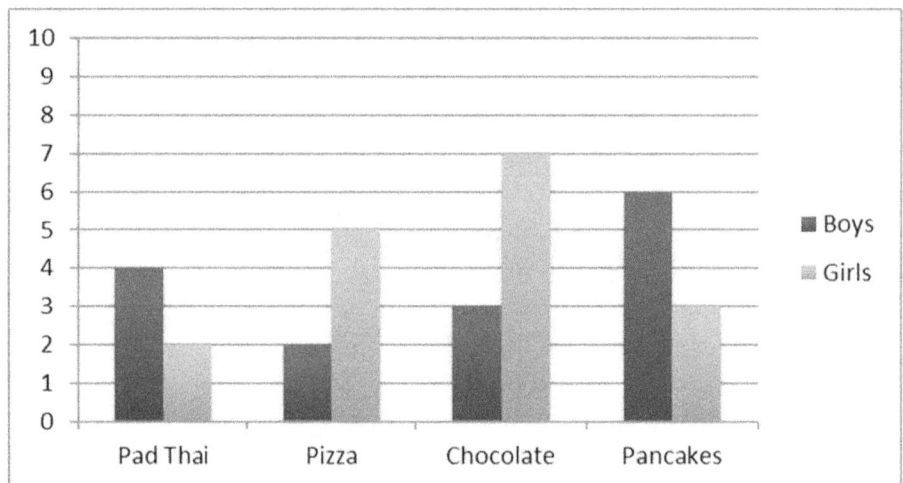

A circle graph, also called a pie chart, displays categorical data with each category representing a percentage of the whole data set. To construct a circle graph, the percent of the data set for each category must be determined. To do so, the frequency of the category is divided by the total number of data points and converted to a percent. For example, if 80 people were asked their favorite pizza topping and 20 responded cheese, then cheese constitutes 25% of the data:

$$\frac{20}{80} = .25 = 25\%$$

Each category in a data set is represented by a *slice* of the circle proportionate to its percentage of the whole.

Choice of Graphs to Display Data

Choosing the appropriate graph to display a data set depends on what type of data is included in the set and what information must be displayed. Histograms and box plots can be used for data sets consisting of individual values across a wide range. Examples include test scores and incomes. Histograms and box plots will indicate the center, spread, range, and outliers of a data set. A histogram will show the shape of the data set, while a box plot will divide the set into quartiles (25% increments), allowing for comparison between a given value and the entire set.

Scatter plots and line graphs can be used to display data consisting of two variables. Examples include height and weight, or distance and time. A correlation between the variables is determined by examining the points on the graph. Line graphs are used if each value for one variable pairs with a distinct value for the other variable. Line graphs show relationships between variables.

Line plots, bar graphs, and circle graphs are all used to display categorical data, such as surveys. Line plots and bar graphs both indicate the frequency of each category within the data set. A line plot is used when the categories consist of numerical values. For example, the number of hours of TV watched by individuals is displayed on a line plot. A bar graph is used when the categories consists of words. For example, the favorite ice cream of individuals is displayed with a bar graph. A circle graph can be used to display either type of categorical data. However, unlike line plots and bar graphs, a circle graph does not indicate the frequency of each category. Instead, the circle graph represents each category as its percentage of the whole data set.

Probability and Statistics

Describing a Set of Data

A set of data can be described in terms of its center, spread, shape and any unusual features. The center of a data set can be measured by its mean, median, or mode. The spread of a data set refers to how far the data points are from the center (mean or median). The spread can be measured by the range or by the quartiles and interquartile range. A data set with all its data points clustered around the center will have a small spread. A data set covering a wide range of values will have a large spread.

When a data set is displayed as a histogram or frequency distribution plot, the shape indicates if a sample is normally distributed, symmetrical, or has measures of skewness or kurtosis. When graphed, a data set with a normal distribution will resemble a bell curve.

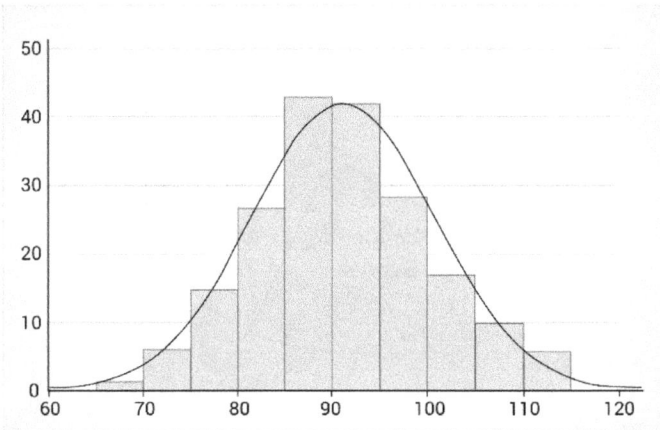

If the data set is symmetrical, each half of the graph when divided at the center is a mirror image of the other. If the graph has fewer data points to the right, the data is skewed right. If it has fewer data points to the left, the data is skewed left.

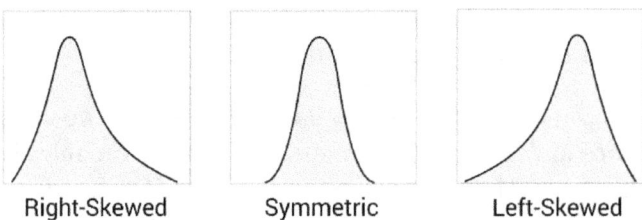

Kurtosis is a measure of whether the data is heavy-tailed with a high number of outliers, or light-tailed with a low number of outliers.

A description of a data set should include any unusual features such as gaps or outliers. A gap is a span within the range of the data set containing no data points. An outlier is a data point with a value either extremely large or extremely small when compared to the other values in the set.

Normal Distribution

A *normal distribution* of data follows the shape of a bell curve. In a normal distribution, the data set's median, mean, and mode are equal. Therefore, 50 percent of its values are less than the mean and 50 percent are greater than the mean. Data sets that follow this shape can be generalized using normal distributions. Normal distributions are described as *frequency distributions* in which the data set is plotted as percentages rather than true data points. A *relative frequency distribution* is one where the y-axis is between zero and 1, which is the same as 0% to 100%. Within a standard deviation, 68 percent of the values are within 1 standard deviation of the mean, 95 percent of the values are within 2 standard deviations of the mean, and 99.7 percent of the values are within 3 standard deviations of the mean.

The number of standard deviations that a data point falls from the mean is called the *z-score*. The formula for the z-score is $Z = \frac{x-\mu}{\sigma}$, where μ is the mean, σ is the standard deviation, and x is the data point. This formula is used to fit any data set that resembles a normal distribution to a standard normal distribution in a process known as **standardizing**. Here is a normal distribution with labelled z-scores:

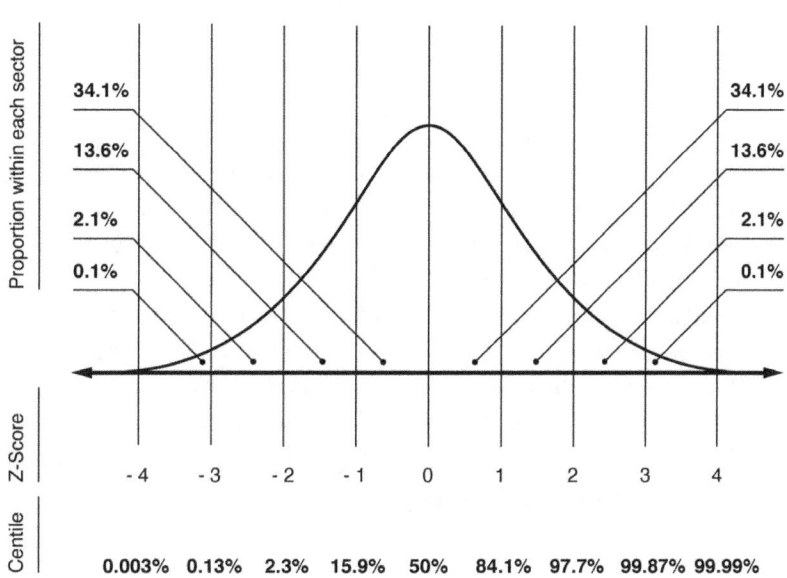

Population percentages can be estimated using normal distributions. For example, the probability that a data point will be less than the mean, or that the z-score will be less than 0, is 50%. Similarly, the probability that a data point will be within 1 standard deviation of the mean, or that the z-score will be between -1 and 1, is about 68.2%. When using a z-table, the left column states how many standard deviations (to one decimal place) away from the mean the point is, and the row heading states the second decimal place. The entries in the table corresponding to each column and row give the probability, which is equal to the area.

Measures of Center and Range

The center of a set of data (statistical values) can be represented by its mean, median, or mode. These are sometimes referred to as measures of central tendency. The mean is the average of the data set.

Probability and Statistics

The mean can be calculated by adding the data values and dividing by the sample size (the number of data points). Suppose a student has test scores of 93, 84, 88, 72, 91, and 77. To find the mean, or average, the scores are added and the sum is divided by 6 because there are 6 test scores:

$$\frac{93 + 84 + 88 + 72 + 91 + 77}{6} = \frac{505}{6} = 84.17$$

Given the mean of a data set and the sum of the data points, the sample size can be determined by dividing the sum by the mean. Suppose you are told that Kate averaged 12 points per game and scored a total of 156 points for the season. The number of games that she played (the sample size or the number of data points) can be determined by dividing the total points (sum of data points) by her average (mean of data points): $\frac{156}{12} = 13$. Therefore, Kate played in 13 games this season.

If given the mean of a data set and the sample size, the sum of the data points can be determined by multiplying the mean and sample size. Suppose you are told that Tom worked 6 days last week for an average of 5.5 hours per day. The total number of hours worked for the week (sum of data points) can be determined by multiplying his daily average (mean of data points) by the number of days worked (sample size):

$$5.5 \times 6 = 33$$

Therefore, Tom worked a total of 33 hours last week.

The median of a data set is the value of the data point in the middle when the sample is arranged in numerical order. To find the median of a data set, the values are written in order from least to greatest. The lowest and highest values are simultaneously eliminated, repeating until the value in the middle remains. Suppose the salaries of math teachers are: $35,000; $38,500; $41,000; $42,000; $42,000; $44,500; $49,000. The values are listed from least to greatest to find the median. The lowest and highest values are eliminated until only the middle value remains. Repeating this step three times reveals a median salary of $42,000. If the sample set has an even number of data points, two values will remain after all others are eliminated. In this case, the mean of the two middle values is the median. Consider the following data set: 7, 9, 10, 13, 14, 14. Eliminating the lowest and highest values twice leaves two values, 10 and 13, in the middle. The mean of these values $\left(\frac{10+13}{2}\right)$ is the median. Therefore, the set has a median of 11.5.

The mode of a data set is the value that appears most often. A data set may have a single mode, multiple modes, or no mode. If different values repeat equally as often, multiple modes exist. If no value repeats, no mode exists. Consider the following data sets:

- A: 7, 9, 10, 13, 14, 14
- B: 37, 44, 33, 37, 49, 44, 51, 34, 37, 33, 44
- C: 173, 154, 151, 168, 155

Set A has a mode of 14. Set B has modes of 37 and 44. Set C has no mode.

The range of a data set is the difference between the highest and the lowest values in the set. The range can be considered the span of the data set. To determine the range, the smallest value in the set is subtracted from the largest value. The ranges for the data sets A, B, and C above are calculated as follows: A: $14 - 7 = 7$; B: $51 - 33 = 18$; C: $173 - 151 = 22$.

Best Description of a Set of Data

Measures of central tendency, namely mean, median, and mode, describe characteristics of a set of data. Specifically, they are intended to represent a *typical* value in the set by identifying a central position of the set. Depending on the characteristics of a specific set of data, different measures of central tendency are more indicative of a typical value in the set.

When a data set is grouped closely together with a relatively small range and the data is spread out somewhat evenly, the mean is an effective indicator of a typical value in the set. Consider the following data set representing the height of sixth grade boys in inches: 61 inches, 54 inches, 58 inches, 63 inches, 58 inches. The mean of the set is 58.8 inches. The data set is grouped closely (the range is only 9 inches) and the values are spread relatively evenly (three values below the mean and two values above the mean). Therefore, the mean value of 58.8 inches is an effective measure of central tendency in this case.

When a data set contains a small number of values either extremely large or extremely small when compared to the other values, the mean is not an effective measure of central tendency. Consider the following data set representing annual incomes of homeowners on a given street: $71,000; $74,000; $75,000; $77,000; $340,000. The mean of this set is $127,400. This figure does not indicate a typical value in the set, which contains four out of five values between $71,000 and $77,000. The median is a much more effective measure of central tendency for data sets such as these. Finding the middle value diminishes the influence of outliers, or numbers that may appear out of place, like the $340,000 annual income. The median for this set is $75,000 which is much more typical of a value in the set.

The mode of a data set is a useful measure of central tendency for categorical data when each piece of data is an option from a category. Consider a survey of 31 commuters asking how they get to work with results summarized below.

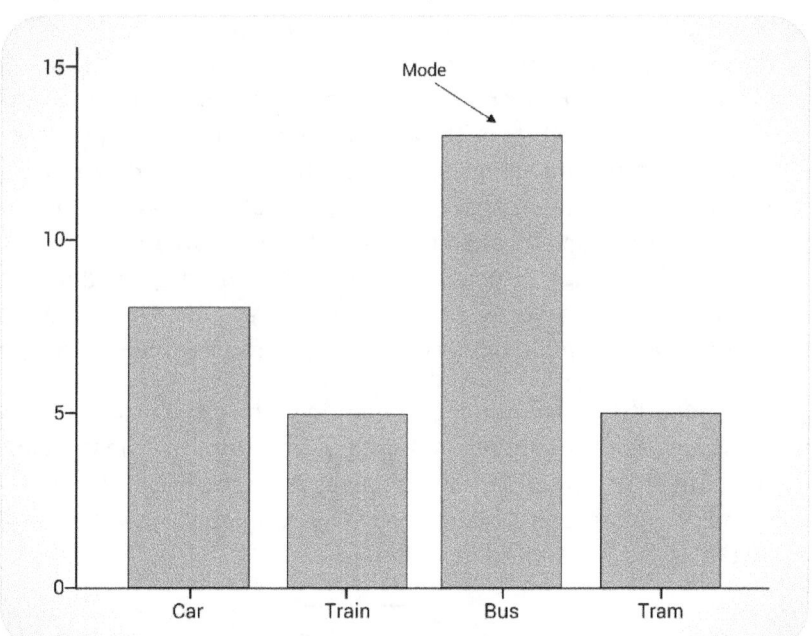

The mode for this set represents the value, or option, of the data that repeats most often. This indicates that the bus is the most popular method of transportation for the commuters.

Effects of Changes in Data

Changing all values of a data set in a consistent way produces predictable changes in the measures of the center and range of the set. A linear transformation changes the original value into the new value by either adding a given number to each value, multiplying each value by a given number, or both. Adding (or subtracting) a given value to each data point will increase (or decrease) the mean, median, and any modes by the same value. However, the range will remain the same due to the way that range is calculated. Multiplying (or dividing) a given value by each data point will increase (or decrease) the mean, median, and any modes, and the range by the same factor.

Consider the following data set, call it set *P*, representing the price of different cases of soda at a grocery store: $4.25, $4.40, $4.75, $4.95, $4.95, $5.15. The mean of set *P* is $4.74. The median is $4.85. The mode of the set is $4.95. The range is $0.90. Suppose the state passes a new tax of $0.25 on every case of soda sold. The new data set, set *T*, is calculated by adding $0.25 to each data point from set *P*. Therefore, set *T* consists of the following values: $4.50, $4.65, $5.00, $5.20, $5.20, $5.40. The mean of set *T* is $4.99. The median is $5.10. The mode of the set is $5.20. The range is $.90. The mean, median and mode of set *T* is equal to $0.25 added to the mean, median, and mode of set *P*. The range stays the same.

Now suppose, due to inflation, the store raises the cost of every item by 10 percent. Raising costs by 10 percent is calculated by multiplying each value by 1.1. The new data set, set *I*, is calculated by multiplying each data point from set *T* by 1.1. Therefore, set *I* consists of the following values: $4.95, $5.12, $5.50, $5.72, $5.72, $5.94. The mean of set *I* is $5.49. The median is $5.61. The mode of the set is $5.72. The range is $0.99. The mean, median, mode, and range of set *I* is equal to 1.1 multiplied by the mean, median, mode, and range of set *T* because each increased by a factor of 10 percent.

Comparing Data

Data sets can be compared by looking at the center and spread of each set. Measures of central tendency involve median, mean, midrange, and mode. The *mode* of a data set is the data value or values that appears the most frequently. The *midrange* is equal to the maximum value plus the minimum value divided by two. The *median* is the value that is halfway into each data set; it splits the data into two intervals. The *mean* is the sum of all data values divided by the number of data points. Two completely different sets of data can have the same mean. For example, a data set having values ranging from 0 to 100 and a data set having values ranging from 44 to 46 could both have means equal to 50. The first data set would have a much wider range, which is known as the *spread* of the data. It measures how varied the data is within each set. Spread can be defined further as either interquartile range or standard deviation. The *interquartile range (IQR)* is the range of the middle fifty percent of the data set.

The *standard deviation, s,* quantifies the amount of variation with respect to the mean. A lower standard deviation shows that the data set does not differ much from the mean. A larger standard deviation shows that the data set is spread out farther away from the mean. The formula used for standard deviation depends on whether it's being used for a population or a sample (a subset of a population). The formula for sample standard deviation is:

$$s = \sqrt{\frac{\sum(x - \bar{x})^2}{n - 1}}$$

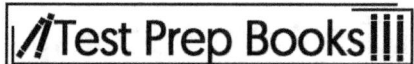

In this formula, s represents the standard deviation value, x is each value in the data set, $\bar{x}$ is the sample mean, and n is the total number of data points in the set. Note that sample standard deviations use *one less than the total* in the denominator. The population standard deviation formula is similar:

$$\sigma = \sqrt{\frac{\sum(x-\mu)^2}{N}}$$

For population standard deviations, sigma (σ) represents the standard deviation, x represents each value in the data set, mu (μ) is the population mean, and N is the total number of data points for the population. The square of the standard deviation is known as the *variance* of the data set. A data set can have outliers, and measures of central tendency that are not affected by outliers are the mode and median. Those measures are labeled as resistant measures of center.

Statistical Questions

A statistical question is answered by collecting data with variability. Data consists of facts and/or statistics (numbers), and variability refers to a tendency to shift or change. Data is a broad term, inclusive of things like height, favorite color, name, salary, temperature, gas mileage, and language. Questions requiring data as an answer are not necessarily statistical questions. If there is no variability in the data, then the question is not statistical in nature. Consider the following examples: what is Mary's favorite color? How much money does your mother make? What was the highest temperature last week? How many miles did your car get on its last tank of gas? How much taller than Bob is Ed?

None of the above are statistical questions because each case lacks variability in the data needed to answer the question. The questions on favorite color, salary, and gas mileage each require a single piece of data, whether a fact or statistic. Therefore, variability is absent. Although the temperature question requires multiple pieces of data (the high temperature for each day), a single, distinct number is the answer. The height question requires two pieces of data, Bob's height and Ed's height, but no difference in variability exists between those two values. Therefore, this is not a statistical question. Statistical questions typically require calculations with data.

Consider the following statistical questions:

How many miles per gallon of gas does the 2016 Honda Civic get? To answer this question, data must be collected. This data should include miles driven and gallons used. Different cars, different drivers, and different driving conditions will produce different results. Therefore, variability exists in the data. To answer the question, the mean (average) value could be determined.

Are American men taller than German men? To answer this question, data must be collected. This data should include the heights of American men and the heights of German men. All American men are not the same height and all German men are not the same height. Some American men are taller than some German men and some German men are taller than some American men. Therefore, variability exists in the data. To answer the question, the median values for each group could be determined and compared.

The following are more examples of statistical questions: What proportion of 4th graders have a favorite color of blue? How much money do teachers make? Is it colder in Boston or Chicago?

Independence and Conditional Probability

Sample Subsets

A sample can be broken up into subsets that are smaller parts of the whole. For example, consider a sample population of females. The sample can be divided into smaller subsets based on the characteristics of each female. There can be a group of females with brown hair and a group of females that wear glasses. There also can be a group of females that have brown hair *and* wear glasses. This "and" relates to the *intersection* of the two separate groups of brunettes and those with glasses. Every female in that intersection group has both characteristics.

Similarly, there also can be a group of females that either have brown hair *or* wear glasses. The "or" relates to the union of the two separate groups of brunettes and glasses. Every female in this group has at least one of the characteristics. Finally, the group of females who do not wear glasses can be discussed. This "not" relates to the *complement* of the glass-wearing group. No one in the complement has glasses. *Venn diagrams* are useful in highlighting these ideas. When discussing statistical experiments, this idea can also relate to events instead of characteristics.

Verifying Independent Events

Two events aren't always independent. For example, having glasses and having brown hair aren't independent characteristics. There definitely can be overlap because people with brown hair can wear glasses. Also, two events that exist at the same time don't have to have a relationship. For example, even if everyone in a given sample is wearing glasses, the characteristics aren't related. In this case, the probability of a brunette wearing glasses is equal to the probability of a person being a brunette multiplied by the probability of a person wearing glasses. This mathematical test of $P(A \cap B) = P(A)P(B)$ verifies that two events are independent.

Conditional Probability

Conditional probability is the probability that event A will happen given that event B has already occurred. An example of this is calculating the probability that a person will eat dessert once they have eaten dinner. This is different than calculating the probability of a person just eating dessert. The formula for the conditional probability of event A occurring given B is $P(A|B) = \frac{P(A \text{ and } B)}{P(B)}$, and it's defined to be the probability of both A and B occurring divided by the probability of event B occurring. If A and B are independent, then the probability of both A and B occurring is equal to $P(A)P(B)$, so $P(A|B)$ reduces to just $P(A)$. This means that A and B have no relationship, and the probability of A occurring is the same as the conditional probability of A occurring given B. Similarly:

$$P(B|A) = \frac{P(B \text{ and } A)}{P(A)} = P(B)$$

if A and B are independent.

Independent Versus Related Events

To summarize, conditional probability is the probability that an event occurs given that another event has happened. If the two events are related, the probability that the second event will occur changes if the other event has happened. However, if the two events aren't related and are therefore independent, the first event to occur won't impact the probability of the second event occurring.

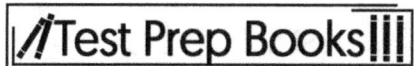

Computing Probabilities of Simple Events, Probabilities of Compound Events, and Conditional Probabilities

Simple and Compound Events

A *simple event* consists of only one outcome. The most popular simple event is flipping a coin, which results in either heads or tails. A *compound event* results in more than one outcome and consists of more than one simple event. An example of a compound event is flipping a coin while tossing a die. The result is either heads or tails on the coin and a number from one to six on the die. The probability of a simple event is calculated by dividing the number of possible outcomes by the total number of outcomes. Therefore, the probability of obtaining heads on a coin is $\frac{1}{2}$, and the probability of rolling a 6 on a die is $\frac{1}{6}$. The probability of compound events is calculated using the basic idea of the probability of simple events. If the two events are independent, the probability of one outcome is equal to the product of the probabilities of each simple event. For example, the probability of obtaining heads on a coin and rolling a 6 is equal to:

$$\frac{1}{2} \times \frac{1}{6} = \frac{1}{12}$$

The probability of either A or B occurring is equal to the sum of the probabilities minus the probability that both A and B will occur. Therefore, the probability of obtaining either heads on a coin or rolling a 6 on a die is:

$$\frac{1}{2} + \frac{1}{6} - \frac{1}{12} = \frac{7}{12}$$

The two events aren't mutually exclusive because they can happen at the same time. If two events are mutually exclusive, and the probability of both events occurring at the same time is zero, the probability of event A or B occurring equals the sum of both probabilities. An example of calculating the probability of two mutually exclusive events is determining the probability of pulling a king or a queen from a deck of cards. The two events cannot occur at the same time.

Sample Spaces

Probabilities are based on observations of events. The probability of an event occurring is equal to the ratio of the number of favorable outcomes over the total number of possible outcomes. The total number of possible outcomes is found by constructing the sample space. The sum of probabilities of all possible distinct outcomes is equal to 1. A simple example of a sample space involves a deck of cards. They contain 52 distinct cards, and therefore the sample space contains each individual card. To find the probability of selecting a queen on one draw from the deck, the ratio would be equal to $\frac{4}{52} = \frac{1}{13}$, which equals 4 possible queens over the total number of possibilities in the sample space.

Probability with Combinations and Permutations

Probability problems require that the total number of simple events is known, which means the entire sample space must be recognized. Different methods can be used to count the number of possible outcomes, depending on whether different arrangements of the same items are counted only once or separately. *Permutations* are arrangements in which different sequences are counted separately. Therefore, order matters in permutations. *Combinations* are arrangements in which different sequences are not counted separately. Therefore, order does not matter in combinations. If the sample space contains n different permutations of n different items and all of them must be selected, there are $n!$ different possibilities. For example, 5 different books can be rearranged 5! = 120 times. The probability of two people ordering the books in the same way is $\frac{1}{120}$. A different calculation is necessary if a number less than n is to be selected or if order does not matter. In general, the notation $P(n,r)$ represents the number of ways to arrange r objects from a set of n if order does not matter, and:

$$P(n,r) = \frac{n!}{(n-r)!}$$

Secondly, $C(n,r)$ represents the total number of r combinations selected out of n items when order does not matter and,

$$C(n,r) = \frac{n!}{(n-r)!\, r!}$$

Therefore, the following relationship exists between permutations and combinations:

$$C(n,r) = \frac{P(n,r)}{n!}$$

Solving Probability Problems Using Geometric Ratios

The ratio between two similar geometric figures is called the *scale factor*. In the following example, there are two similar triangles. The scale factor from figure A to figure B is 2 because the length of the corresponding side of the larger triangle, 14, is twice the corresponding side on the smaller triangle, 7.

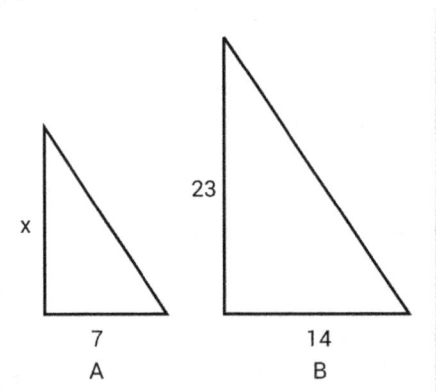

This scale factor can also be used to find the value of X. Since the scale factor from small to large is 2, the larger number, 23, can be divided by 2 to find the missing side: X = 11.5. The scale factor can also be represented in the equation $2A = B$ because two times the lengths of A gives the corresponding lengths of B. This is the idea behind similar triangles.

Ratios can be used to solve problems that concern length, volume, and other units. If the following graphic of a cone is given, the problem may ask for the volume to be found.

Referring to the formulas provided on the test, the volume of a cone is given as: $V = \pi r^2 \frac{h}{3}$, where r is the radius, and h is the height.

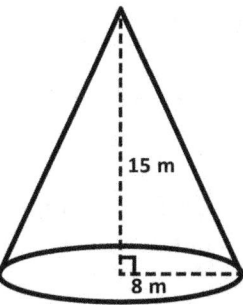

Plugging $r = 7$ and $h = 16$ from the graphic in to the formula, the following is obtained:
$$V = \pi(7^2)\frac{16}{3}$$

Therefore, the volume of the cone is found to be approximately 821m³. Sometimes, answers in different units are sought. If this problem wanted the answer in liters, 821m³ would need to be converted. Using the equivalence statement 1m³ = 1,000L, the following ratio would be used to solve for liters: $821m^3 * \frac{1,000L}{1m^3}$. Cubic meters in the numerator and denominator cancel each other out, and the answer is converted to 821,000 liters, or $8.21 * 10^5$ L.

Other conversions can also be made between different given and final units. If the temperature in a pool is 30°C, what is the temperature of the pool in degrees Fahrenheit? To convert these units, an equation is used relating Celsius to Fahrenheit. The following equation is used:

$$T_{°F} = 1.8 T_{°C} + 32$$

Plugging in the given temperature and solving the equation for T yields the result:

$$T_{°F} = 1.8(30) + 32 = 86°F$$

Units in both the metric system and U.S. customary system are widely used.

Probability Axioms
The *addition rule* is necessary to find the probability of event A or event B occurring, or both occurring at the same time. If events A and B are mutually exclusive, which means they cannot occur at the same time,
$$P(A \text{ or } B) = P(A) + P(B)$$

If events A and B are not mutually exclusive, $P(A \text{ or } B) = P(A) + P(B) - P(A \text{ and } B)$, where $P(A \text{ and } B)$ represents the probability of event A and B both occurring at the same time. The *multiplication rule* is necessary to find the probability that both A and B occur in two separate trials. This rule differs if the events are independent or dependent. Two events, A and B, are labeled as *independent* if the occurrence of one event does not affect the probability that the other event will occur. If A and be are not independent, they are *dependent*. If events A and B are independent, $P(A \text{ and } B) = P(A)P(B)$, and if events A and B are dependent, $P(A \text{ and } B) = P(A)P(B|A)$ where

Probability and Statistics

$P(B|A)$ represents the probability event B occurs given that event A has already occurred. $P(B|A)$ represents *conditional probability*. $P(B|A)$ can be found using the formula:

$$P(B|A) = \frac{P(A \text{ and } B)}{P(A)}$$

and represents the total number of outcomes remaining for B to occur after A occurs.

Probability Distributions

Probability is a measure of the likelihood of something happening or being the case. The probability of an event A is written P(A) and is assigned a value between zero (can't happen) and one (is certain to happen): $0 \leq P(A) \leq 1$.

Probabilities can be objectively assigned by sampling or reviewing historical data to determine how frequently the outcome has occurred in the past.

If the probability of a parameter's value is calculated and plotted along its entire possible range, a probability distribution function (PDF) can be determined. The normal probability distribution is a continuous PDF.

The binomial probability distribution is an important discrete PDF giving the probability of getting exactly k successes in n trials of a "yes-no," or *binomial*, test: $P(k) = \binom{n}{k} p^k (1-p)^{n-k}$, where p is the probability of success for each trial. The binomial coefficient $\binom{n}{k}$ is the number of possible ways k values can be selected from a group of n items and is calculated as n!/(k!(n − k)!, where k! = k × (k − 1) × (k − 2) × ... × 2 × 1. The value of 0! is defined as 1 to allow calculation of the probability of zero occurrences of the event in a time interval.

For example, to determine the probability of getting exactly 4 heads in 10 tosses of a fair coin: p(H) = p(T) = 0.5 and:

$$P(4) = \binom{10}{4} 0.5^4 (1 - 0.5)^6 = 0.2051$$

The Poisson discrete PDF is used for modeling the number of times a discrete event occurs in an interval of time. It is valid for events occurring with a known average rate, λ, and probability independent of the time since the last event: $P(k \text{ events}) = \frac{\lambda^k e^{-\lambda}}{k!}$, where λ is the average number of events per interval, e is the base of natural logarithms (2.7182...), and k! is calculated as discussed above.

Discrete and Continuous Random Variables

A *discrete random variable* consists of a collection of values that is either finite or countable. If there are infinitely many values, being countable means that each individual value can be counted. For example, the number of coin tosses before getting heads could potentially be infinite, but the total number of tosses is countable. A continuous random variable has infinitely many values and is not countable. The individual items cannot be counted, and an example is a measurement. Because of the use of decimals, there are infinitely many heights of human beings. Each type of variable has its own *probability distribution*, which is a description that shows the probability for each potential value of the random variable. They are usually seen in tables, formulas, or graphs.

The *expected value* of a random variable represents what the mean value should be in either a large sample size or after many trials. According to the Law of Large Numbers, after many trials, the actual mean and that of the probability distribution should be approximately equal to the expected value. The expected value is a weighted average that is calculated as $E(X) = \sum x_i p_i$, where x_i represent the value of each outcome and p_i represent the probability of each outcome. The expected value if all probabilities are equal is:

$$E(X) = \frac{x_1 + x_2 + \cdots + x_n}{n}$$

Expected value is often called the mean of the random variable and is also a measure of central tendency. A **binomial probability distribution** is a probability distribution in which there is a fixed number of trials, all trials are independent, each trial has an outcome classified as either a success or a failure, and the probability of a success is the same in each trial. Within any binomial experiment, x is the number of resulting successes, n is the number of trials, P is the probability of success within each trial, and $Q = 1 - P$ is the probability of failure within each trial. The probability of obtaining x successes within n trials is:

$$\binom{n}{x} P^x (1 - P)^{n-x}$$

The combination

$$\binom{n}{x} = \frac{n!}{x!\,(n-x)!}$$

is called the **binomial coefficient** and represents the number of possible outcomes where exactly x many successes occur out of n trials.

A *geometric probability distribution* is a binomial probability distribution where the number of trials is not fixed. A *uniform probability distribution* exists when there is constant probability. Each random variable has equal probability and its graph is a rectangle. Finally, a *uniform probability distribution* has a graph that is symmetric and bell-shaped.

Population percentages can be estimated using normal distributions. For example, the probability that a data point will be less than the mean is 50%. Similarly, the probability that a data point will be within one standard deviation of the mean, or that the z-score will be between -1 and 1, is about 68.2%. When using a z-table, the left column states how many standard deviations (to one decimal place) away from the mean the point lies, and the row heading states the second decimal place. The entries in the table corresponding to each column and each row gives the probability, which is equal to the area under the curve. The area under the entire curve of a standard normal distribution is equal to 1.

Making Inferences and Justifying Conclusions from Samples, Experiments, and Observational Studies

Data Gathering Techniques

Statistics involves making decisions and predictions about larger sets of data based on smaller data sets. The information from a small subset can help predict what happens in the entire set. The smaller data set is called a *sample* and the larger data set for which the decision is being made is called a *population*. The three most common types of data gathering techniques are sample surveys, experiments, and observational studies.

Sample surveys involve collecting data from a random sample of people from a desired population. The measurement of the variable is only performed on this set of people. To have accurate data, the sampling must be unbiased and random. For example, surveying students in an advanced calculus class on how much they enjoy math classes is not a useful sample if the population should be all college students based on the research question. There are many methods to form a random sample, and all adhere to the fact that every sample that could be chosen has a predetermined probability of being chosen. Once the sample is chosen, statistical experiments can then be carried out to investigate real-world problems.

An **experiment** is the method by which a hypothesis is tested using a controlled process called the scientific method. A cause and the effect of that cause are measured, and the hypothesis is accepted or rejected. Experiments are usually completed in a controlled environment where the results of a control population are compared to the results of a test population. The groups are selected using a randomization process in which each group has a representative mix of the population being tested. Finally, an *observational study* is similar to an experiment. However, this design is used when circumstances prevent or do not allow for a designated control group and experimental group (e.g., lack of funding or unrealistic expectations). Instead, existing control and test populations must be used, so this method has a lack of randomization.

Interpreting Statistical Information

To make decisions concerning populations, data must be collected from a sample. The sample must be large enough to be able to make conclusions. A common way to collect data is via surveys and polls. Every survey and poll must be designed so that there is no bias. An example of a biased survey is one with loaded questions, which are either intentionally worded or ordered to obtain a desired response. Once the data is obtained, conclusions should not be made that are not justified by statistical analysis. One must make sure the difference between correlation and causation is understood. Correlation implies there is an association between two variables, and correlation does not imply causation.

Population Mean and Proportion

Both the population mean and proportion can be calculated using data from a sample. The *population mean (μ)* is the average value of the parameter for the entire population. Due to size constraints, finding the exact value of μ is impossible, so the mean of the sample population is used as an estimate instead. The larger the sample size, the closer the sample mean gets to the population mean. An alternative to finding μ is to find the *proportion* of the population, which is the part of the population with the given characteristic. The proportion can be expressed as a decimal, a fraction, or a percentage, and can be given as a single value or a range of values. Because the population mean and proportion are both estimates, there's a *margin of error*, which is the difference between the actual value and the expected value.

T-Tests

A *randomized experiment* is used to compare two treatments by using statistics involving a *t-test*, which tests whether two data sets are significantly different from one another. To use a t-test, the test statistic must follow a normal distribution. The first step of the test involves calculating the *t* value, which is given as:

$$t = \frac{\overline{x_1} - \overline{x_2}}{s_{\bar{x}_1 - \bar{x}_2}}$$

Probability and Statistics

where $\bar{x}_1$ and $\bar{x}_2$ are the averages of the two samples. Also:

$$s_{\bar{x}_1 - \bar{x}_2} = \sqrt{\frac{s_1^2}{n_1} + \frac{s_2^2}{n_2}}$$

where s_1 and s_2 are the standard deviations of each sample and n_1 and n_2 are their respective sample sizes. The *degrees of freedom* for two samples are calculated as:

$$df = \frac{(n_1 - 1) + (n_2 - 1)}{2}$$

rounded to the lowest whole number. Also, a significance level α must be chosen, where a typical value is $\alpha = 0.05$. Once everything is compiled, the decision is made to use either a *one-tailed test* or a *two-tailed test*. If there's an assumed difference between the two treatments, a one-tailed test is used. If no difference is assumed, a two-tailed test is used.

Analyzing Test Results

Once the type of test is determined, the t-value, significance level, and degrees of freedom are applied to the published table showing the *t* distribution. The row is associated with degrees of freedom and each column corresponds to the probability. The t-value can be exactly equal to one entry or lie between two entries in a row.

For example, consider a t-value of 1.7 with degrees of freedom equal to 30. This *test statistic* falls between the *p* values of 0.05 and 0.025. For a one-tailed test, the corresponding *p* value lies between 0.05 and 0.025. For a two-tailed test, the *p* values need to be doubled so the corresponding *p* value falls between 0.1 and 0.05. Once the probability is known, this range is compared to α. If $p < \alpha$, the hypothesis is rejected. If $p > \alpha$, the hypothesis isn't rejected. In a two-tailed test, this scenario means the hypothesis is accepted that there's no difference in the two treatments. In a one-tailed test, the hypothesis is accepted, indicating that there's a difference in the two treatments.

Evaluating Completed Tests

In addition to applying statistical techniques to actual testing, evaluating completed tests is another important aspect of statistics. Reports can be read that already have conclusions, and the process can be evaluated using learned concepts. For example, deciding if a sample being used is appropriate. Other things that can be evaluated include determining if the samples are randomized or the results are significant. Once statistical concepts are understood, the knowledge can be applied to many applications.

Sample Statistics

A *point estimate* is a single point used to estimate a population parameter. It is used because it is an *unbiased estimator,* meaning that it is a statistic that targets the value of the population parameter by assuming the mean of the sampling distribution is equal to the mean of the population distribution. Other unbiased estimators include the mean and variance. *Biased estimators* do not target the value of the population parameter, and such values include median, range, and standard deviation. A *confidence interval* consists of a range of values that is utilized to approximate the true value of a population parameter. The *confidence level* is the probability that the confidence interval does contain the population parameter, assuming the estimation process is repeated many times.

Probability and Statistics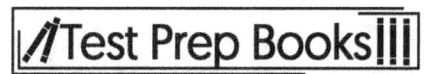

Population Inferences Using Distributions

Samples are used to make inferences about a population. The sampling distribution of a sample mean is a distribution of all sample means for a fixed sample size, n, which is part of a population. Depending on different criteria, either a binomial, normal, or geometric distribution can be used to determine probabilities. A normal distribution uses a continuous random variable, and is bell-shaped and symmetric. A binomial distribution uses a discrete random variable, has a finite number of trials, and only has two possible outcomes: a success and a failure. A geometric distribution is very similar to a binomial distribution; however, the number of trials does not have to be finite.

Creating and Interpreting Linear Regression Models

Linear Regression

Regression lines are a way to calculate a relationship between the independent variable and the dependent variable. A straight line means that there's a linear trend in the data. Technology can be used to find the equation of this line (e.g., a graphing calculator or Microsoft Excel®). In either case, all of the data points are entered, and a line is "fit" that best represents the shape of the data. Other functions used to model data sets include quadratic and exponential models.

Estimating Data Points

Regression lines can be used to estimate data points not already given. For example, if an equation of a line is found that fit the temperature and beach visitor data set, its input is the average daily temperature and its output is the projected number of visitors. Thus, the number of beach visitors on a 100-degree day can be estimated. The output is a data point on the regression line, and the number of daily visitors is expected to be greater than on a 96-degree day because the regression line has a positive slope.

Plotting and Analyzing Residuals

Once the function is found that fits the data, its accuracy can be calculated. Therefore, how well the line fits the data can be determined. The difference between the actual dependent variable from the data set and the estimated value located on the regression line is known as a *residual*. Therefore, the residual is known as the predicted value $\hat{y}$ minus the actual value y. A residual is calculated for each data point and can be plotted on the scatterplot. If all the residuals appear to be approximately the same distance from the regression line, the line is a good fit. If the residuals seem to differ greatly across the board, the line isn't a good fit.

Interpreting the Regression Line

The formula for a regression line is $y = mx + b$, where m is the slope and b is the y-intercept. Both the slope and y-intercept are found in the *Method of Least Squares*, which is the process of finding the equation of the line through minimizing residuals. The slope represents the rate of change in y as x gets larger. Therefore, because y is the dependent variable, the slope actually provides the predicted values given the independent variable. The y-intercept is the predicted value for when the independent variable equals zero. In the temperature example, the y-intercept is the expected number of beach visitors for a very cold average daily temperature of zero degrees.

Correlation Coefficient

The *correlation coefficient (r)* measures the association between two variables. Its value is between -1 and 1, where -1 represents a perfect negative linear relationship, 0 represents no relationship, and 1 represents a perfect positive linear relationship. A *negative linear relationship* means that as x values

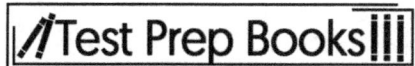

Probability and Statistics

increase, y values decrease. A *positive linear relationship* means that as x values increase, y values increase. The formula for computing the correlation coefficient is (n is the number of data points):

$$r = \frac{n(\sum xy) - (\sum x)(\sum y)}{\sqrt{n(\sum x^2) - (\sum x)^2}\sqrt{n(\sum y^2) - (\Sigma y)^2}}$$

Both Microsoft Excel® and a graphing calculator can evaluate this easily once the data points are entered. A correlation greater than 0.8 or less than -0.8 is classified as "strong" while a correlation between -0.5 and 0.5 is classified as "weak."

Correlation Versus Causation

Correlation and causation have two different meanings. If two values are correlated, there is an association between them. However, correlation doesn't necessarily mean that one variable causes the other. *Causation* (or "cause and effect") occurs when one variable causes the other. Average daily temperature and number of beachgoers are correlated and have causation. If the temperature increases, the change in weather causes more people to go to the beach. However, alcoholism and smoking are correlated but don't have causation. The more someone drinks the more likely they are to smoke, but drinking alcohol doesn't cause someone to smoke.

Regression Models

Regression lines are straight lines that calculate a relationship between nonlinear data involving an independent variable and a dependent variable. A regression line is of the form $y = mx + b$, where m is the slope and b is the y-intercept. Both the slope and y-intercept are found using the *Method of Least Squares*, which involves minimizing residuals – the difference between the dependent variable from the data set and the estimated value located on the regression line. The slope represents the rate of change in y as x increases. The y-intercept is the predicted value when the independent variable is equal to 0. Technology, such as a graphing calculator or Microsoft Excel®, can also be utilized to find the equation of this line. In either case, the data points are entered, and a line is "fit" that best represents the shape of the data.

Here is an example of a data set and its regression line:

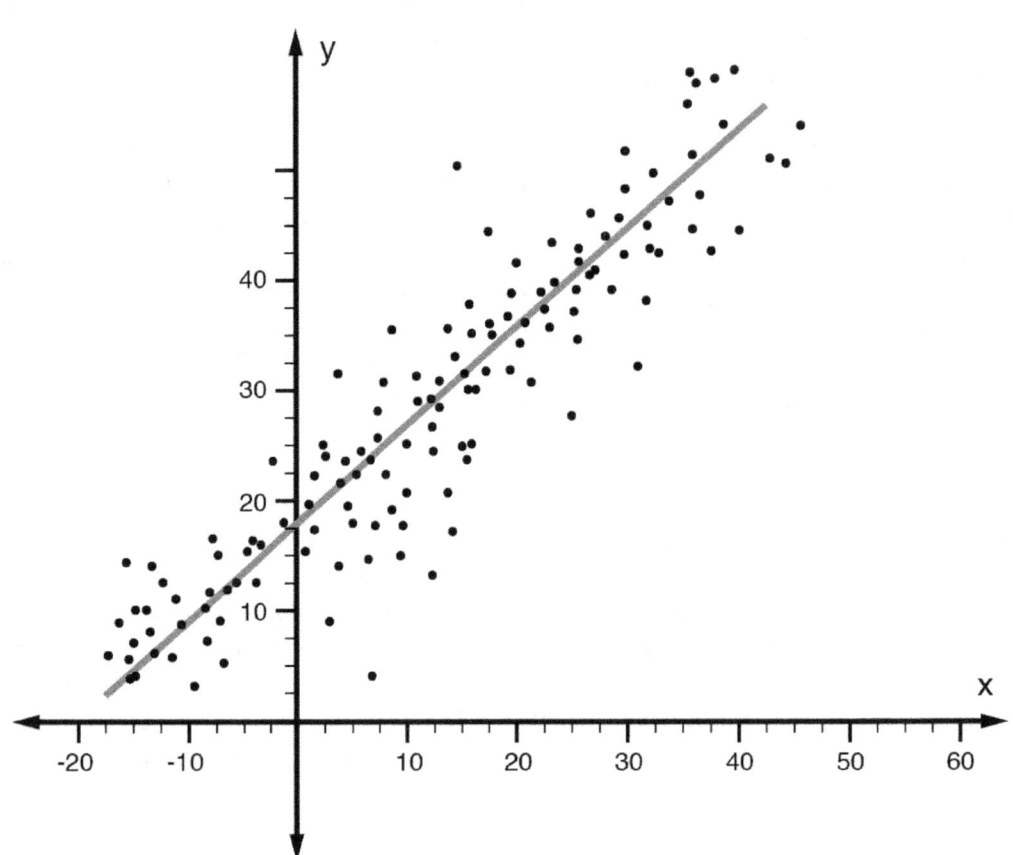

Regression models are highly used for forecasting, and linear regression techniques are the simplest models. If the nonlinear data follows the shape of exponential, logarithmic, or power functions, those types of functions can be used to more accurately model the data rather than lines.

Here is an example of both an exponential regression and a logarithmic regression model:

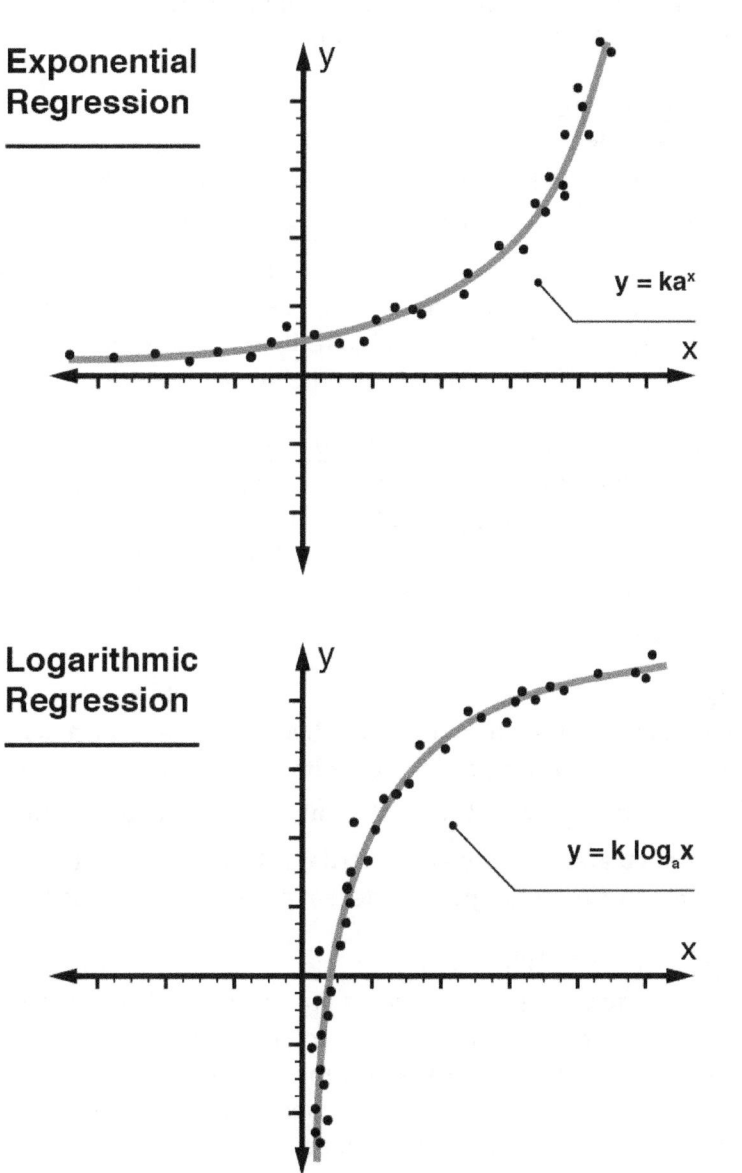

The Law of Large Numbers and the Central Limit Theorem

The Law of Large Numbers states that as the number of experiments increases, the actual ratio of outcomes will approach the theoretical probability. The *Central Limit Theorem* states that through using a sufficiently large sample size N, meaning over 30, the sampling distribution of the mean approaches a normal distribution with a mean of μ and variance of σ^2/N. The variance of the actual population is σ^2 and its mean is μ. In other words, as the sample size increases, the distribution will behave normally.

Estimating Parameters

A point estimate of a population parameter is a single statistic. For example, the sample mean is a point estimate of the population mean. Once all calculations are made, a confidence interval is used to express the accuracy of the sampling method used. The confidence interval consists of a confidence level, the statistic, and a margin of error. A 95% confidence level indicates that 95% of all confidence intervals will contain the population parameter. Also, the margin of error gives a range of values above and below the sample statistic, which helps to form a confidence interval.

The Principles of Hypotheses Testing

The *P*-value approach to hypothesis testing involves assuming a null hypothesis is true and then determining the probability of a test statistic in the direction of the alternative hypothesis. The test statistic is defined as the *t*-statistic $t^* = \frac{\bar{x} - \mu}{s/\sqrt{n}}$, which follows a *t*-distribution with *n*-1 degrees of freedom. The *P*-value is then calculated as the probability that if the null hypothesis is true, a more extreme test statistic in the direction of the alternative hypothesis would be observed. A significance level, α, is set (usually at 0.05 or 0.001) and the *P*-value is compared to α. If $P \leq \alpha$, one rejects the null hypothesis and accepts the alternative hypothesis. If $P > \alpha$, one accepts the null hypothesis.

Measuring Probabilities with Two-Way Frequency Tables

When measuring event probabilities, two-way frequency tables can be used to report the raw data and then used to calculate probabilities. If the frequency tables are translated into relative frequency tables, the probabilities presented in the table can be plugged directly into the formulas for conditional probabilities. By plugging in the correct frequencies, the data from the table can be used to determine if events are independent or dependent.

Differing Probabilities

The probability that event A occurs differs from the probability that event A occurs given B. When working within a given model, it's important to note the difference. $P(A|B)$ is determined using the formula $P(A|B) = \frac{P(A \text{ and } B)}{P(B)}$ and represents the total number of A's outcomes left that could occur after B occurs. $P(A)$ can be calculated without any regard for B. For example, the probability of a student finding a parking spot on a busy campus is different once class is in session.

Uniform and Non-Uniform Probability Models

A *uniform probability model* is one where each outcome has an equal chance of occurring, such as the probabilities of rolling each side of a die. A *non-uniform probability model* is one where each result has a different chance of taking place. In a uniform probability model, the conditional probability formulas for $P(B|A)$ and $P(A|B)$ can be multiplied by their respective denominators to obtain two formulas for $P(A \text{ and } B)$. Therefore, the multiplication rule is derived as:

$$P(A \text{ and } B) = P(A)P(B|A) = P(B)P(A|B)$$

In a model, if the probability of either individual event is known and the corresponding conditional probability is known, the multiplication rule allows the probability of the joint occurrence of A and B to be calculated.

Binomial Experiments

In statistics, a *binomial experiment* is an experiment that has the following properties. The experiment consists of *n* repeated trial that can each have only one of two outcomes. It can be either a success or a failure. The probability of success, p, is the same in every trial. Each trial is also independent of all other trials. An example of a binomial experiment is rolling a die 10 times with the goal of rolling a 5. Rolling a 5 is a success while any other value is a failure. In this experiment, the probability of rolling a 5 is $\frac{1}{6}$. In any binomial experiment, x is the number of resulting successes, n is the number of trials, p is the probability of success in each trial, and $q = 1 - p$ is the probability of failure within each trial. The probability of obtaining x successes within n trials is:

$$P(X = x) = \frac{n!}{x!\,(n-x)!} p^x (1-p)^{n-x}$$

With the following being the *binomial coefficient*:

$$\binom{n}{x} = \frac{n!}{x!\,(n-x)!}$$

Within this calculation, $n!$ is n factorial that's defined as:

$$n \cdot (n-1) \cdot (n-2) \ldots 1$$

Let's look at the probability of obtaining 2 rolls of a 5 out of the 10 rolls.

Start with $P(X = 2)$, where 2 is the number of successes. Then fill in the rest of the formula with what is known, n=10, x=2, p=1/6, q=5/6:

$$P(X = 2) = \left(\frac{10!}{2!\,(10-2)!}\right)\left(\frac{1}{6}\right)^2 \left(1 - \frac{1}{6}\right)^{10-2}$$

Which simplifies to:

$$P(X = 2) = \left(\frac{10!}{2!\,8!}\right)\left(\frac{1}{6}\right)^2 \left(\frac{5}{6}\right)^8$$

Then solve to get:

$$P(X = 2) = \left(\frac{3628800}{80640}\right)(.0277)(.2325) = .2898$$

Statistical Processes

Samples and Populations

Statistics involves making decisions and predictions about larger data sets based on smaller data sets. Basically, the information from one part or subset can help predict what happens in the entire data set or population at large. The entire process involves guessing, and the predictions and decisions may not be 100 percent correct all of the time; however, there is some truth to these predictions, and the decisions do have mathematical support. The smaller data set is called a *sample* and the larger data set (in which the decision is being made) is called a *population*. A *random sample* is used as the sample, which is an unbiased collection of data points that represents the population as well as it can. There are many methods of forming a random sample, and all adhere to the fact that every potential data point has a predetermined probability of being chosen.

Probability and Statistics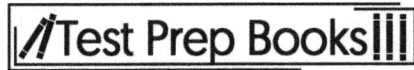

Goodness of Fit

Goodness of fit tests show how well a statistical model fits a given data set. They allow the differences between the observed and expected quantities to be summarized to determine if the model is consistent with the results. The *Chi-Squared Goodness of Fit Test* (or *Chi-Squared Test* for short) is used with one categorical variable from one population, and it concludes whether or not the sample data is consistent with a hypothesized distribution. Chi-Squared is evaluated using the following formula: $\chi^2 = \sum \frac{(O-E)^2}{E}$, where O is the observed frequency value and E is the expected frequency value. Also, the *degree of freedom* must be calculated, which is the number of categories in the data set minus one. Then a Chi-Squared table is used to test the data. The *degree of freedom value* and a *significance value*, such as 0.05, are located on the table. The corresponding entry represents a critical value.

If the calculated χ^2 is greater than the critical value, the data set does not work with the statistical model. If the calculated χ^2 is less than the critical value, the statistical model can be used.

Making Informed Decisions Using Probabilities and Expected Values

Graphical Displays

Graphical displays are used to visually represent probability distributions in statistical experiments. Specific displays representing probability distributions illustrate the probability of each event. Histograms are typically used to represent probability distributions, and the actual probability can be thought of as $P(x)$, where x is the independent variable.

Expected Value

The *expected value* of a random variable represents the mean value in either a large sample size or after a large number of trials. According to the law of large numbers, after a large number of trials, the actual mean (and that of the probability distribution) is approximately equal to the expected value. The expected value is a weighted average and is calculated as $E(X) = \sum x_i p_i$, where x_i represents the value of each outcome and p_i represents the probability of each outcome. If all probabilities are equal, the expected value is:

$$E(X) = \frac{x_1 + x_2 + \cdots + x_n}{n}$$

Expected value is often called the *mean of the random variable* and is also a measure of central tendency.

Calculating Theoretical Probabilities

Given a statistical experiment, a theoretical probability distribution can be calculated if the theoretical probabilities are known. The theoretical probabilities are plugged into the formula for both the binomial probability and the expected value. An example of this is any scenario involving rolls of a die or flips of a coin. The theoretical probabilities are known without any observed experiments. Another example of this is finding the theoretical probability distribution for the number of correct answers obtained by guessing a specific number of multiple choice questions on a class exam.

Determining Unknown Probabilities

Empirical data is defined as real data. If real data is known, approximations concerning samples and populations can be obtained by working backwards. This scenario is the case where theoretical probabilities are unknown, and experimental data must be used to make decisions. The sample data (including actual probabilities) must be plugged into the formulas for both binomial probability and the expected value. The actual probabilities are obtained using observation and can be seen in a probability distribution. An example of this scenario is determining a probability distribution for the number of televisions per household in the United States, and determining the expected number of televisions per household as well.

Weighing Outcomes

Calculating if it's worth it to play a game or make a decision is a critical part of probability theory. Expected values can be calculated in terms of payoff values, and deciding whether to make a decision or play a game can be done based on the actual expected value. Applying this theory to gambling and card games is fairly typical. The payoff values in these instances are the actual monetary totals.

Fairness

Fairness can be used when making decisions given different scenarios. For example, a game of chance can be deemed fair if every outcome has an equal probability of occurring. Also, a decision or choice can be labeled as fair if each possible option has an equal probability of being chosen. Using basic probability knowledge allows one to make decisions based on fairness. Fairness helps determine if an event's outcome is truly random and no bias is involved in the results. Random number generators are a good way to ensure fairness. An example of an event that isn't fair is the rolling of a weighted die.

Practice Quiz

1. The table below shows tickets purchased during the week for entry to the local zoo. What is the mean number of adult tickets sold for the week?

Day of the Week	Age	Tickets Sold
Monday	Adult	22
Monday	Child	30
Tuesday	Adult	16
Tuesday	Child	15
Wednesday	Adult	24
Wednesday	Child	23
Thursday	Adult	19
Thursday	Child	26
Friday	Adult	29
Friday	Child	38

    a. 24.2
    b. 21
    c. 22
    d. 26.4

2. A local candy store reports that, of the 100 customers that bought suckers, 35 of them bought cherry. If all 100 sucker wrappers are put in a jar, and 2 are drawn at random, what is the probability that both are cherry? Enter your answer in lowest terms.

    a. $\frac{119}{990}$

    b. $\frac{35}{100}$

    c. $\frac{49}{400}$

    d. $\frac{69}{99}$

3. A data set is comprised of the following values: 30, 33, 33, 26, 27, 32, 33, 35, 29, 27. Which of the following has the greatest value?
    a. Mean
    b. Median
    c. Mode
    d. Range

4. 250 students were asked their favorite flavor of ice cream. The results are presented in the pie chart below. What is the probability of choosing a student who likes vanilla or strawberry ice cream to receive a free ice cream cone?

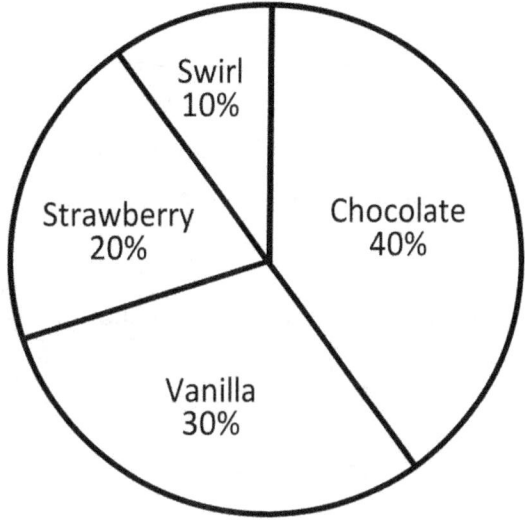

Favorite Ice Cream Flavor

a. $\frac{3}{10}$
b. $\frac{2}{10}$
c. $\frac{1}{2}$
d. $\frac{1}{20}$

5. The table below displays the number of three-year-olds at Kids First Daycare who are potty-trained and those who still wear diapers.

	Potty-trained	Wear diapers	
Boys	26	22	48
Girls	34	18	52
	60	40	

If a three-year-old girl is randomly selected from this school, what is the probability that she is potty-trained?

a. 52%
b. 34%
c. 65%
d. 57%

See answers on the next page.

Answer Explanations

1. C: To find the mean, or average, of a set of values, add the values together and then divide by the total number of values. We will need to add up the number of adult tickets sold for the week. The equation is as follows:

$$\frac{22 + 16 + 24 + 19 + 29}{5} = 22$$

2. A: The probability of choosing a cherry wrapper with the first selection is $\frac{35}{100}$. If the first selection is cherry, then the probability of getting cherry the second time is $\frac{34}{99}$. So, the chance that both are cherry would be: $\frac{34}{99}$.

So, the probability of choosing 2 customers simultaneously that both bought cherry would be:

$$\frac{35}{100} \times \frac{34}{99}$$

$$\frac{1,190}{9,900}$$

$$\frac{119}{990}$$

3. C: Each value can be calculated so that they can be compared to find which one is the greatest. The mean is equal to:

$$\frac{26 + 27 + 27 + 29 + 30 + 32 + 33 + 33 + 33 + 35}{10} = 30.5$$

The median is equal to:

$$\frac{30 + 32}{2} = 31$$

The mode is equal to 33 because that number occurs 3 times in the data set. The range is equal to:

$$35 - 26 = 9$$

Therefore, the mode is the greatest value of the answer choices.

4. C: These two events are mutually exclusive because the students only picked one flavor of ice cream as the favorite so a student can't have chosen two flavors. Therefore, the probability of choosing a student who likes each flavor of interest (vanilla and strawberry) should be added together. 30% of students chose vanilla, and 20% of the students chose strawberry. Expressed as percentages the probabilities are $\frac{3}{10}$ and $\frac{2}{10}$ which can be added together to find:

$$\frac{3}{10} + \frac{2}{10} = \frac{5}{10} = \frac{1}{2}$$

5. C: There are 34 girls who are potty-trained out of a total of 52 girls:

$$34 \div 52 \approx 0.65 = 65\%$$

Mathematical Processes and Perspectives

Proofs

A proof is a deductive argument that supports a mathematical statement. Other previously established mathematical statements, such as theorems and axioms, are used within proofs. A proof shows that the concept is always true, and does not just give specific examples and cases. In direct proofs, the conclusion is found by combining the axioms, theorems, and possibly definitions in a specific and logical order. An indirect proof involves showing that the mathematical statement can never be false. However, it still involves a logical order of theorems, definitions, and axioms.

Deductive Rand Inductive Reasoning

Deductive reasoning involves starting with stating a general rule, and then moving forward with logic to obtain a desired conclusion. If the original statements are true, then the conclusion is true. Most of mathematics involves deductive reasoning. For example, if $x = 2$ and $y = 4$ then $x + y = 6$. Also, if x is an even number and y is an odd number, then $x + y$ is an odd number.

Inductive reasoning involves starting with specific observations, but due to the nature of those observations, conclusions are classified as likely but not guaranteed. This process behaves similarly to probability in which nothing is completely certain. As opposed to deductive reasoning, a general conclusion can be drawn by observing specific examples. Note that inductive reasoning is not the same as proof by induction. Once a statement is found using inductive logic, specific examples can be found to be true or false using deductive reasoning. A counterexample is an example that shows a mathematical statement is false.

Using Reasoning to Justify Mathematical Ideas

A difference exists between formal and informal proofs. A formal proof involves the steps listed above, which include very structured deductive reasoning through the application of a specific order of theorems, axioms, and definitions. However, sometimes a formal proof is cumbersome and an informal proof might be used instead. These proofs are more applicable for everyday use and include high-level summaries that provide enough information to formulate the formal proof if given enough time.

The Problem-Solving Process

Overall, the problem-solving process in mathematics involves a step-by-step procedure that one must follow when deciding what approach to take. First, one must understand the problem by deciding what is being sought, if enough information is given, and what units are necessary in the solution. Then, the plan of action must be determined. In some cases, there might be many options. Therefore, one should begin with one approach and if the strategy does not fit, he or she should move on to another. In some cases, a combination of approaches can be used. A beginning estimate is always useful for comparison once a solution is found. The answer must be reasonable and must fulfill all requirements of the problem.

Mathematical Models to Represent Real-World Situations

A mathematical model is a representation in mathematical terms of a real-world situation, and is widely used in science and engineering. Formulas are derived that model phenomena such as population

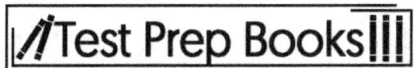

growth and decay. In any model, simplifications must be made to create such formulas, and parameters within the model usually do not represent the physical world exactly. Once the model is formulated, its output can be compared to real-world scenarios to judge how valid the model is. If a model is deemed to be inaccurate, original assumptions and restrictions can be lifted that initially simplified the model.

Using Multiple Representations of a Mathematical Concept

There are many different areas of mathematics, and a single mathematical concept can have meaning in more than one area. Some of the main divisions of math include arithmetic, algebra, calculus, geometry, and statistics. A concept that spans across those divisions is *area*. Many different formulas in geometry involve calculating the area of different shapes. For example, area of a circle $A = \pi r^2$ is a quadratic function in r, the radius of the circle. In calculus, an area problem can involve calculating the area under a curve from two points on the x-axis, which is known as the definite integral. Also, the area between two curves is discussed. Finally, in statistics, the area under a density curve is defined to be probability.

Using Math in Other Disciplines

As discussed previously, a mathematical model translates a real-world scenario into mathematical terms. Many disciplines involve the use of mathematical models. Usual disciplines that require the use of models are science and business, with their most widely-known models being population growth and compound interest. However, other disciplines such as art, music, and social science also can employ the use of mathematics. The keys are to first understand the problem needed to be solved, then to define variables, make assumptions and simplifications, and translate the concepts into mathematical formulas and equations. Once the model is built, different scenarios can be tested for accuracy and reasonableness.

Translating Between Verbal and Symbolic Forms

Being able to translate verbal scenarios into symbolic forms is a critical skill in mathematics. This idea is seen mostly when solving word problems. First, the problem needs to be read carefully several times until one can state clearly what is being sought. Then, variables that represent the unknown quantities need to be defined. Equations can be defined using those variables that model the verbal conditions of the given problem. The equations then need to be solved to answer the problem's questions. The problem-solving skills learned in these types of problems is an invaluable skill, and is ultimately more important than finding the answer to each individual problem.

Communicating Mathematical Ideas

Many different types of representations are useful in mathematics, and the most widely-used are written symbols, pictures or diagrams, models, spoken words, and real-world experiences. Real-world experiences and spoken words are both representations that can be expressed by written symbols that impart mathematical meaning to the situation being discussed. Pictures or diagrams, including graphs and geometric figures, allow for visual representations of mathematical concepts. These external representations are widely used and have been developed for centuries. Similarly, written representations, such as symbolic methods like equations and functions, are also widely used and are used the most in math classes.

Mathematical Processes and Perspectives

Using Visual Media

Students benefit from the use of visual media that represents mathematical information, and teachers should be able to go back and forth between each type. They should know which type of representation is useful in given a scenario. For example, a function can be represented by a diagram, a table, a graph, and a set of numbers simultaneously. Here is such an example:

Multiple Representations of a Function

Mapping

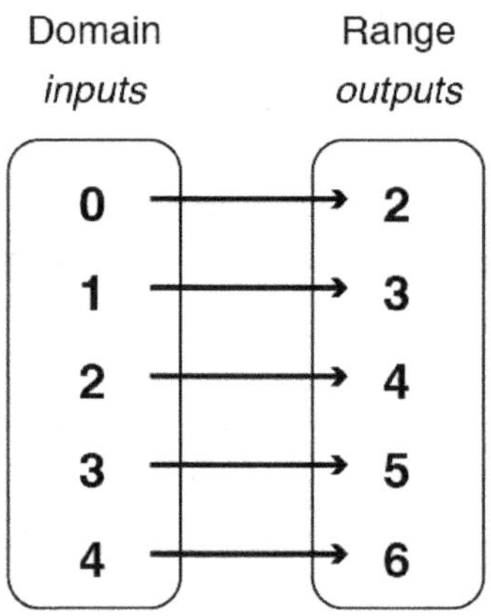

Domain inputs → Range outputs

0 → 2
1 → 3
2 → 4
3 → 5
4 → 6

Table

x	y
0	2
1	3
2	4
3	5
4	6

Graph

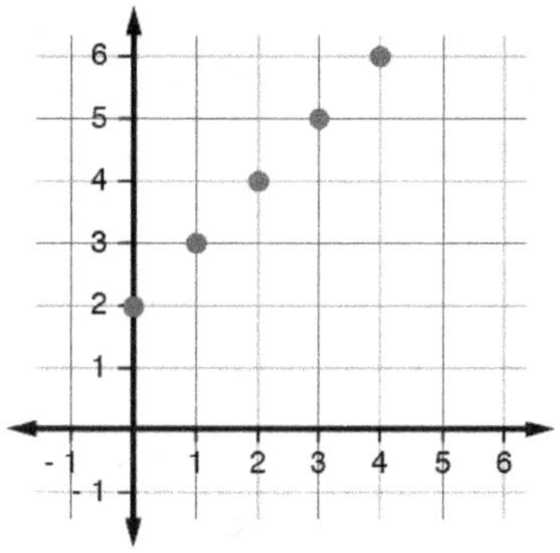

(points plotted: (0,2), (1,3), (2,4), (3,5), (4,6))

Ordered Pairs

{(0,2),(1,3),(2,4),(3,5),(4,6)}

Using Math Terminology

Using appropriate vocabulary that represents mathematical ideas is a critical skill in both being able to teach mathematics and use mathematical techniques to solve real-world situations. Each area in mathematics has its own set of definitions, and the translation of ideas onto paper requires a deep understanding of all the terminology. An important application of this idea is being able to translate word problems into equations that can be solved.

Practice Quiz

1. Katie works at a clothing company and sold 192 shirts over the weekend. One third of the shirts that were sold were patterned and the rest were solid. Which mathematical expression would calculate the number of solid shirts Katie sold over the weekend?
    a. $192 \times \frac{1}{3}$
    b. $192 \div \frac{1}{3}$
    c. $192 \times (1 - \frac{1}{3})$
    d. $192 \div 3$

2. If $a > b$ and $b = c$, then which of the following is true?
    a. $a < c$
    b. $c < a$
    c. $c = a$
    d. $a < c$

3. Which of the following could be used to visually show $\frac{3}{7} < \frac{5}{6}$ is a true statement?
    a. A bar graph
    b. A number line
    c. An area model
    d. Base 10 blocks

4. Let p equal "Alex is an engineering major," q equal "Alex is not an English major," r equal "Alex's sister is a history major," s equal "Alex's sister has been to Germany," and t equal "Alex's sister has been to Austria." Which of the following answers represents the statement, "Alex is an engineering and English major, but his sister is a history major who hasn't been to either Germany or Austria"?
    a. $p \wedge \sim q \wedge (r \vee (\sim s \vee \sim t))$
    b. $p \wedge q \wedge r \vee (\sim s \wedge \sim t)$
    c. $p \wedge \sim q \wedge r \wedge (\sim s \vee \sim t)$
    d. $p \wedge q \wedge (r \vee (\sim s \wedge \sim t))$

5. Which of the following is a counterexample that disproves the statement, "All prime numbers are also odd numbers"?
    a. 1
    b. 2
    c. 100
    d. There is no counterexample because it is a true statement.

See answers on the next page.

Answer Explanations

1. C: $\frac{1}{3}$ of the shirts sold were patterned. Therefore, $1 - \frac{1}{3}$ (that is, $\frac{2}{3}$) of the shirts sold were solid. A fraction of something is calculated with multiplication, so $192 \times \left(1 - \frac{1}{3}\right)$ solid shirts were sold. (We could calculate that this equals 128, but that's not necessary for this question.)

2. B: Since $a > b$ and $b = c$, through deductive reasoning, a has to be greater than c (and c is less than a). No other case is possible.

3. B: This inequality can be seen with the use of a number line. $\frac{3}{7}$ is close to $\frac{1}{2}$. $\frac{5}{6}$ is close to 1, but less than 1, and $\frac{8}{7}$ is greater than 1. Therefore, $\frac{3}{7}$ is less than $\frac{5}{6}$.

4. C: "Alex is an engineering and English major, but his sister is a history major who hasn't been to either Germany or Austria," can be rewritten as, "p and not q and r and not s or not t." Using logical symbols, this is written as:

$$p \wedge \sim q \wedge r \wedge (\sim s \vee \sim t)$$

5. B: A counterexample is a specific example that shows the statement is not true. 2 is prime and an even number.

Mathematical Learning, Instruction and Assessment

Planning Appropriate Instructional Activities

In planning instructional activities for students, it is important to apply research-based theories of learning mathematics in order to ensure that the lessons are both appropriate and informative. There are a number of theories regarding learning mathematics, including behaviorism, cognitive learning theory, and constructivism. The behaviorism learning theory deals with stimulus and response. In the classroom, it is applied through a set of practices that help students learn through positive reinforcement when they do well. Cognitive learning theory was developed following behaviorism with the intention of developing a theory regarding both external and internal processes that are used within learning. In this theory, students first take in information, which they then store in their minds after cognitively processing it. Examples of the application of cognitivism in the classroom include having students reflect on a past unit and what they learned or encouraging them to first explore newer topics and their connections on their own or with the help of the instructor. The constructivist view of learning approaches learning as a construction—adding new knowledge that builds on previously understood information. This theory focuses on students learning through active work. In the classroom, this could be applied by them solving problems or completing experiments that build on their previous knowledge to incorporate new information.

Differences in Approaches

In different areas of study, students vary in their approach to learning. This includes the way they approach learning mathematics. It is important to not just acknowledge this but to understand it in a way that allows teachers to apply it within their classroom. It is also important in considering the needs of each student individually. There are many different approaches to learning mathematics, including kinesthetic, visual, and auditory. Students who approach learning through a kinesthetic (also known as hands-on) style learn best when they are able to do things physically. This can include tasks that help them to physically carry out a problem/process or with flashcards. Students who prefer a visual learning style approach learning through viewing. They learn best through pictures and reading and best recall things using sight. Some students prefer to approach learning aurally. These students learn best through listening to instruction and speaking. An example of a task for a student with an auditory approach to learning is pairing two students together and having them work through problems by sharing their thought process aloud. It is important to know how to best help students as individuals, and this includes understanding how different students approach learning.

Building on Prior Knowledge and Strengths

In instructing students, it is important to create links with their knowledge that build on previous knowledge and strengths while also considering potential areas of improvement. To build on students' existing mathematical knowledge, teachers should help students make connections as they learn new information. This can be connections to past knowledge and references to what will be learned next. Another way to help students create these connections within their existing knowledge is to have them reflect and draw connections between the different mathematical concepts they have learned. Concerning individual students' strengths and areas of improvement, there are many ways to accommodate different needs through planning instruction. One area of accommodation is considering different students' preferred learning methods. Showing students mathematical concepts using a few different methods (visually, aurally, working hands-on, etc.) allows different students' preferences to be met. This helps more students understand the new information as opposed to going through the information using just one of these methods. Another way to ensure that students' strengths and needs are being met is to include some form of reflection or knowledge check. This lets instructors see both generally and individually what knowledge students have best absorbed and what they are still working to understand and may need additional instruction on.

Manipulatives, Technology and Other Tools

Many mathematical concepts can be instructed using various manipulatives, tools, and technology. When planning, it is important to introduce a new concept to consider different ways of teaching it to students to allow for the most thorough understanding possible among each individual learner. Letting students work with a new concept hands-on through using tools is an engaging way for them to learn and potentially work together to not only learn new information but to understand it as well. There are many ways that manipulatives, technology, and tools can be used in the classroom. One example of a manipulative is using dice to conduct an experiment about probability. An example of a tool is students using stop watches to measure time, which can then be used to measure speed. Another example is using a ruler to measure side lengths of different shapes. Technology can be a helpful aid as well. It can be used to help provide additional information through a visual and entertaining way. Technology can be used not only to show visual examples through different videos but also through interactive activities that can also be found online. These interactive activities can be useful in allowing students to do things hands-on that could not be realistically done within the classroom setting.

Providing Instruction from Concrete to Abstract

To instruct students thoroughly about mathematical concepts as well as their connections, there should be a variety in lessons consisting of both concrete and abstract concepts as they apply. This should be done along a continuum and through building new information on existing knowledge. In planning instruction, lessons regarding more concrete aspects of mathematical concepts can be used in a way that builds toward the students learning about more abstract concepts. A general example that could be applied to various concepts would be to start with an activity that allows students to work with concrete things. This could include doing a hands-on task that uses manipulatives or tools or a collaborative task that incorporates something that applies to daily life. Once students have a basic understanding of the mathematical concept that is being taught as it applies to the concrete, more abstract concepts can be introduced. This can expand upon the previous concrete task through using something that is not wholly unfamiliar but retains some connection to the previous concrete work. From here, more abstract problems can be introduced for students to apply the knowledge they have gained from the previous steps.

Promoting Students' Mathematical Abilities

When planning instruction, both the instruction and the information within TEKS are important to consider. There are many different ways of approaching instruction, including direct versus interactive instruction, hands-on tasks/experiments, and independent versus collaborative instruction/tasks. These strategies each have varying levels of active and passive learning, both of which can be important in the learning process. Direct instruction is led by the teacher and includes things such as lectures, whereas interactive instruction involves more student interaction and can include using discussion groups of varying sizes. Direct instruction is an example of more passive learning, whereas interactive instruction is more active. These can be incorporated together as well—for example, setting aside a lecture time and then allowing students to discuss the concept in smaller groups and make note of what they understand and what they would like more clarification on. Hands-on tasks or experiments can be very helpful not only for students who prefer that method of learning but also to help all students develop a deeper understanding of different topics. Creating a situation in which students can actively work through problems can help them to better retain the information. Independent instruction or study includes students working individually to help them focus on their unique strengths and needs. This is in contrast to collaborative work such as working on tasks together or discussing things in small groups. Collaborative work can be beneficial because different students' strengths can be aspects that other students need help understanding. Individual work, however, is important in ensuring that students retain knowledge and are able to apply it themselves without the aid of others.

Learning Environments

The environment that surrounds students can have a great impact on how well they are able to learn. Each student is unique and has different needs when it comes to learning. It is important for the learning environment to be inclusive of all students and their individual needs in order to best foster their development in their mathematical knowledge. Patience and using a variety of techniques and tasks can be beneficial in creating a positive and educational learning environment. It is important to instruct students using clear explanations and a variety of methods. An example of this is first giving students a general explanation of a concept, then doing an example, including visual aids and walking through the process slowly, and finally, letting students work through an example together in groups while going around the room and addressing individual or small-group concerns and questions. This example allows for direct instruction, as well as visual aids and collaborative work, while also allowing room for individual concerns to be addressed. Many of these details, including various methods of instruction (especially visual), ensuring the use of clear language, and including room for individual and small-group interactions, are all important for the accommodation of English-language learners in the classroom.

Encouraging Mathematical Discourse and Analysis

Analysis and evaluation are important in the process of learning how to think mathematically. To encourage students to improve their mathematical thinking, it is important to learn how to use different questioning strategies when interacting with students. One way to do this is to ask questions that have the intention of inciting a certain type of thinking that allows for a more in-depth analysis or evaluation. An example of this is asking a question that inspires insightful thought into the bigger picture of a mathematical concept. This would include questions about hypotheticals as well as questions that use "why" or "how." Another strategy to use could be to ask questions that deal with evaluation. There are many different things that students could evaluate, including an experiment/task conducted during class or their process of learning a new mathematical concept. Another questioning strategy that could inspire a greater depth of mathematical thinking is providing students with a set of questions designed for critical thought and having them discuss it with one another. This allows students to develop not only their own line of thought but also to use the thought processes of other students to further deepen their discussion of mathematical discourse.

Relating Mathematics to Students' Lives and Careers

In order to improve students' knowledge and interest in mathematics, it can be beneficial to relate mathematics to their lives and various careers or professions. There are some careers or professions that have an obvious correlation to mathematics, such as various scientific and mathematical careers, including environmental scientists, chemists, and statisticians. However, it is also important to be able to relate mathematics to real life. A teacher could use an example like students getting a job and learning about personal finance or using probability and statistics while playing sports to try to make winning decisions. Mathematics can also be applied to creative careers such as music and art. Proportionality is, at times, important when creating art. Music is based on numbers and can include various subdivisions that can be difficult to understand without at least a basic understanding of different mathematical concepts.

Assessments in Mathematics

One way of measuring the information that has been learned by students is through assessments, such as formative and summative assessments. Both of these have different purposes and are important to understand. Formative assessments are generally more flexible assessments that are designed to discover how well students are learning. These assessments can be quizzes or a number of different group activities and can be graded or not graded. They can be done throughout a unit to find areas that need improvement as well as to make adjustments for when that subject is taught again in the future. When done regularly, formative assessments can allow for both individual and class-wide measures of what material is being absorbed and what tasks work best for students to learn. Summative assessments, however, are tests, exams, papers, and so forth, that are designed to measure how well individual students have retained information. They are generally given toward either the end of the semester or the end of a unit, depending on the instructors' choice. These assessments measure what students have learned and whether or not they are ready to move forward in their mathematical knowledge.

Selecting and Developing Assessments

Assessments should be designed to accurately measure students' knowledge and retention. In order to do this, it is useful to consider which type of assessment is most appropriate as well as the content of the assessment and how it is presented. If the goal is to assess cumulative knowledge, a test may be fitting, whereas if the goal is to assess where students currently are, a quiz may be a better fit. The assessment should ask students to complete problems that are relevant to the mathematical concept they have been learning. They should be familiar enough that students are able to recognize which processes to use, while also being novel enough that they test the students' understanding. It is important for the problems to be presented in a way that is consistent with how the concepts have been taught because the way that students are taught is what aids them in developing their understanding.

Assessments and Scoring Procedures

When using assessments to measure knowledge, teachers should look for mathematical understanding, common misconceptions, and error patterns. Mathematical understanding can be assessed for using questions based on what is taught in class to find students' strengths and needs. Common misconceptions are ideas that are false but are accepted by many as true. An example of a common misconception in math is mistaking the variable x with the use of × as an operation for multiplication. An instructor should prepare a list of common misconceptions of the mathematical concept being taught in order to identify them as they come up. It is important to have students show their work because they can reach a correct answer while performing a misconception. To compensate for this, grading can be based on both the answer and the work shown. Error patterns, which are any mistakes that are made consistently, should also be looked for. An example of an error pattern is a student consistently confusing complementary and supplementary angles. Error patterns noted among a class can then be addressed in instruction.

Designing, Monitoring, and Modifying Instruction

The relationship between instruction and the assessments that follow are important to use to the benefit of the mathematical knowledge of all students, including English-language learners. It is important to know how to reflect on students' assessment results to modify future instruction regarding information and/or how the information is presented, including adjusting based on which learning methods seem to be the most effective. Formative assessments are a great way to measure students' learning, both in being able to assess which tasks have allowed for the best understanding among students (individually and as a group) as well as which information needs additional work. These assessments are flexible and can be done as a group or individually, although using the individual assessments may be more beneficial to get a better understanding of how well each student is learning rather than a general idea of how the group is learning. This allows instruction to be modified to include measures that consider the individual needs of different students to be met while also instructing the class as a group. Using these assessments can also help improve the lesson for future students because these changes can be incorporated during each new semester.

Practice Quiz

1. Students are being asked to flip a coin and note how many times they have a success across fifty flips, with tails being a success. They are then using the formula $P_x = \binom{n}{x} p^x q^{n-x}$ to find the probabilities of various numbers of successes when flipping a coin. What learning method is being used during this task?
    a. Hands-on
    b. Visual
    c. Aural
    d. Direct

2. Students are tasked with measuring the angles of different shapes on a piece of paper. Which tool is the most appropriate for them to use to find these measurements?
    a. Measuring tape
    b. Compass
    c. Protractor
    d. Ruler

3. Which of the following is the most appropriate exercise for students to demonstrate an understanding of proportionality?
    a. Students measuring the side lengths of various shapes
    b. Students finding the corresponding side lengths of similar shapes
    c. Students finding the slope of triangles
    d. Students solving for the area of different shapes

4. Which of the following tasks follows the behaviorism learning theory?
    a. Students playing a game during which correct answers gain points toward a prize
    b. Giving students a worksheet of problems to work on independently
    c. Giving students a group project to create 3-D shapes when learning about volume
    d. Instructing students to find connections from the previous unit to the current unit they're learning

5. An instructor wants to give their students a summative assessment to test their individual retention. Which of the following is an example of this kind of assessment?
    a. A weekly quiz that tests students' understanding of the past week's material
    b. A quiz game in which students are grouped together
    c. A collaborative quiz during which small groups work on a larger problem together
    d. A test that covers the material of a whole unit

See answers on the next page.

Answer Explanations

1. A: Choice *A* is correct because having the students conduct the trials and work the problem themselves is having them work hands-on. Choice *B* is incorrect because it is not creating a visual lesson with photos or video. Choice *C* is incorrect because it is not an aural lesson, and students are not expected to listen to a lesson about it. Choice *D* is incorrect because direct instruction would be something like a lecture rather than running an experiment.

2. C: Choice *C* is correct because a protractor is used to measure angles. Choice *A* is incorrect because measuring tape would be used to find length. Choice *B* is incorrect because compasses are used to draw circles. Choice *D* is incorrect because rulers are also used to find length.

3. B: Choice *B* is correct because it involves using the proportionality of similar shapes to find corresponding side lengths. Choice *A* is incorrect because measuring side lengths independently does not involve proportionality. Choice *C* is incorrect because although the slopes of a triangle could be used in a proportionality problem, simply measuring the slopes independently is not an exercise in proportionality. Choice *D* is incorrect because solving for area is also not inherently an exercise in proportionality.

4. A: Choice *A* is correct because behaviorism involves students receiving positive reinforcement for correct answers in order to learn the material. Students winning points toward a prize of their choice would be the positive reinforcement in this scenario. Choice *B* is incorrect because students working on a worksheet does not involve positive reinforcement. Choice *C* is incorrect because students creating 3-D shapes is a hands-on collaborative task that does not involve positive reinforcement and fits more with cognitive learning theory than behaviorism. Choice *D* is incorrect because students making connections between units fits more with the connectivism learning theory rather than behaviorism.

5. D: Choice *D* is correct because a summative assessment is something that tests students' knowledge of a unit or semester and is generally done through something such as a final exam or test. Each of the other choices are more formative assessments and some also involve collaboration. Choice *A* checks students' understanding of the past week, Choice *B* is a way to check students' knowledge in a collaborative and engaging way, and Choice *C* is also collaborative.

Practice Test #1

Number Concepts

1. Which of the following numbers has the greatest value?
    a. 1.43785
    b. 1.07548
    c. 1.43592
    d. 0.89409

2. The value of 6 × 12 is the same as:
    a. 2 × 4 × 4 × 2
    b. 7 × 4 × 3
    c. 6 × 6 × 3
    d. 3 × 3 × 4 × 2

3. This chart indicates how many sales of CDs, vinyl records, and MP3 downloads occurred over the last year. Approximately what percentage of the total sales was from CDs?

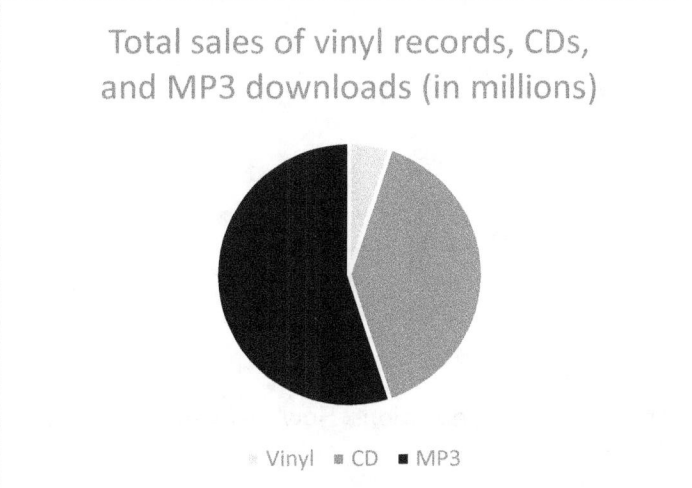

    a. 55%
    b. 25%
    c. 40%
    d. 5%

4. After a 20% sale discount, Frank purchased a new refrigerator for $850. How much did he save compared to the original price?
    a. $170
    b. $212.50
    c. $105.75
    d. $200

Practice Test #1

5. Which of the following is largest?
   a. 0.45
   b. 0.096
   c. 0.3
   d. 0.313

6. What is the value of b in this equation?

$$5b - 4 = 2b + 17$$

   a. 13
   b. 24
   c. 7
   d. 21

7. In 2015, it was estimated that there were 7,350,000,000 people living on Earth. Express this value in scientific notation.
   a. 7.35×10^7
   b. 7.35×10^9
   c. 73.5×10^8
   d. 73.5×10^9

8. Express the following in decimal form:

$$\frac{3}{5} \times \frac{7}{10} \div \frac{1}{2}$$

   a. 0.042
   b. 84%
   c. 0.84
   d. 0.42

9. A student gets an 85% on a test with 20 questions. How many questions did the student answer correctly?
   a. 15
   b. 16
   c. 17
   d. 18

10. The Roman numeral CCXLVII equals:
    a. 377
    b. 301
    c. 251
    d. 247

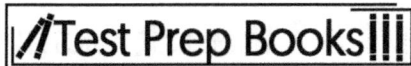

11. Alan currently weighs 200 pounds, but he wants to lose weight to get down to 175 pounds. What is this difference in kilograms? (1 pound is approximately equal to 0.45 kilograms.)
    a. 9 kg
    b. 11.25 kg
    c. 78.75 kg
    d. 90 kg

12. Johnny earns $2,334.50 from his job each month. He pays $1,437 for monthly expenses and saves the rest. Johnny is planning a vacation in 3 months that he estimates will cost $1,750 total. How much will Johnny have left over from 3 months of saving once he pays for his vacation?
    a. $948.50
    b. $584.50
    c. $852.50
    d. $942.50

13. What is $\frac{420}{98}$ rounded to the nearest integer?
    a. 3
    b. 4
    c. 5
    d. 6

14. What is $4 \times 7 + (25 - 21)^2 \div 2$?
    a. 512
    b. 36
    c. 60.5
    d. 22

Patterns and Algebra

1. Simplify:

$$\frac{4a^{-1}b^3}{a^4 b^{-2}} \times \frac{3a}{b}$$

   a. $12a^3 b^5$
   b. $12\frac{b^4}{a^4}$
   c. $\frac{12}{a^4}$
   d. $7\frac{b^4}{a}$

2. What is the product of two irrational numbers?
    a. Irrational
    b. Rational
    c. Irrational or rational
    d. Complex and imaginary

Practice Test #1

3. Which of the following augmented matrices represents the system of equations below?

$$2x - 3y + z = -5$$
$$4x - y - 2z = -7$$
$$-x + 2z = -1$$

a. $\begin{bmatrix} 2 & -3 & 1 & -5 \\ 4 & -1 & -2 & -7 \\ -1 & 0 & 2 & -1 \end{bmatrix}$

b. $\begin{bmatrix} 2 & 4 & -1 \\ -3 & -1 & 0 \\ 1 & -2 & 2 \\ -5 & -7 & -1 \end{bmatrix}$

c. $\begin{bmatrix} 2 & 4 & -1 & -5 \\ -3 & -1 & 0 & -7 \\ 2 & -2 & 2 & -1 \end{bmatrix}$

d. $\begin{bmatrix} 2 & -3 & 1 \\ 4 & -1 & -2 \\ -1 & 0 & 2 \end{bmatrix}$

4. What are the zeros of the function: $f(x) = x^3 + 4x^2 + 4x$?
   a. -2
   b. 0, -2
   c. 2
   d. 0, 2

5. If $g(x) = x^3 - 3x^2 - 2x + 6$ and $f(x) = 2$, then what is $g(f(x))$?
   a. -26
   b. 6
   c. $2x^3 - 6x^2 - 4x + 12$
   d. -2

6. What is the solution to the following system of equations?

$$x^2 - 2x + y = 8$$
$$x - y = -2$$

   a. $(-2, 3)$
   b. There is no solution.
   c. $(-2, 0) (1, 3)$
   d. $(-2, 0) (3, 5)$

7. Which of the following shows the correct result of simplifying the following expression?

$$(7n + 3n^3 + 3) + (8n + 5n^3 + 2n^4)$$

   a. $9n^4 + 15n - 2$
   b. $2n^4 + 5n^3 + 15n - 2$
   c. $9n^4 + 8n^3 + 15n$
   d. $2n^4 + 8n^3 + 15n + 3$

8. What is the product of the following expression?

$$(4x - 8)(5x^2 + x + 6)$$

   a. $20x^3 - 36x^2 + 16x - 48$
   b. $6x^3 - 41x^2 + 12x + 15$
   c. $20x^3 + 11x^2 - 37x - 12$
   d. $2x^3 - 11x^2 - 32x + 20$

9. How could the following equation be factored to find the zeros?

$$y = x^3 - 3x^2 - 4x$$

   a. $0 = x^2(x - 4), x = 0, 4$
   b. $0 = 3x(x + 1)(x + 4), x = 0, -1, -4$
   c. $0 = x(x + 1)(x + 6), x = 0, -1, -6$
   d. $0 = x(x + 1)(x - 4), x = 0, -1, 4$

10. What is the simplified quotient of $\frac{5x^3}{3x^2y} \div \frac{25}{3y^9}$?

   a. $\frac{125x}{9y^{10}}$
   b. $\frac{x}{5y^8}$
   c. $\frac{5}{xy^8}$
   d. $\frac{xy^8}{5}$

11. What is the solution for the following equation?

$$\frac{x^2 + x - 30}{x - 5} = 11$$

   a. $x = -6$
   b. There is no solution.
   c. $x = 16$
   d. $x = 5$

12. Mom's car drove 72 miles in 90 minutes. How fast did she drive in feet per second?
    a. 0.8 feet per second
    b. 48.9 feet per second
    c. 0.009 feet per second
    d. 70.4 feet per second

13. What is the domain for the function $y = \sqrt{x}$?
    a. All real numbers
    b. $x \geq 0$
    c. $x > 0$
    d. $y \geq 0$

14. The phone bill is calculated each month using the equation $c = 50g + 75$. The cost of the phone bill per month is represented by c, and g represents the gigabytes of data used that month. What is the value and interpretation of the slope of this equation?
    a. 75 dollars per day
    b. 75 gigabytes per day
    c. 50 dollars per day
    d. 50 dollars per gigabyte

15. Which of the following functions has a graph equivalent to $y = \cos(x)$?
    a. $y = \tan(x)$
    b. $y = \csc(x)$
    c. $y = \sin(x + \frac{\pi}{2})$
    d. $y = \sin(x - \frac{\pi}{2})$

16. What is the solution for the equation $\tan(\theta) + 1 = 0$, where $0 \leq \theta < 2\pi$?
    a. $\theta = \frac{3\pi}{4}, \frac{5\pi}{4}$
    b. $\theta = \frac{3\pi}{4}, \frac{\pi}{4}$
    c. $\theta = \frac{5\pi}{4}, \frac{7\pi}{4}$
    d. $\theta = \frac{3\pi}{4}, \frac{7\pi}{4}$

17. What is the inverse of the function $f(x) = 3x - 5$?
    a. $f^{-1}(x) = \frac{x}{3} + 5$
    b. $f^{-1}(x) = \frac{5x}{3}$
    c. $f^{-1}(x) = 3x + 5$
    d. $f^{-1}(x) = \frac{x+5}{3}$

18. What are the zeros of $f(x) = x^2 + 4$?
    a. $x = -4$
    b. $x = \pm 2i$
    c. $x = \pm 2$
    d. $x = \pm 4i$

19. What is the y-intercept for $y = x^2 + 3x - 4$?
    a. $y = 1$
    b. $y = -4$
    c. $y = 3$
    d. $y = 4$

20. Is the following function even, odd, neither, or both?

$$y = \frac{1}{2}x^4 + 2x^2 - 6$$

    a. Even
    b. Odd
    c. Neither
    d. Both

21. Which equation is NOT a function of x?
    a. $y = |x|$
    b. $y = x^2$
    c. $x = 3$
    d. $y = 4$

22. How could the following function be rewritten to identify the zeros?

$$y = 3x^3 + 3x^2 - 18x$$

    a. $y = 3x(x+3)(x-2)$
    b. $y = x(x-2)(x+3)$
    c. $y = 3x(x-3)(x+2)$
    d. $y = (x+3)(x-2)$

23. What is the slope of the line tangent to the graph of $y = x^3 - 4$ at the point where $x = 2$?
    a. $3x^2$
    b. 4
    c. -4
    d. 12

Practice Test #1

24. Let $f(x) = \begin{cases} \frac{x^2-4}{x-2} & if\ x \neq 2 \\ 0 & if\ x = 2 \end{cases}$. Which of the following statements is/are true?

   I. $\lim_{x \to 2} exists$
   II. $f(2) exists$
   III. $f\ is\ continuous\ at\ x = 2$

   a. Choice I only
   b. Choice II only
   c. Choices I and II
   d. Choices I and III

25. What is $\lim_{x \to 4} \frac{x^2-16}{x-4}$?

   a. 0
   b. 1
   c. 8
   d. Nonexistent

26. What are the first four terms of the sequence $\left\{ \frac{(-1)^{n+1}}{n^2+5} \right\}_{n=0}^{\infty}$?

   a. $\frac{1}{6}, \frac{1}{9}, \frac{1}{14}, \frac{1}{19}$
   b. $\frac{1}{6}, \frac{-1}{9}, \frac{1}{14}, \frac{-1}{19}$
   c. $\frac{-1}{5}, \frac{1}{6}, \frac{-1}{9}, \frac{1}{14}$
   d. $\frac{1}{5}, \frac{1}{6}, \frac{1}{9}, \frac{1}{14}$

27. A particle moves along the x-axis so that at any time $t \geq 0$, its velocity is given by $v(t) = \frac{6}{t+3}$. What is the acceleration of the particle at time $t = 5$?

   a. $-\frac{2}{3}$
   b. $-\frac{3}{32}$
   c. $\frac{3}{4}$
   d. $\frac{2}{3}$

190

28. Given the graph of the derivative of $f(x)$, on what interval(s) is the graph of $f(x)$ increasing?

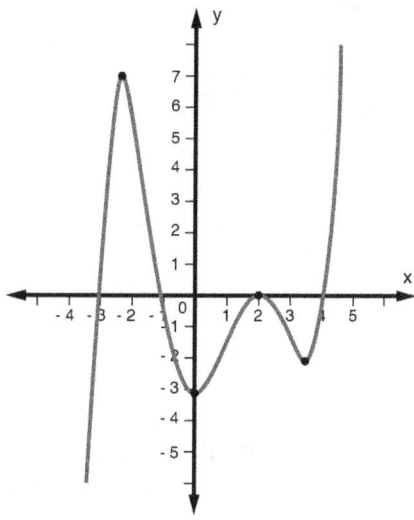

a. $(-3, -1)(4, \infty)$
b. $(-\infty, -2.4)(0, 2)(3.4, \infty)$
c. $(-\infty, -3)(-1, 4)$
d. $(0, \infty)$

29. What is the trapezoidal approximation for the integral $\int_0^4 \sqrt{x}\, dx$, using 4 subintervals?

a. 5.333
b. 12.293
c. 10.293
d. 5.146

30. What is the definite integral that represents the area of the region bounded by the graphs of $y_1 = 5 - x^2$ and $y_2 = -3x - 5$?

a. $\int_{-\sqrt{5}}^{\sqrt{5}} (5 - x^2)\, dx$

b. $\int_{-\sqrt{5}}^{\sqrt{5}} (x^2 - 3x - 10)\, dx$

c. $\int_{-2}^{5} (-x^2 + 3x + 10)\, dx$

d. $\int_{-2}^{5} [(5 - x^2) + (-3x - 5)]\, dx$

Practice Test #1

31. What type of function is modeled by the values in the following table?

x	$f(x)$
1	2
2	4
3	8
4	16
5	32

a. Linear
b. Exponential
c. Quadratic
d. Cubic

32. An investment of $2,000 is made into an account with an annual interest rate of 5%, compounded continuously. What is the total value for the investment after eight years?
a. $2,954.91
b. $3,000
c. $2,983.65
d. $2,800

33. Is the series $\sum_{k=0}^{\infty}(-1)^k \left(\frac{2}{3}\right)^k$ convergent or divergent? If convergent, find its sum.
a. Divergent
b. Convergent, $\frac{3}{5}$
c. Convergent, $\frac{5}{3}$
d. Convergent, $\frac{2}{3}$

Geometry and Measurement

1. For the following similar triangles, what are the values of x and y (rounded to one decimal place)?

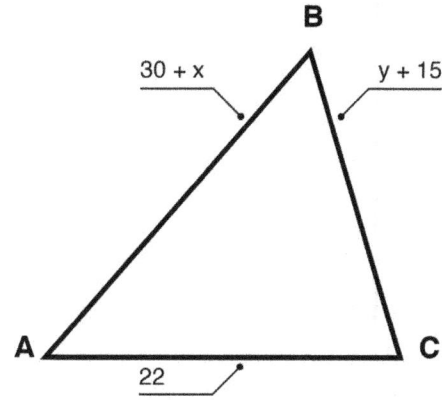
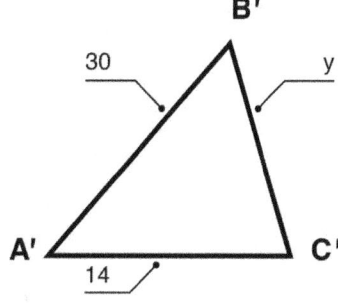

a. $x = 16.5, y = 25.1$
b. $x = 19.5, y = 24.1$
c. $x = 17.1, y = 26.3$
d. $x = 26.3, y = 17.1$

2. What are the center and radius of a circle with equation $4x^2 + 4y^2 - 16x - 24y + 51 = 0$?
a. Center $(3, 2)$ and radius $1/2$
b. Center $(2, 3)$ and radius $1/2$
c. Center $(3, 2)$ and radius $1/4$
d. Center $(2, 3)$ and radius $1/4$

3. If the point $(-3, -4)$ is reflected over the x-axis, what new point does it make?
a. $(-3, -4)$
b. $(3, -4)$
c. $(3, 4)$
d. $(-3, 4)$

4. If the volume of a sphere is $288\,\pi$ cubic meters, what are the radius and surface area of the same sphere?
a. Radius: 6 meters, surface area: $144\,\pi$ square meters
b. Radius: 36 meters, surface area: $144\,\pi$ square meters
c. Radius: 6 meters, surface area: $12\,\pi$ square meters
d. Radius: 36 meters, surface area: $12\,\pi$ square meters

5. The triangle shown below is a right triangle. What's the value of x?

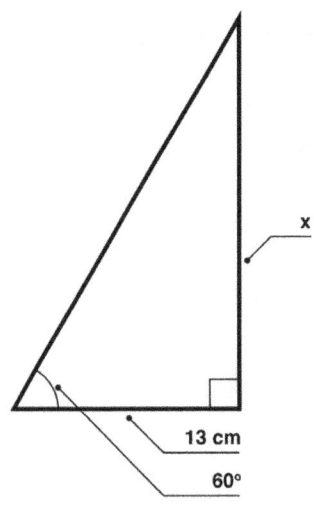

a. $x = 1.73$
b. $x = 0.57$
c. $x = 13$
d. $x = 22.52$

6. What's the midpoint of a line segment with endpoints $(-1, 2)$ and $(3, -6)$?
a. $(1, 2)$
b. $(1, 0)$
c. $(-1, 2)$
d. $(1, -2)$

7. A sample data set contains the following values: 1, 3, 5, 7. What's the standard deviation of the set?
a. 2.58
b. 4
c. 6.23
d. 1.1

8. Given the following triangle, what's the length of the missing side? Round the answer to the nearest tenth.

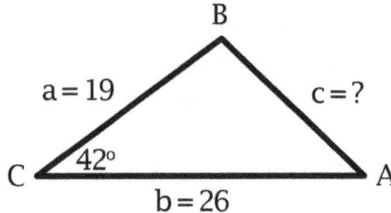

a. 17.0
b. 17.4
c. 18.0
d. 18.4

9. What are the coordinates of the focus of the parabola $y = -9x^2$?
   a. $(-3, 0)$
   b. $\left(-\frac{1}{36}, 0\right)$
   c. $(0, -3)$
   d. $\left(0, -\frac{1}{36}\right)$

10. The total perimeter of a rectangle is 36 cm. If the length is 12 cm, what is the width?
    a. 3 cm
    b. 12 cm
    c. 6 cm
    d. 8 cm

11. Using the following diagram, calculate the total circumference, rounding to the nearest tenths place.

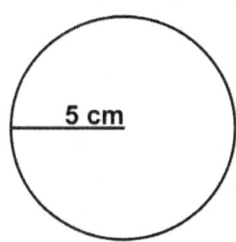

   a. 25.0 cm
   b. 15.7 cm
   c. 78.5 cm
   d. 31.4 cm

12. Which of the following figures is NOT a polygon?
    a. Decagon
    b. Cone
    c. Triangle
    d. Rhombus

13. What is the area of the regular hexagon shown below?

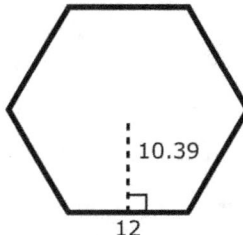

   a. 72
   b. 124.68
   c. 374.04
   d. 748.08

14. The area of a given rectangle is 24 square centimeters. If the measure of each side is multiplied by 3, what is the area of the new figure?
   a. 48 cm²
   b. 72 cm²
   c. 216 cm²
   d. 13,824 cm²

15. A cereal box has a base 3 inches by 5 inches and is 10 inches tall. Another box has a base 5 inches by 6 inches. Students are trying to calculate how tall the second box must be to hold the same amount of cereal as the first box. What formula should they use?
   a. Area of a rectangle
   b. Volume of a rectangular solid
   c. Volume of a cube
   d. Perimeter of a square

16. An angle measures 54 degrees. In order to correctly determine the measure of its complementary angle, what concept is necessary?
   a. Two complementary angles sum up to 180 degrees.
   b. Complementary angles are always acute.
   c. Two complementary angles sum up to 90 degrees.
   d. Complementary angles sum up to 360 degrees.

17. The diameter of a circle measures 5.75 centimeters. What would be the best tool in the classroom to draw such a circle?
   a. Ruler
   b. Meter stick
   c. Compass
   d. Protractor

18. What unit is used to describe the volume of the following 3-dimensional shape?

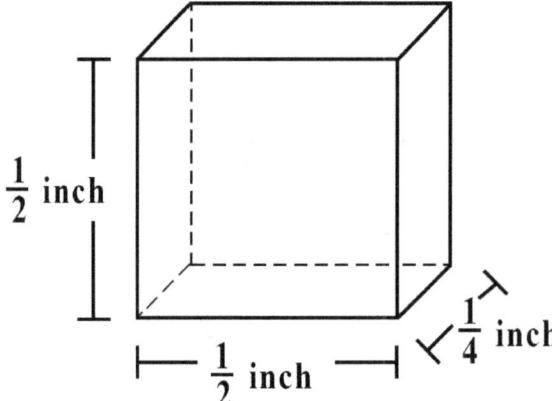

   a. Square inches
   b. Inches
   c. Cubic inches
   d. Squares

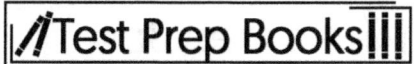

19. The perimeter of a 6-sided polygon is 56 cm. The lengths of three sides are 9 cm each. The lengths of two other sides are 8 cm each. What is the length of the final side?
    a. 11 cm
    b. 12 cm
    c. 13 cm
    d. 10 cm

Probability and Statistics

1. A ball is drawn at random from a ball pit containing 8 red balls, 7 yellow balls, 6 green balls, and 5 purple balls. What's the probability that the ball drawn is yellow?
    a. $\frac{1}{26}$
    b. $\frac{19}{26}$
    c. $\frac{7}{26}$
    d. 1

2. A shuffled deck of 52 cards contains 4 kings. One card is drawn, and is not put back in the deck. Then a second card is drawn. What's the probability that both cards are kings?
    a. $\frac{1}{169}$
    b. $\frac{1}{221}$
    c. $\frac{1}{13}$
    d. $\frac{4}{13}$

3. What's the probability of rolling a 6 exactly once in two rolls of a die?
    a. $\frac{1}{3}$
    b. $\frac{1}{36}$
    c. $\frac{1}{6}$
    d. $\frac{5}{18}$

4. Given the sets $A = \{1, 2, 3, 4, 5, 6, 7, 8, 9, 10\}$ and $B = \{1, 2, 3, 4, 5\}$, what is $A - (A \cap B)$?
    a. $\{6, 7, 8, 9, 10\}$
    b. $\{1, 2, 3, 4, 5\}$
    c. $\{1, 2, 3, 4, 5, 6, 7, 8, 9, 10\}$
    d. $\emptyset$

5. A six-sided die is rolled. What is the probability that the roll is 1 or 2?
   a. $\frac{1}{6}$
   b. $\frac{1}{4}$
   c. $\frac{1}{3}$
   d. $\frac{1}{2}$

6. For a group of 20 men, the median weight is 180 pounds and the range is 30 pounds. If each man gains 10 pounds, which of the following would be true?
   a. The median weight will increase, and the range will remain the same.
   b. The median weight and range will both remain the same.
   c. The median weight will stay the same, and the range will increase.
   d. The median weight and range will both increase.

7. A pair of dice is thrown, and the sum of the two scores is calculated. What's the expected value of the roll?
   a. 5
   b. 6
   c. 7
   d. 8

8. How many possible two-number pairs are there for the numbers 1, 2, 3, 4, and 5 if each number can only be used once and order DOES matter?
   a. 120
   b. 60
   c. 20
   d. 10

9. In a statistical experiment, 29 college students are given an exam during week 11 of the semester, and 30 college students are given an exam during week 12 of the semester. Both groups are being tested to determine which exam week might result in a higher grade. The two groups have equal variances. What's the degree of freedom in this experiment?
   a. 29
   b. 30
   c. 59
   d. 28

10. Which measure for the center of a small sample set is most affected by outliers?
    a. Mean
    b. Median
    c. Mode
    d. None of the above

11. Given the value of a particular stock at monthly intervals, which graph should be used to best represent the trend of the stock?
   a. Box plot
   b. Line plot
   c. Line graph
   d. Circle graph

12. Before a race of four horses, you make a random guess of which horse will get first place and which will get second place. What is the probability that both your guesses will be correct?
   a. $\frac{1}{4}$
   b. $\frac{1}{2}$
   c. $\frac{1}{16}$
   d. $\frac{1}{12}$

13. In Jim's school, there are a total of 650 boys and girls. There are 3 girls for every 2 boys. How many students are girls?
   a. 260
   b. 130
   c. 65
   d. 390

14. Five of six numbers have a sum of 25. The average of all six numbers is 6. What is the sixth number?
   a. 8
   b. 10
   c. 11
   d. 12

Mathematical Processes and Perspectives

1. Which of the following proves that a mathematical statement is true?
   a. Deductive reasoning
   b. Counterexample
   c. Inductive reasoning
   d. None of the above

2. If $a = b$ and $b = c$, then which of the following is true?
   a. $a < c$
   b. $c < a$
   c. $c = a$
   d. $b < a$

3. Which of the following is a counterexample that disproves the statement, "The product of two even numbers is an odd number"?
   a. $2 \times 3 = 6$
   b. $3 \times 5 = 15$
   c. $4 \times 6 = 24$
   d. $0 \times 1 = 0$

4. Students are working with the formula that the sum of the first n integers is equal to $\frac{n(n+1)}{2}$. They are plugging in specific values for n to show some examples in which the formula holds. Which of the following is being used?
   a. A formal proof
   b. Deductive reasoning to prove the formula
   c. A counterexample to disprove the formula
   d. Inductive reasoning to make conclusions

5. Which of the following is a counterexample that disproves the statement, "If one pair of opposite sides of a quadrilateral is parallel, then the quadrilateral is a parallelogram"?
   a. Trapezoid
   b. Square
   c. Rhombus
   d. Rectangle

6. Mathematical models provide which of the following?
   a. Wrong results
   b. Approximate results
   c. Exact results
   d. Unrealistic results

7. Which of the following can be used to find the definite integral $\int_0^2 x \, dx$?
   I. Area of a triangle
   II. Fundamental Theorem of Calculus
   III. Riemann Sums
   IV. Poisson's Ratio

   a. Choices I and II
   b. Choice II only
   c. Choices I, II, and III
   d. All of the above

8. 40 gallons of milk was poured into two containers of different sizes. Which of the following represents the amount of milk poured into the smaller container in terms of the amount m poured into the larger container?
   a. $40 + m$
   b. $m - 40$
   c. $40 - m$
   d. $40/m$

9. The growth model $A = 3.9e^{0.02t}$ describes Australia's population, A, in millions, t years after 2010. What is Australia's growth rate?
   a. 3.9%
   b. 2%
   c. 2
   d. e

10. Which of the following statements is correct regarding the equation $(a + b)^2 = a^2 + b^2$?
    a. It is false for all real numbers a and b
    b. It is true for all real numbers a and b
    c. It is true for only $a = b = 1$
    d. It is true for only $a = b = 0$

Mathematical Learning, Instruction and Assessment

1. Some students in a precalculus class are struggling to apply the Law of Sines when doing their work. These students generally find real-world examples to be helpful in understanding new concepts. Which of the following tasks is most appropriate to help these students?
   a. Finding the missing degree of a triangle using given angles and side lengths
   b. Measuring the length of a tree's shadow
   c. Finding the missing length of a side using given angles and side lengths
   d. Giving students a number of practice problems to work on as a class

2. A teacher had her students take a non-graded quiz to check their knowledge regarding one-variable equations and inequalities. In checking their work, she noticed that many of the students combined non-like terms. Which of the following is most appropriate to help correct this error?
   a. Working with students individually to discover why they misunderstand this topic
   b. Instructing students using a lecture-style lesson to correct this error
   c. Making a note on the paper of each student who made this error and allowing them to make the change on their own
   d. Instructing the students as a class regarding the error using multiple methods (hands-on, visual, aural)

3. Students are given the task of calculating how many tiles are on the floor of the classroom through measuring the room and the size of individual tiles. Which of the following is most appropriate to push students' knowledge toward a more abstract lesson?
   a. Students completing the same task in a room within their home
   b. Students completing a series of problems calculating the area of various shapes given on a worksheet
   c. Students using the same geometric concepts to calculate how many ceramic tiles are needed to fill a bathroom floor after being given the layout of a bathroom on paper
   d. Students completing problems in which they have to calculate geometric means of various problems on a given worksheet

Practice Test #1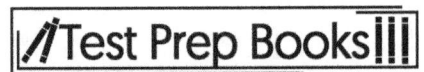

4. A teacher has instructed students on patterns and structure in algebraic reasoning primarily through having them work individually on practice problems in which they discover and explain the key attributes of functions. Which of the following is the most appropriate way this teacher could build an assessment according to how the students have been instructed?
    a. Students modeling various attributes from a given set of problems
    b. Creating a larger problem that involves students comparing and contrasting various attributes of three different functions
    c. Asking students to determine quotients of polynomial functions
    d. Students solving problems about linear equations and matrices

5. In solving a trigonometry problem, a student answered incorrectly with $\tan(30) = \frac{1}{\sqrt{3}}$. This error was likely due to which of the following errors?
    a. The answer is in degrees instead of radians.
    b. The answer is in radians instead of degrees.
    c. The answer is not correct in degrees or radians.
    d. There is not enough information regarding why the answer is incorrect.

6. A teacher gives students the task of working together to complete geometric proofs. This is an example of what kind of instructional strategy?
    a. Direct
    b. Inquiry-guided
    c. Independent
    d. Collaborative

7. A teacher is creating an assessment for a unit on inference for a statistics class. Which of the following is the LEAST appropriate option for this assessment?
    a. Including problems that involve calculating confidence intervals
    b. Asking students to explain the impact of Type II errors
    c. Students explaining different sampling techniques
    d. Students constructing both null and alternative hypotheses

8. Students are given the instruction to reflect on the connections between the unit circle and different geometric functions (of sine, cosine, etc.). Which of the following is this an example of?
    a. Students strengthening their mathematical knowledge through creating links
    b. Measuring the way that students best learn
    c. Behaviorism
    d. A hands-on task

9. A teacher is creating an exercise for students to learn about the unit circle, most of whom prefer to learn using the hands-on method. Which of the following is the most appropriate option that also allows for the inclusion of other learning methods?
    a. Giving students a lecture so they can take notes about the unit circle
    b. Showing students the visual of a unit circle for them to gain a visual understanding of it
    c. Leading the students through creating their own unit circle using paper and a protractor
    d. None of these options

10. In a problem regarding exponents, a student wrote $x^4 x^5 = x^{20}$. This student made an error in regard to which property of exponents?
   a. The product of powers
   b. The quotient of powers
   c. The power of a product
   d. The power to a power

Answer Explanations #1

Number Concepts

1. A: Compare each number after the decimal point to figure out which overall number is greatest. In Choices A (1.43785) and C (1.43592), both have the same tenths place (4) and hundredths place (3). However, the thousandths place is greater in Choice A (7), so A has the greatest value overall.

2. D: By rearranging and grouping the factors in Choice D, we can notice that $3 \times 3 \times 4 \times 2 = (3 \times 2) \times (4 \times 3) = 6 \times 12$, which is what we were looking for.

3. C: The total percentage of a pie chart equals 100%. We can see that CD sales make up less than half of the chart (50%) but more than a quarter (25%), and the only answer choice that meets these criteria is Choice C, 40%.

4. B: Since $850 is the price after a 20% discount, $850 represents 80% (or 0.8) of the original price. In other words, $850 = 0.8x$ (where x is the original price). Solving this, we find $x = \frac{850}{0.8} = 1{,}062.5$. Now, to find the savings, calculate the original price minus the sale price: $\$1{,}062.50 - \$850 = \$212.50$.

5. A: To figure out which is largest, look at the first nonzero digits. Choice B's first nonzero digit is in the hundredths place. The other three all have nonzero digits in the tenths place, so it must be A, C, or D. Of these, A's first nonzero digit is the largest.

6. C: To solve for the value of b, isolate the variable b on one side of the equation.

Start by moving the lower value of -4 to the other side by adding 4 to both sides:

$$5b - 4 = 2b + 17$$

$$5b - 4 + 4 = 2b + 17 + 4$$

$$5b = 2b + 21$$

Then subtract $2b$ from both sides:

$$5b - 2b = 2b + 21 - 2b$$

$$3b = 21$$

Then divide both sides by 3 to get the value of b:

$$\frac{3b}{3} = \frac{21}{3}$$

$$b = 7$$

7. B: Scientific notation takes the form $a \times 10^n$, where a is any decimal number between 1 and 10 and n is the number of decimal places it takes to reach the first digit. In this case, take the first digit 7, add a decimal point, and then include each non-zero digit after that to determine the value of a as 7.35. Next, count the place values from the position of the decimal point in standard form to the position in

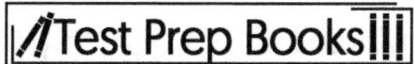

scientific notation in order to determine the value of n, which would be 9. Therefore, this number expressed in scientific notation would be 7.35×10^9.

8. C: The first step in solving this problem is expressing the result in fraction form. Multiplication and division are typically performed in order from left to right, but they can be performed in any order. For this problem, let's start with the division operation between the last two fractions. When dividing one fraction by another, invert or flip the second fraction and then multiply the numerators and denominators.

$$\frac{7}{10} \times \frac{2}{1} = \frac{14}{10}$$

Next, multiply the first fraction by this value:

$$\frac{3}{5} \times \frac{14}{10} = \frac{42}{50}$$

In this instance, to find the decimal form, we can multiply the numerator and denominator by 2 to get 100 in the denominator. In decimal form, this would be expressed as 0.84.

9. C: To find what 85% of 20 questions is, multiply 20 by .85:

$$20 \times .85 = 17 \text{ questions}$$

10. D: In Roman numerals, C is 100, L is 50, X is 10, V is 5, and I is 1. To prevent four identical letters in a row, a lesser number is put before a larger one, and the lesser number is subtracted from the larger one. In this case, an X (10) is put before an L (50), which equals 40. Written in Arabic form, the numerals are:

$$200 + 40 + 5 + 2 = 247$$

11. B: Using the conversion rate, multiply the projected weight loss of 25 lb. by $0.45 \frac{\text{kg}}{\text{lb}}$ to get the amount in kilograms (11.25 kg).

12. D: First, subtract $1,437 from $2,334.50 to find Johnny's monthly savings; this equals $897.50. Then, multiply this amount by 3 to find out how much he will have (in 3 months) before he pays for his vacation; this equals $2,692.50. Finally, subtract the cost of the vacation ($1,750) from this amount to find how much Johnny will have left: $942.50.

13. B: Dividing by 98 can be approximated by dividing by 100, which would mean shifting the decimal point of the numerator to the left by 2. The result is 4.2, which rounds to 4.

14. B: To solve this correctly, keep in mind the order of operations with the mnemonic PEMDAS (Please Excuse My Dear Aunt Sally). This stands for Parentheses, Exponents, Multiplication & Division, Addition & Subtraction. Taking it step by step, solve inside the parentheses first:

$$4 \times 7 + (4)^2 \div 2$$

Then, apply the exponent:

$$4 \times 7 + 16 \div 2$$

Answer Explanations #1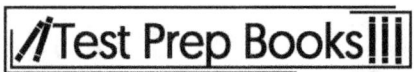

Multiplication and division are both performed next:

$$28 + 8$$

And then finally, addition:

$$28 + 8 = 36$$

Patterns and Algebra

1. B: The first step is to make all exponents positive by moving the terms with negative exponents to the opposite side of the fraction. This expression becomes:

$$\frac{4b^3 b^2}{a^1 a^4} \times \frac{3a}{b}$$

Then the rules for exponents can be used to simplify. Multiplying the same bases means the exponents can be added. Dividing the same bases means the exponents are subtracted. Thus, after multiplying the exponents in the first fraction, the expression becomes:

$$\frac{4b^5}{a^5} \times \frac{3a}{b}$$

Therefore, we can first multiply to get:

$$\frac{12ab^5}{a^5 b}$$

Then, simplifying yields:

$$12 \frac{b^4}{a^4}$$

2. C: The product of two irrational numbers can be rational or irrational. Sometimes, the irrational parts of the two numbers cancel each other out, leaving a rational number. For example, $\sqrt{2} \times \sqrt{2} = 2$ because the roots cancel each other out. Technically, the product of two irrational numbers is a complex number, because real numbers are a type of complex number. However, Choice D is incorrect because the product of two irrational numbers is not an imaginary number.

3. A: The augmented matrix that represents the system of equations has dimensions 4×3 because there are three equations with three unknowns. The coefficients of the variables make up the first three columns, and the last column is made up of the numbers to the right of the equals sign. This system can be solved by reducing the matrix to row-echelon form, where the last column gives the solution for the unknown variables.

4. B: There are two zeros for the given function. They are $x = 0, -2$. The zeros can be found several ways, but this particular equation can be factored into:

$$f(x) = x(x^2 + 4x + 4) = x(x + 2)(x + 2)$$

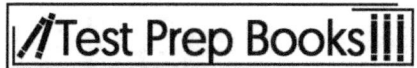

Answer Explanations #1

By setting each factor equal to zero and solving for x, there are two solutions: $x = 0$ and $x = -2$. On a graph, these zeros can be seen where the line crosses the x-axis.

5. D: This problem involves a composition function, where one function is plugged into the other function. In this case, the $f(x)$ function is plugged into the g(x) function for each x value. Since $f(x) = 2$, the composition equation becomes:

$$g(f(x)) = g(2) = (2)^3 - 3(2)^2 - 2(2) + 6$$

6. D: This system of equations involves one quadratic equation and one linear equation. One way to solve this is through substitution.

Solving for y in the second equation yields:

$$y = x + 2$$

Plugging this equation in for the y of the quadratic equation yields:

$$x^2 - 2x + x + 2 = 8$$

Simplify the equation:

$$x^2 - x + 2 = 8$$

Set this equal to zero and factor:

$$x^2 - x - 6 = 0 = (x - 3)(x + 2)$$

Solving these two factors for x gives the zeros:

$$x = 3, -2$$

To find the y-value for the point, plug in each number to either original equation. Solving each one for y yields the points $(3,5)$ and $(-2,0)$.

7. D: The expression is simplified by collecting like terms. Terms with the same variable and exponent are like terms, and their coefficients can be added.

8. A: Finding the product means distributing one polynomial to the other so that each term in the first is multiplied by each term in the second. Then, like terms can be collected. Multiplying the factors yields the expression:

$$20x^3 + 4x^2 + 24x - 40x^2 - 8x - 48$$

Collecting like terms means adding the x^2 terms and adding the x terms. The final answer after simplifying the expression is:

$$20x^3 - 36x^2 + 16x - 48$$

9. D: Finding the zeros for a function by factoring is done by setting the equation equal to zero, then completely factoring. Since there is a common x for each term in the provided equation, that should be factored out first. Then the quadratic that is left can be factored into two binomials, which are $(x + 1)(x - 4)$. Setting each factor equal to zero and solving for x yields three zeros.

Answer Explanations #1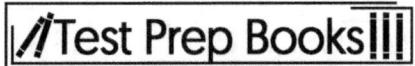

10. D: Dividing rational expressions follows the same rule as dividing fractions. The division is changed to multiplication by the reciprocal of the second fraction. This turns the expression into:

$$\frac{5x^3}{3x^2y} \times \frac{3y^9}{25}$$

This can be simplified by finding common factors in the numerators and denominators of the two fractions.

$$\frac{x^3}{x^2y} \times \frac{y^9}{5}$$

Multiplying across creates:

$$\frac{x^3y^9}{5x^2y}$$

Simplifying leads to the final expression of:

$$\frac{xy^8}{5}$$

11. B: We can try to solve the equation by factoring the numerator into $(x+6)(x-5)$. Since (x-5) is on the top and bottom, that factor cancels out. This leaves the equation $x + 6 = 11$. Solving the equation gives the answer $x = 5$. When this value is plugged into the equation, it yields a zero in the denominator of the fraction. Since this is undefined, there is no solution.

12. D: This problem can be solved by using unit conversion. The initial units are miles per minute. The final units need to be feet per second. Converting miles to feet uses the equivalence statement 1 mi = 5,280 ft. Converting minutes to seconds uses the equivalence statement 1 min = 60 s. Setting up the ratios to convert the units is shown in the following equation:

$$\frac{72 \text{ mi}}{90 \text{ min}} \times \frac{1 \text{ min}}{60 \text{ s}} \times \frac{5,280 \text{ ft}}{1 \text{ mi}} = 70.4 \frac{\text{ft}}{\text{s}}$$

The initial units cancel out, and the new units are left.

13. B: The domain is all possible input values, or x-values. For this equation, the domain is every number greater than or equal to zero. There are no negative numbers in the domain because taking the square root of a negative number results in an imaginary number.

14. D: The slope from this equation is 50, and it is interpreted as the cost per gigabyte used. Since the g-value represents the number of gigabytes and the equation is set equal to the cost in dollars, the slope relates these two values. For every gigabyte used on the phone, the bill goes up 50 dollars.

15. C: Graphing the function $y = \cos(x)$ shows that the curve starts at $(0, 1)$ and has an amplitude of 1 and a period of 2π. This same curve can be constructed using the sine graph, by shifting the graph to the left $\frac{\pi}{2}$ units. This equation is in the form $y = \sin\left(x + \frac{\pi}{2}\right)$.

16. D: Using SOHCAHTOA reminds us that tangent equals the opposite side over the adjacent side. Since $tan(\theta) + 1 = 0$, we are looking for $tan(\theta) = -1$. On the unit circle, "opposite over adjacent" equals 1

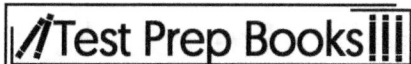

Answer Explanations #1

or −1 when the angle with the x-axis is 45°, or $\frac{\pi}{4}$ This value is negative in the second and fourth quadrant, which corresponds to $\frac{3\pi}{4}$ and $\frac{7\pi}{4}$.

17. D: The inverse of a function is found by following these steps:

1. Change $f(x)$ to y.

2. Switch the x and y in the equation.

3. Solve for y. In the given equation, solving for y is done by adding 5 to both sides, then dividing both sides by 3.

This answer can be checked on the graph by verifying the lines are reflected over $y = x$.

18. B: The zeros of this function can be found by using the quadratic formula:

$$x = \frac{-b \pm \sqrt{b^2 - 4ac}}{2a}$$

This formula is for a function of the form $f(x) = ax^2 + bx + c$. Our function can be written in that form as follows: $f(x) = (1)x^2 + (0)x + 4$. In other words, $a = 1$, $b = 0$, and $c = 4$. The formula becomes:

$$x = \frac{0 \pm \sqrt{0^2 - 4(1)(4)}}{2(1)} = \frac{\sqrt{-16}}{2}$$

Since there is a negative underneath the radical, the answer is a complex number:

$$x = \pm 2i$$

19. B: The y-intercept of an equation is found where the x-value is zero. Plugging in zero for x in the equation, we get $0^2 + 3(0) - 4 = -4$.

20. A: The definition of an even function is that $f(-x) = f(x)$. We can plug in $-x$ to our function to see what we get:

$$f(-x) = \frac{1}{2(-x)^4} + 2(-x)^2 - 6$$

Since $(-x)^4 = x^4$ and $(-x)^2 = x^2$, we see that $f(-x)$ is equal to the original function, so our function is even. The definition of an odd function is that $f(-x) = -f(x)$. We can calculate $-f(x)$:

$$-f(x) = -1\left(\left(\frac{1}{2}\right)x^4 + 2x^2 - 6\right) = \left(-\frac{1}{2}\right)x^4 - 2x^2 + 6$$

This does not equal $f(-x)$ (which, remember, is the same as our original function), so our function is not odd.

21. C: The equation $x = 3$ is not a function of x because it does not pass the vertical-line test: if any vertical line can intersect the equation's graph at more than one point, the equation is not a function. This test comes from the definition of a function, in which each x value in the domain must be mapped

Answer Explanations #1

to no more than one y value. This equation is a vertical line, so the x value of 3 is mapped to an infinite number of y values.

22. A: The function can be factored to identify the zeros. First, the term $3x$ is factored out to the front because each term contains $3x$. Then, the quadratic is factored into $(x + 3)(x - 2)$.

23. D: The first derivative of a function gives the slope of the function's tangent line at any point. This function's first derivative is $y' = 3x^2$. Since $x = 2$, we calculate the slope as $3(2^2) = 12$.

24. C: The limit exists because $\lim_{x \to 2} f(x) = 4$. The limit as x approaches two is four, and the function value $f(2) = 0$; thus, they are not equal. Because they are not the same, the function is not continuous, and the first and second statements are the only ones that are true.

25. C: The numerator can be factored into $(x + 4)(x - 4)$. Since there is a factor of $(x - 4)$ in the numerator and denominator, these factors cancel, leaving the $(x + 4)$. Plugging in $x = 4$ into this function yields $4 + 4 = 8$.

26. C: The numerator in the sequence:

$$\left\{\frac{(-1)^{n+1}}{n^2 + 5}\right\}_{n=0}^{\infty}$$

indicates that the sign of each term changes from term to term. The first term is negative because $n = 0$ and:

$$-1^{n+1} = -1^1 = -1$$

Therefore, the second term is positive, the third term is negative, etc. The denominator is evaluated like a function for plugging in various n values. For example, the denominator of the first term, when $n = 0$, is $0^2 + 5 = 5$.

27. B: The acceleration of the particle can be found by taking the derivative of the velocity equation:

$$v'(t) = \frac{0 - 6(1)}{(t + 3)^2} = \frac{-6}{(t + 3)^2}$$

The acceleration at time $t = 5$ can be found by plugging 5 in for the variable t in the derivative:

$$v'(5) = \frac{-6}{(5 + 3)^2} = \frac{-6}{64} = \frac{-3}{32}$$

28. A: The graph of $f'(x)$ is positive on the intervals $(-3, -1)$ and $(4, \infty)$, meaning that $f(x)$ is increasing on the same intervals.

29. D: The graph of $f(x) = \sqrt{x}$ can be split into four trapezoids to approximate the integral. These subintervals can be represented in the expression:

$$\frac{4 - 0}{2(4)}[f(0) + 2f(1) + 2f(2) + 2f(3) + f(4)]$$

The area of a trapezoid is equal to one-half the sum of the two bases multiplied by the height. Each function value in the brackets represents the sum of the bases of the trapezoids. The fraction outside

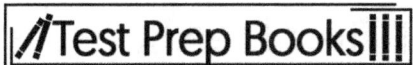
Answer Explanations #1

the brackets represents the height of the trapezoids, dividing by two for the one-half. Finding the function values and simplifying the expression leads to the answer 5.146.

30. C: Setting the y-values of each equation equal to one another finds the point where they meet. The equation $5 - x^2 = -3x - 5$ can be simplified by solving for 0,

$$0 = x^2 - 3x - 10$$

This equation can be factored into:

$$0 = (x + 2)(x - 5)$$

The zeros are $x = -2$ and $x = 5$, between $x = -2$ and $x = 5$, $y_1 > y_2$.

31. B: The table shows values that are increasing exponentially. The differences between the inputs are the same, while the differences in the outputs are changing by a factor of 2. The values in the table can be modeled by the equation $f(x) = 2^x$.

32. C: The formula for continually compounded interest is:

$$A = Pe^{rt}$$

Plugging in the given values to find the total amount in the account yields the equation:

$$A = 2000e^{0.05 \times 8} = 2983.65$$

Choice A is incorrect because it uses annually compounded interest instead of continuous,

$$A = 2000 \times 1.05^8 = 2954.91$$

Choice B is incorrect because it fails to apply the formula for continuously compounded interest. Choice D is incorrect because it simply adds 40% (or eight times 5%) to the original investment rather than compounding annually.

33. B: The given series is a geometric series because it can be written as $\sum_{k=0}^{\infty} \left(\frac{-2}{3}\right)^k$, and it is convergent because $|r| = \frac{2}{3} < 1$. Its sum is:

$$\frac{1}{1-(-\frac{2}{3})} = \frac{3}{5}$$

Geometry and Measurement

1. C: Because the triangles are similar, the lengths of the corresponding sides are proportional. Therefore:

$$\frac{30+x}{30} = \frac{22}{14} = \frac{y+15}{y}$$

Using cross multiplication on the first two terms results in the equation:

$$14(30 + x) = 22 \times 30$$

Answer Explanations #1

When solved, this gives:

$$x \approx 17.1$$

Using cross multiplication on the last two terms results in the equation:

$$14(y + 15) = 22y$$

When solved, this gives:

$$y \approx 26.3$$

2. B: The technique of completing the square must be used to change the equation below into the standard equation of a circle:

$$4x^2 + 4y^2 - 16x - 24y + 51 = 0$$

First, the constant must be moved to the right-hand side of the equals sign and each term must be divided by the coefficient of the x^2-term (which is 4). The x- and y- terms must be grouped together to obtain:

$$x^2 - 4x + y^2 - 6y = -\frac{51}{4}$$

Then, the process of completing the square must be completed for each variable. This gives:

$$(x^2 - 4x + 4) + (y^2 - 6y + 9) = -\frac{51}{4} + 4 + 9$$

The equation can be written as:

$$(x - 2)^2 + (y - 3)^2 = \frac{1}{4}$$

Therefore, the center of the circle is $(2, 3)$ and the radius is:

$$\sqrt{\frac{1}{4}} = \frac{1}{2}$$

3. D: When a point is reflected over an axis, the sign of at least one of the coordinates must change. When it's reflected over the x-axis, the sign of the y coordinate must change. The x value remains the same. Therefore, the new point is $(-3, 4)$.

4. A: The volume of the sphere is 288π cubic meters. Using the formula for sphere volume, we see that:

$$\frac{4}{3}\pi r^3 = 288\pi$$

We solve this equation for r to obtain a radius of 6 meters. The formula for surface area is $4\pi r^2$, so:

$$SA = 4\pi \, 6^2 = 144\pi \text{ square meters}$$

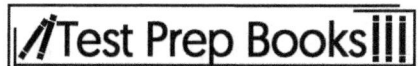

Answer Explanations #1

5. D: We are given an angle (60°), the length of the opposite side (x), and the length of the adjacent side (13 cm). We can use the mnemonic "SOHCAHTOA," where the "TOA" reminds us that tangent equals the opposite side over the adjacent side. In other words, $tan\ 60° = \frac{x}{13}$. Since $tan\ 60° = \sqrt{3}$, we can calculate:

$$x = 13\ tan\ 60° = 13 \times \sqrt{3} \approx 22.52\ \text{cm}$$

6. D: The midpoint formula should be used to get the average of both points.

$$M = \left(\frac{x_1 + x_2}{2}, \frac{y_1 + y_2}{2}\right) = \left(\frac{-1 + 3}{2}, \frac{2 + (-6)}{2}\right) = (1, -2)$$

7. A: First, the sample mean must be calculated. $\bar{x} = \frac{1}{4}(1 + 3 + 5 + 7) = 4$. The sample standard deviation of the data set is:

$$s = \sqrt{\frac{\sum(x - \bar{x})^2}{n - 1}}$$

$n = 4$ represents the number of data points.

Therefore, the sample standard deviation is:

$$s = \sqrt{\frac{1}{3}[(1 - 4)^2 + (3 - 4)^2 + (5 - 4)^2 + (7 - 4)^2]}$$

$$s = \sqrt{\frac{1}{3}(9 + 1 + 1 + 9)} = 2.58$$

8. B: Because this isn't a right triangle, the SOHCAHTOA mnemonic can't be used. However, the law of cosines can be used:

$$c^2 = a^2 + b^2 - 2ab\cos C$$

$$c^2 = 19^2 + 26^2 - 2 \times 19 \times 26 \times \cos 42° = 302.773$$

Taking the square root and rounding to the nearest tenth results in $c = 17.4$.

9. D: A parabola of the form $y = \frac{1}{4f}x^2$ has a focus $(0, f)$. Because $y = -9x^2$, set $-9 = \frac{1}{4f}$. Solving this equation for f results in $f = -\frac{1}{36}$. Therefore, the coordinates of the focus are $\left(0, -\frac{1}{36}\right)$.

10. C: The formula for the perimeter of a rectangle is $P = 2L + 2W$, where P is the perimeter, L is the length, and W is the width. The first step is to substitute all of the data into the formula:

$$36 = 2(12) + 2W$$

Simplify by multiplying 2×12:

$$36 = 24 + 2W$$

Simplifying this further by subtracting 24 on each side gives:

$$36 - 24 = 24 - 24 + 2W$$

$$12 = 2W$$

Divide by 2:

$$6 = W$$

The width is 6 cm. Remember to test this answer by substituting this value into the original formula:

$$36 = 2(12) + 2(6)$$

11. D: To calculate the circumference of a circle, use the formula $2\pi r$, where r equals the radius (half of the diameter) of the circle and $\pi \approx 3.14$. Substitute the given information to get:

$$2 \times 3.14 \times 5 = 31.4$$

12. B: A polygon is a closed two-dimensional figure consisting of 3 or more sides. A decagon is a polygon with 10 sides. A triangle is a polygon with 3 sides. A rhombus is a type of polygon with 4 sides. A cone is a three-dimensional figure and is classified as a solid.

13. C: The formula for finding the area of a regular polygon is $A = \frac{1}{2} \times a \times P$ where a is the length of the apothem (the distance from the center to any side at a right angle), and P is the perimeter of the figure. The apothem a is given as 10.39, and the perimeter can be found by multiplying the length of one side by the number of sides (since the polygon is regular):

$$P = 12 \times 6 = 72$$

To find the area, substitute the values for a and P into the formula:

$$A = \frac{1}{2} \times a \times P = \frac{1}{2} \times 10.39 \times 72 = 374.04$$

14. C: The area of a rectangle is $A = lw$. We don't know the length or width of this rectangle, but the area is 24, so we can say that $lw = 24$. Length and width are each multiplied by 3, so the area of our new rectangle is $3l \times 3w$, or $9lw$. Since we know that $lw = 24$, the area of the new rectangle is $9lw = 9 \times 24 = 216$ cm^2.

15. B: The formula for the volume of a rectangular solid would need to be used. The volume of the first box is:

$$V = 3 \times 5 \times 10 = 150 \text{ cubic inches}$$

The second box needs to hold cereal that would take up the same space. The volume of the second box is:

$$V = 5 \times 6 \times h = 30 \times h$$

In order for this to equal 150, h must equal 5 inches.

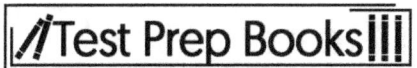

Answer Explanations #1

16. C: The measure of two complementary angles sums up to 90 degrees. Subtracting one angle from 90 gives the complimentary angle:

$$90 - 54 = 36$$

Therefore, the complementary angle is 36 degrees.

17. C: A compass is the ideal tool for drawing a circle. The circle would be drawn by using the length of the radius, which is half of the diameter. Rulers and yard sticks measure distance, and protractors are used to measure angles.

18. C: The volume of this 3-dimensional figure is calculated using $length \times width \times height$. Each of these three measurements is in inches. Therefore, the answer would be labeled in cubic inches.

19. C: The perimeter is found by calculating the sum of all sides of the polygon:

$$9 + 9 + 9 + 8 + 8 + s = 56$$

where s is the missing side length. Therefore, $43 + s = 56$. The missing side length is 13 cm.

Probability and Statistics

1. C: The sample space is made up of $8 + 7 + 6 + 5 = 26$ balls. The probability of pulling each individual ball is $1/26$. Since there are 7 yellow balls, the probability of pulling a yellow ball is $7/26$.

2. B: For the first card drawn, the probability of a king being pulled is $\frac{4}{52}$. Since this card isn't replaced, if a king is drawn first, the probability of a king being drawn second is $\frac{3}{51}$. The probability of a king being drawn in both the first and second draw is the product of the two probabilities:

$$\frac{4}{52} \times \frac{3}{51} = \frac{12}{2,652}$$

To reduce this fraction, divide the top and bottom by 12 to get $\frac{1}{221}$.

3. D: If we roll a die twice, there are 6 possibilities for the first roll and 6 for the second roll, which gives $6 \times 6 = 36$ total possibilities. Now, how many ways are there to roll exactly one 6? We could get a 6 & 1, or 6 & 2, or 6 & 3, or 6 & 4, or 6 & 5. Or the 6 could come on the second roll; we could get a 1 & 6, or 2 & 6, or 3 & 6, or 4 & 6, or 5 & 6. Counting these up, we find a total of 10 different ways to roll exactly one 6. That means our event happens in 10 out of 36 possible rolls, so the probability is $\frac{10}{36}$, which reduces to $\frac{5}{18}$.

4. A: $(A \cap B)$ is equal to the intersection of the two sets A and B, which is $\{1, 2, 3, 4, 5\}$. $A - (A \cap B)$ is equal to the elements of A that are *not* included in the set $(A \cap B)$. Therefore, $A - (A \cap B) = \{6, 7, 8, 9, 10\}$.

5. C: When a die is rolled, each outcome is equally likely. Since it has six sides, each outcome has a probability of $\frac{1}{6}$. The chance of a 1 or a 2 is therefore:

$$\frac{1}{6} + \frac{1}{6} = \frac{1}{3}$$

Answer Explanations #1

6. A: If each man gains 10 pounds, every original data point will increase by 10 pounds. Therefore, the man with the original median will still have the median value, but that value will increase by 10. The smallest value and largest value will also increase by 10, so the difference between the two (the range) will remain the same.

7. C: To find the expected value, take the product of each individual sum and the probability of rolling the sum, then add together the products for each sum. There are 36 possible rolls.

The probability of rolling a 2 is $\frac{1}{36}$.

The probability of rolling a 3 is $\frac{2}{36}$.

The probability of rolling a 4 is $\frac{3}{36}$.

The probability of rolling a 5 is $\frac{4}{36}$.

The probability of rolling a 6 is $\frac{5}{36}$.

The probability of rolling a 7 is $\frac{6}{36}$.

The probability of rolling an 8 is $\frac{5}{36}$.

The probability of rolling a 9 is $\frac{4}{36}$.

The probability of rolling a 10 is $\frac{3}{36}$.

The probability of rolling an 11 is $\frac{2}{36}$.

Finally, the probability of rolling a 12 is $\frac{1}{36}$.

Each possible outcome is multiplied by the probability of it occurring. Like this:

$$2 \times \frac{1}{36} = a$$

$$3 \times \frac{2}{36} = b$$

$$4 \times \frac{3}{36} = c$$

And so forth.

Then, all of those results are added together:

$$a + b + c \ldots = expected\ value = 252/36$$

In this case, it equals 7, which makes sense considering it is the value that has the highest probability of being rolled.

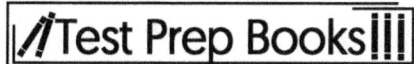

Answer Explanations #1

8. C: Because order *does* matter, the total number of permutations needs to be computed. $P(5,2) = \frac{5!}{(5-2)!} = \frac{120}{6} = 20$ represents the number of ways that two objects can be arranged from a set of five.

9. D: The degree of freedom for two samples is calculated as $df = \frac{(n_1-1)+(n_2-1)}{2}$ rounded to the lowest whole number. For this example, $df = \frac{(29-1)+(30-1)}{2} = \frac{28+29}{2} = 28.5$ which, rounded to the lowest whole number, is 28.

10. A: An outlier is a data value that is either far above or far below the majority of values in a sample set. The mean is the average of all the values in the set. In a small sample set, a very high or very low number could drastically change the average (or mean) of the data points. Outliers will have no more of an effect on the median (the middle value when arranged from lowest to highest) than any other value above or below the median. If the same outlier does not repeat, outliers will have no effect on the mode (value that repeats most often).

11. C: The scenario involves data consisting of two variables: month and stock value. Box plots display data consisting of values for one variable. Therefore, a box plot is not an appropriate choice. Both line plots and circle graphs are used to display frequencies within categorical data. Neither can be used for the given scenario. Line graphs display two numerical variables on a coordinate grid and show trends among the variables, so this is the correct choice.

12. D: The probability of picking the winner of the race is $\frac{1}{4}$, or $\left(\frac{\text{number of favorable outcomes}}{\text{number of total outcomes}}\right)$. Assuming the winner was picked on the first selection, three horses remain from which to choose the runner-up (these are dependent events). Therefore, the probability of picking the runner-up is $\frac{1}{3}$. To determine the probability that multiple events all happen, multiply the probabilities of the events:

$$\frac{1}{4} \times \frac{1}{3} = \frac{1}{12}$$

13. D: Three girls for every two boys can be expressed as a ratio: $3:2$. This can be visualized as splitting the school into 5 groups: 3 girl groups and 2 boy groups. The number of students that are in each group can be found by dividing the total number of students by 5:

$$\frac{650 \text{ students}}{5 \text{ groups}} = \frac{130 \text{ students}}{\text{group}}$$

To find the total number of girls, multiply the number of students per group (130) by the number of girl groups in the school (3). This equals 390, Choice D.

14. C: If the average of all six numbers is 6, that means:

$$\frac{a+b+c+d+e+x}{6} = 6$$

The sum of the first five numbers is 25, so this equation can be simplified to $\frac{25+x}{6} = 6$. Multiplying both sides by 6 gives $25 + x = 36$, and x, or the sixth number, is found to equal 11.

Answer Explanations #1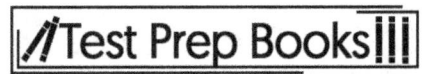

Mathematical Processes and Perspectives

1. A: A counterexample disproves a statement, and inductive reasoning does not prove something with full certainty. Deductive reasoning is the only way listed to prove something is true.

2. C: Since $a = b$ and $b = c$, through deductive reasoning, a has to be equal to c. No other case is possible.

3. C: A counterexample is a specific example that shows the statement is not true. $4 \times 6 = 24$ is an example of a product of two even numbers that is in an even number.

4. D: Students are using specific examples to make a conclusion. However, no proving method is employed, so they are neither trying to disprove the formula or prove it with a formal deductive reasoning method. They are using inductive reasoning.

5. A: A trapezoid is a quadrilateral with only one set (a pair) of parallel sides, but it does not have two sets of parallel sides, which it would have to contain to be a parallelogram. Therefore, a trapezoid is a counterexample that shows why the statement is not true. It disproves the statement.

6. B: Mathematical models involve representing real-world situations with derived equations. The process involves assumptions and simplifications, so the results are approximate and estimations. They are neither wrong nor exact.

7. C: Within calculus, a definite integral can be calculated using both the fundamental theorem of calculus and Riemann sums. However, a geometric formula can also be used. The integral is equal to the area under the line $y = x$ from $x = 0$ to $x = 2$, which is a triangle. The formula $A = \frac{1}{2}bh$ can be used to calculate the area, as this is the formula to calculate the area of a triangle. Poisson's ratio has to do with strains on stress concentrations.

8. C: Because the two amounts add up to 40, each amount can be found by subtracting the other from 40. If the larger amount is m, the smaller amount is $40 - m$.

9. B: The growth rate, r, is included in the formula $P = P_0 e^{rt}$, where P_0 is the initial population. Therefore, the growth rate is 0.02, which is the same as 2%.

10. D: This problem involves a combination of using inductive reasoning and counterexamples. The only case where this equation is true is when $a = b = 0$. Any other values for a and b are counterexamples.

Mathematical Learning, Instruction and Assessment

1. B: Choice B is correct because measuring the length of a tree's shadow is a real-life example that can help students better visualize the Law of Sines. The other choices all give students practice problems but do not involve relating the problems to a real-life scenario, which is the best way these students learn. Choice A gives students a practice problem with a triangle that does not relate to real life. Choice C also gives students a practice problem with a triangle that does not relate to real life. Choice D gives students a number of practice problems but does not specify what is included within these problems.

2. D: Choice D is correct because many of the students misunderstood this concept, and therefore it is best to clarify with them generally and in a way that allows them to receive the information again in

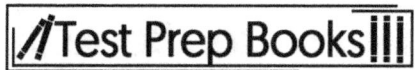

Answer Explanations #1

their preferred learning method. Choice *A* is incorrect because many of the students made this error; going through individually and finding out why they misunderstand it is not the most efficient way to approach this scenario. Choice *B* is incorrect because it involves instructing students in only one way, which may not help some students who prefer a different learning method. Choice *C* is incorrect because students may also not understand their mistake by simply getting a note about it.

3. C: Choice *C* is correct because it takes the same problem but makes it move toward the abstract—they are using similar concepts and applying them to a hypothetical room that will have different qualities than a classroom. Choice *A* is incorrect because students are performing the same task, which is not moving their understanding toward the abstract. Choice *B* is incorrect because it is moving the students too far toward the abstract and not allowing for a middle step that moves them from concrete to abstract. Choice *D* is incorrect because it is not related to the problem they completed in class and is also too abstract without any connection to the original concrete problem.

4. B: Choice *B* is correct because it asks students to complete a problem that is relevant in terms of its content and also structured in a way that is similar to how they were instructed. The other choices have content that is related to algebraic reasoning but are not entirely appropriate for the intended assessment. Choice *A* is incorrect because students were not instructed regarding modeling various attributes, which makes this choice inappropriate for the intended assessment. Choice *C* is incorrect because asking students to find quotients of polynomial functions is also not wholly relevant to the content the instructor would like to assess students on. Choice *D* is incorrect because linear equations and matrices are not the relevant content either.

5. A: Choice *A* is correct because the answer was given in degrees rather than radians. Choice *B* is incorrect because the answer wasn't given in radians. Choice *C* is incorrect because the answer was correct in degrees but not in radians. Choice *D* is incorrect because there is a given choice that is correct.

6. D: Choice *D* is correct because asking students to work together is a form of collaborative instruction. Choice *A* is incorrect because an example of direct instruction is a lecture, which is not what students are being given in the scenario. Choice *B* is incorrect because inquiry-guided instruction involves using questions to guide a lesson. Choice *C* is incorrect because students are working in a collaborative way, not independently.

7. C: Choice *C* is correct because sampling techniques would not be included within a unit about inference but rather about process sampling and is therefore the least appropriate of all the choices to include on an exam about inference. Choices *A*, *B*, and *D* could all be included in a lesson on statistical inference.

8. A: Choice *A* is correct because in the task given, students are creating links in their knowledge, which will strengthen their mathematical understanding. Choice *B* is incorrect because it does not measure how students learn but what connections they've made in the process of learning and what they understand. Choice *C* is incorrect because behaviorism would involve students receiving some type of positive reinforcement in each correct connection they make. Choice *D* is incorrect because although students are working on something, it is not a hands-on task because they are not creating a physical activity as it relates to the topic.

9. C: Choice *C* is correct because having students create the unit circle on their own best suits this class's preferred learning method and can then be used as a visual reference throughout various lessons, and they will be led through the lesson aurally. Choice *A* is incorrect because it doesn't suit the general

Answer Explanations #1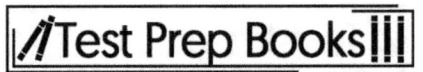

preferred learning style of this class or allow for as thorough of a visual reference for future lessons. Choice *B* is incorrect because it only provides a visual idea of the unit circle and doesn't let students to work hands-on or have a future reference. Choice *D* is incorrect because one of the options does suit the class and the goal the teacher has.

10. A: Choice *A* is correct because the product of powers states that when two exponentials that have the same base are multiplied, the exponents are added together, not multiplied (which is what this student did). Choice *B* is incorrect because the exponentials are being multiplied, not divided, so this property is not relevant. Choice *C* is incorrect because the power of a product involves simplification rather than the multiplication of two exponentials. Choice *D* is incorrect because an exponent is not being raised to another exponent, so this property is also not relevant.

Practice Test #2

Number Concepts

1. Four people split a bill. The first person pays for $\frac{1}{5}$, the second person pays for $\frac{1}{4}$, and the third person pays for $\frac{1}{3}$. What fraction of the bill does the fourth person pay?
    a. $\frac{13}{60}$
    b. $\frac{47}{60}$
    c. $\frac{1}{4}$
    d. $\frac{4}{15}$

2. Simplify $(1.2 \times 10^{12} \div 3.0 \times 10^{8)}$ and write the result in scientific notation.
    a. 0.4×10^4
    b. 4.0×10^4
    c. 4.0×10^3
    d. 3.6×10^{20}

3. A closet is filled with red, blue, and green shirts. If $\frac{1}{3}$ of the shirts are green and $\frac{2}{5}$ are red, what fraction of the shirts are blue?
    a. $\frac{4}{15}$
    b. $\frac{1}{5}$
    c. $\frac{7}{15}$
    d. $\frac{1}{2}$
    e. $\frac{1}{3}$

4. In an office, there are 50 workers. A total of 60% of the workers are women. 50% of the women (and none of the other workers) are wearing skirts. How many workers are wearing skirts?
    a. 12
    b. 15
    c. 16
    d. 20
    e. 21

5. Which of the following is NOT a way to write 40 percent of N?
   a. $(0.4)N$
   b. $\frac{2}{5}N$
   c. $40N$
   d. $\frac{4N}{10}$
   e. $\frac{8N}{20}$

6. Apples cost $2 each, while oranges cost $3 each. Maria purchased 10 fruits in total and spent $22. How many apples did she buy?
   a. 5
   b. 6
   c. 7
   d. 4
   e. 8

7. What would the equation be for the following problem?

   3 times the sum of a number and 7 is greater than or equal to 32
   a. $3(7n) > 32$
   b. $3 \times n + 7 \geq 32$
   c. $3n + 21 > 32$
   d. $3(n + 7) \geq 32$
   e. $3 \times x + 7 \geq 32$

8. A factor of 36 is defined as:
   a. A whole number that can be divided by 36 and have no remainder
   b. A number that can be added to 36 with no remainder
   c. A prime number that is multiplied times 36
   d. A whole number that 36 can be divided by and have no remainder
   e. A number that 36 can be multiplied by and have no remainder

9. If Sarah reads at an average rate of 21 pages in four nights, how long will it take her to read 140 pages?
   a. 6 nights
   b. 26 nights
   c. 8 nights
   d. 27 nights

10. You measure the width of your door to be 36 inches. The true width of the door is 35.75 inches. What is the relative error in your measurement?
    a. 0.7%
    b. 0.007%
    c. 0.99%
    d. 0.1%

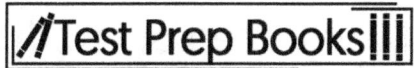

11. Chris walks $\frac{4}{7}$ of a mile to school and Tina walks $\frac{5}{9}$ of a mile. Which student covers more distance on the walk to school?

    a. Chris, because $\frac{4}{7} > \frac{5}{9}$

    b. Chris, because $\frac{4}{7} < \frac{5}{9}$

    c. Tina, because $\frac{5}{9} > \frac{4}{7}$

    d. Tina, because $\frac{5}{9} < \frac{4}{7}$

12. Find the magnitude of the complex number $8 - 10i$.
    a. 4
    b. $2\sqrt{41}$
    c. $\sqrt{41}$
    d. $\sqrt{18}$

13. How many ways can you arrange 4 letters from the word WONDER?
    a. 120
    b. 720
    c. 360
    d. 60

14. Find the product of these two complex numbers: $(3 - 8i)(5 + 10i)$.
    a. $95 - 10i$
    b. $-95 - 10i$
    c. $15 - 90i$
    d. $15 - 40i$

Patterns and Algebra

1. On Monday, Robert mopped the floor in 4 hours. On Tuesday, he did it in 3 hours. If on Monday, his average rate of mopping was p sq. ft. per hour, what was his average rate on Tuesday?

    a. $\frac{4}{3}p$ sq. ft. per hour

    b. $\frac{3}{4}p$ sq. ft. per hour

    c. $\frac{5}{4}p$ sq. ft. per hour

    d. $p + 1$ sq. ft. per hour

2. Solve for x, if $x^2 - 2x - 8 = 0$.
    a. $2 \pm \frac{\sqrt{30}}{2}$
    b. $2 \pm 4\sqrt{2}$
    c. 1 ± 3
    d. $4 \pm \sqrt{2}$

Practice Test #2

3. Which of the following is a factor of both $x^2 + 4x + 4$ and $x^2 - x - 6$?
   a. $x - 3$
   b. $x + 2$
   c. $x - 2$
   d. $x + 3$

4. A line goes through the point $(-4, 0)$ and the point $(0, 2)$. What is the slope of the line?
   a. 2
   b. 4
   c. $\frac{3}{2}$
   d. $\frac{1}{2}$

5. If $4x - 3 = 5$, what is the value of x?
   a. 1
   b. 2
   c. 3
   d. 4

6. For which of the following are $x = 4$ and $x = -4$ solutions?
   a. $x^2 + 16 = 0$
   b. $x^2 + 4x - 4 = 0$
   c. $x^2 - 2x - 2 = 0$
   d. $x^2 - 16 = 0$

7. Which of the following inequalities is equivalent to $3 - \frac{1}{2}x \geq 2$?
   a. $x \geq 2$
   b. $x \leq 2$
   c. $x \geq 1$
   d. $x \leq 1$

8. 7. If $f(x) = 4x + 2$, and $f^{-1}(x)$ is the inverse function for f, then what is $f^{-1}(6)$?
   a. 0
   b. $\frac{1}{2}$
   c. 1
   d. $\frac{3}{2}$

9. What is the slope of this line?

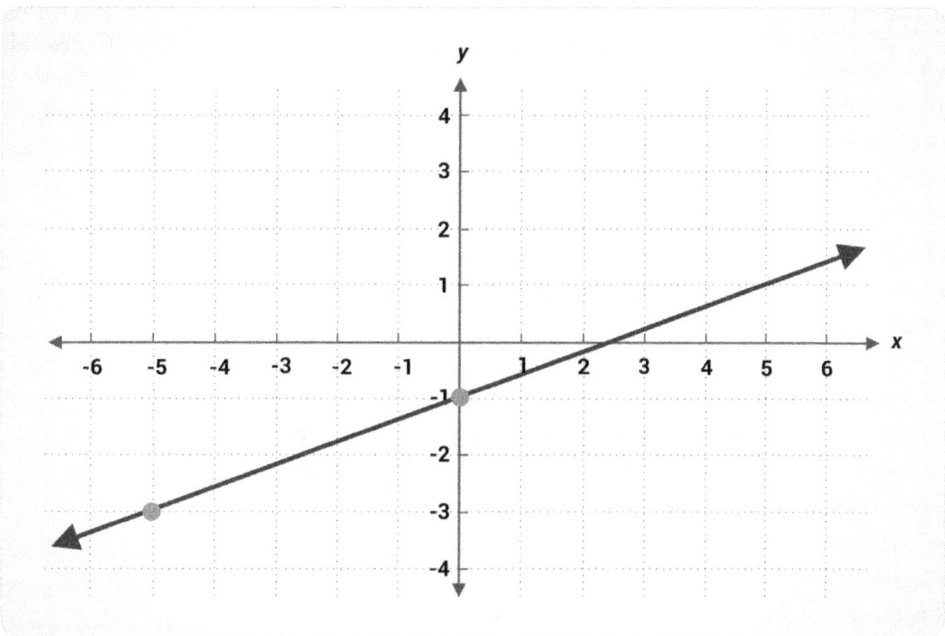

a. 2
b. $\frac{5}{2}$
c. $\frac{1}{2}$
d. $\frac{2}{5}$

10. There are $4x + 1$ treats in each party favor bag. If a total of $60x + 15$ treats are distributed, how many bags are given out?

a. 15
b. 16
c. 20
d. 22
e. 24

11. What is the next number in the following series: $1, 3, 6, 10, 15, 21, \ldots$?

a. 26
b. 27
c. 28
d. 29
e. 30

12. The Cross family is planning a trip to Florida. They will be taking two cars for the trip. One car gets 18 miles to the gallon of gas. The other car gets 25 miles to the gallon. If the total trip to Florida is 450 miles, and the cost of gas is $2.49/gallon, how much will the gas cost for both cars to complete the trip?
    a. $43.00
    b. $44.82
    c. $107.07
    d. $32.33
    e. $62.50

13. If Amanda can eat two times as many mini cupcakes as Marty, what would the missing values be for the following input-output table?

Input (number of cupcakes eaten by Marty)	Output (number of cupcakes eaten by Amanda)
1	2
3	
5	10
7	
9	18

  a. 6, 10
  b. 3, 11
  c. 6, 14
  d. 4, 12
  e. 1.5, 3.5

14. The graph shows the position of a car over a 10-second time interval. Which of the following is the correct interpretation of the graph for the interval 1 to 3 seconds?

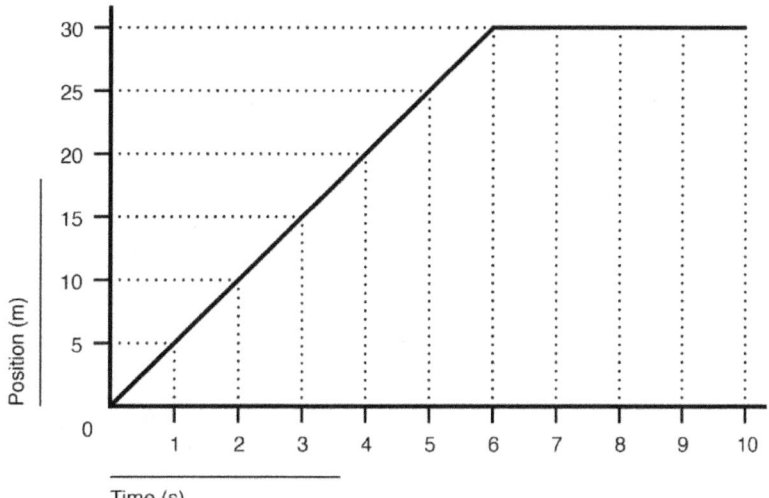

   a. The car remains in the same position.
   b. The car is traveling at a speed of 5 m/s.
   c. The car is traveling up a hill.
   d. The car is traveling at 5 mph.

15. $(2x - 4y)^2 =$
   a. $4x^2 - 16xy + 16y^2$
   b. $4x^2 - 8xy + 16y^2$
   c. $4x^2 - 16xy - 16y^2$
   d. $2x^2 - 8xy + 8y^2$

16. If $\sqrt{1 + x} = 4$, what is x?
   a. 10
   b. 15
   c. 20
   d. 25

17. The height, in feet, of a baseball falling t seconds after it has reached its peak after being hit by a bat can be found by $-16t^2 + 170$. What is the baseball's altitude 1.5 seconds after it has reached its peak?
   a. 134 ft
   b. 154 ft
   c. 206 ft
   d. 184 ft

Practice Test #2

18. Solve the following radical equation: $\sqrt{16-x} - x = 4$.
    a. {0}
    b. {4}
    c. {0, -9}
    d. ∅

19. $2x(3x+1) - 5(3x+1) =$
    a. $10x(3x+1)$
    b. $10x^2(3x+1)$
    c. $(2x-5)(3x+1)$
    d. $(2x+1)(3x-5)$

20. If $x > 3$, then $\frac{x^2-6x+9}{x^2-x-6} =$
    a. $\frac{x+2}{x-3}$
    b. $\frac{x-2}{x-3}$
    c. $\frac{x-3}{x+3}$
    d. $\frac{x-3}{x+2}$

21. If x is not zero, then $\frac{3}{x} + \frac{5u}{2x} - \frac{u}{4} =$
    a. $\frac{12+10u-ux}{4x}$
    b. $\frac{3+5u-ux}{x}$
    c. $\frac{12x+10u+ux}{4x}$
    d. $\frac{12+10u-u}{4x}$

22. What is the simplified form of the expression $tan\theta \, cos\theta$?
    a. $sin\theta$
    b. 1
    c. $csc\theta$
    d. $\frac{1}{sec\theta}$

23. If $-3(x+4) \geq x+8$, what is the value of x?
    a. $x = 4$
    b. $x \geq 2$
    c. $x \geq -5$
    d. $x \leq -5$

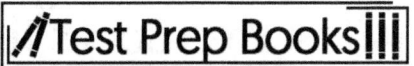

Practice Test #2

24. If $a \neq b$, solve for x if $\frac{1}{x} + \frac{2}{a} = \frac{2}{b}$
   a. $\frac{a-b}{ab}$
   b. $\frac{ab}{2(a-b)}$
   c. $\frac{2(a-b)}{ab}$
   d. $\frac{a-b}{2ab}$

25. Find $\frac{d}{dx} 2x^3$.
   a. $8x^2$
   b. $5x$
   c. $6x^2$
   d. $\frac{x^4}{2}$

26. Which of the following would be the result of a horizontal shift 7 units to the left of the function $f(x) = x^3 - x + 3$?
   a. $x^3 - x + 10$
   b. $x^3 - x - 4$
   c. $x^3 - 21x^2 + 146x - 333$
   d. $x^3 + 21x^2 + 146x + 339$

27. Find the equation for a line running through the point $(-4, 6)$ and parallel to the line $4x + y = 10$.
   a. $y = -4x - 10$
   b. $y = 4x + 10$
   c. $y = \frac{1}{4}x - 2$
   d. $y = -4x + 6$

28. What are the zeros of the function $f(x) = 2x^2 + 5x - 1$?
   a. $\frac{1}{2}$ and -1
   b. $\frac{5 \pm \sqrt{33}}{4}$
   c. $\frac{-5 \pm \sqrt{33}}{4}$
   d. $-\frac{1}{5}$ and 1

29. Solve the following logarithmic equation: $\log_7(4x + 1) = 3$.
   a. 171
   b. $\frac{171}{2}$
   c. 12
   d. $\frac{9}{4}$

30. What is the domain of the function $g(x) = \sqrt{x^2 + 5x + 25}$?
   a. $(-\infty, \infty)$
   b. $(5, \infty)$
   c. $[0, 8)$
   d. $(-\infty, 0) \cup (0, \infty)$

31. Over what interval is the function $f(x) = x^3 - 4x + 2$ concave down?
   a. $(2, \infty)$
   b. $(-\infty, \infty)$
   c. $(-\infty, 0)$
   d. $(0, \infty)$

32. If a $1,200 deposit is made into a bank account that pays 1.5% per year compounded annually, how long will it take the investment to reach $1,250? Round to the nearest hundredth of a year.
   a. 3.24 years
   b. 0.29 years
   c. 1.74 years
   d. 2.74 years

33. The following image shows a right triangle. Find the missing angle, rounding to the nearest tenth if applicable.

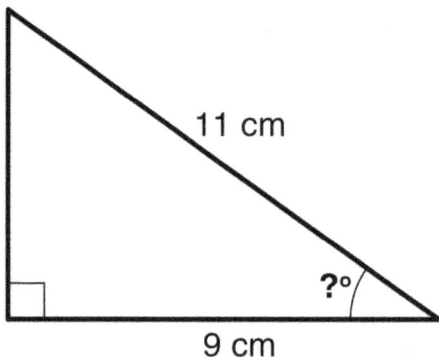

   a. 1°
   b. 35.1°
   c. 54.9°
   d. 39.3°

Geometry and Measurement

1. The square and circle have the same center. The circle has a radius of r. What is the area of the shaded region?

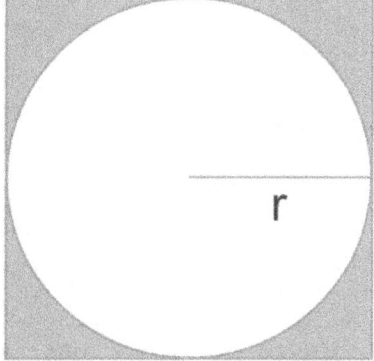

a. $r^2 - \pi r^2$
b. $4r^2 - 2\pi r$
c. $(4 - \pi)r^2$
d. $(\pi - 1)r^2$

2. An equilateral triangle has a perimeter of 18 feet. The sides of a square have the same length as the triangle's sides. What is the area of the square?
   a. 6 square feet
   b. 36 square feet
   c. 256 square feet
   d. 1,000 square feet

3. A rectangle has a length that is 5 feet longer than three times its width. If the perimeter is 90 feet, what is the length in feet?
   a. 10
   b. 20
   c. 25
   d. 35

Practice Test #2

4. What is the perimeter of the figure below? Note that the solid outer line is the perimeter.

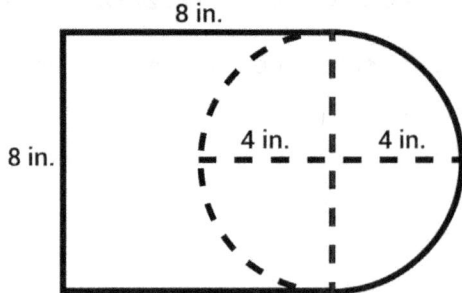

   a. 48.565 in
   b. 36.565 in
   c. 39.78 in
   d. 39.565 in

5. A right triangle has a hypotenuse of 10 inches, and one leg is 8 inches. How long is the other leg?
   a. 6 in
   b. 18 in
   c. 80 in
   d. 13 in

6. In the image below, what is demonstrated by the two triangles?

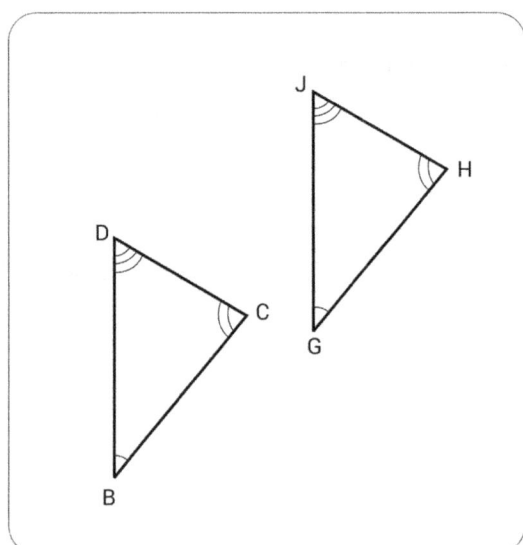

   a. According to Side-Side-Side, the triangles are congruent.
   b. According to Angle-Angle-Angle, the triangles are congruent.
   c. According to Angle-Side-Angle, the triangles are congruent.
   d. According to Side-Side-Angle, the triangles are congruent.
   e. There is not enough information to prove the two triangles are congruent.

7. In the figure below, what is the area of the shaded region?

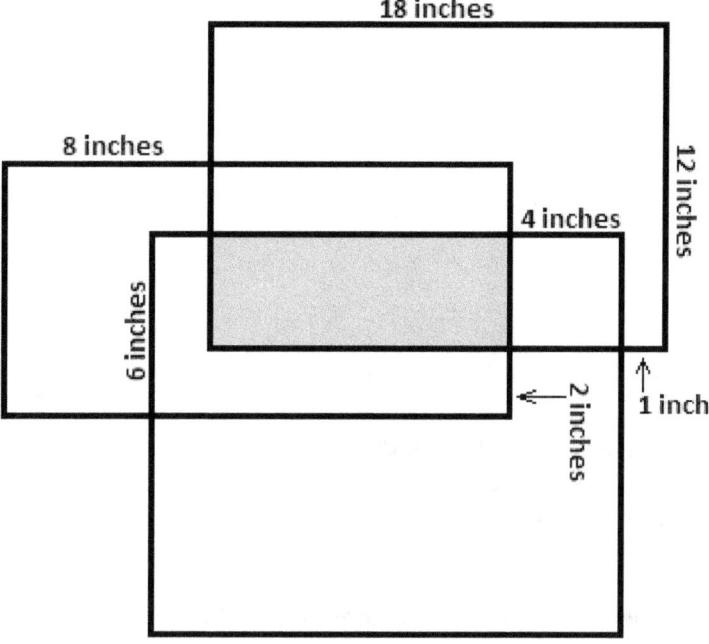

a. 48 sq. inches
b. 52 sq. inches
c. 44 sq. inches
d. 56 sq. inches
e. 50 sq. inches

8. A box with rectangular faces is 5 feet long, 6 feet wide, and 3 feet high. What is its volume?
a. 60 cubic feet
b. 75 cubic feet
c. 80 cubic feet
d. 14 cubic feet
e. 90 cubic feet

9. A truck is carrying three cylindrical barrels. Their bases have a diameter of 2 feet, and they have a height of 3 feet. What is the total volume of the three barrels in cubic feet?
a. 3π
b. 9π
c. 12π
d. 15π
e. 18π

Practice Test #2

10. If the sides of a cube are 5 centimeters long, what is its volume?
    a. $10\ cm^3$
    b. $15\ cm^3$
    c. $50\ cm^3$
    d. $125\ cm^3$

11. Which of the following statements is true about the two lines below?

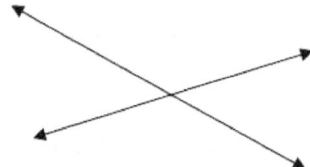

   a. The two lines are parallel but not perpendicular.
   b. The two lines are perpendicular but not parallel.
   c. The two lines are both parallel and perpendicular.
   d. The two lines are neither parallel nor perpendicular.

12. What is the area of a circle with a radius of 10 centimeters, in terms of π?
    a. $10\pi\ cm^2$
    b. $20\pi\ cm^2$
    c. $100\pi\ cm^2$
    d. $200\pi\ cm^2$

13. Find the volume of a cone with a height of 12 inches and a diameter of 10 inches. Use 3.14 for π.
    a. 314 cubic inches
    b. 942 cubic inches
    c. 62 cubic inches
    d. 100 cubic inches

14. A rectangular garden has a length of 14 feet and a width of 9 feet. Find the length of its diagonal, rounding to the nearest tenth of an inch.
    a. 10.7 inches
    b. 11 inches
    c. 16.6 inches
    d. 18.2 inches

15. What is the measure of a single interior angle of an octagon?
    a. 135°
    b. 105°
    c. 80°
    d. 90°

16. Find the distance between $(4, -1)$ and $(3, -3)$ on the coordinate plane. Round to the nearest hundredth if applicable.
   a. 5
   b. 2.23
   c. 3.23
   d. 1.64

17. Find the value of x in the following image. The two horizontal lines are parallel.

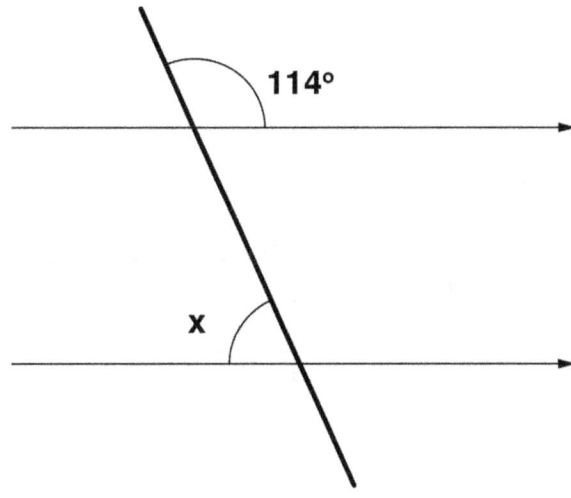

   a. 114°
   b. 66°
   c. 33°
   d. 24°

18. Find the area of the missing sector of the following circle. Round to the nearest tenth.

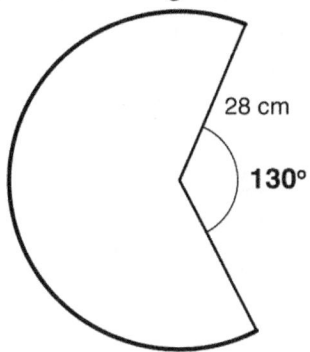

   a. 3,640 cm²
   b. 615.9 cm²
   c. 320,191.1 cm²
   d. 889.4 cm²

Practice Test #2

19. Which of the following represents the new coordinates of the ordered pair A if the triangle was reflected over the y-axis and then shifted down 3 units?

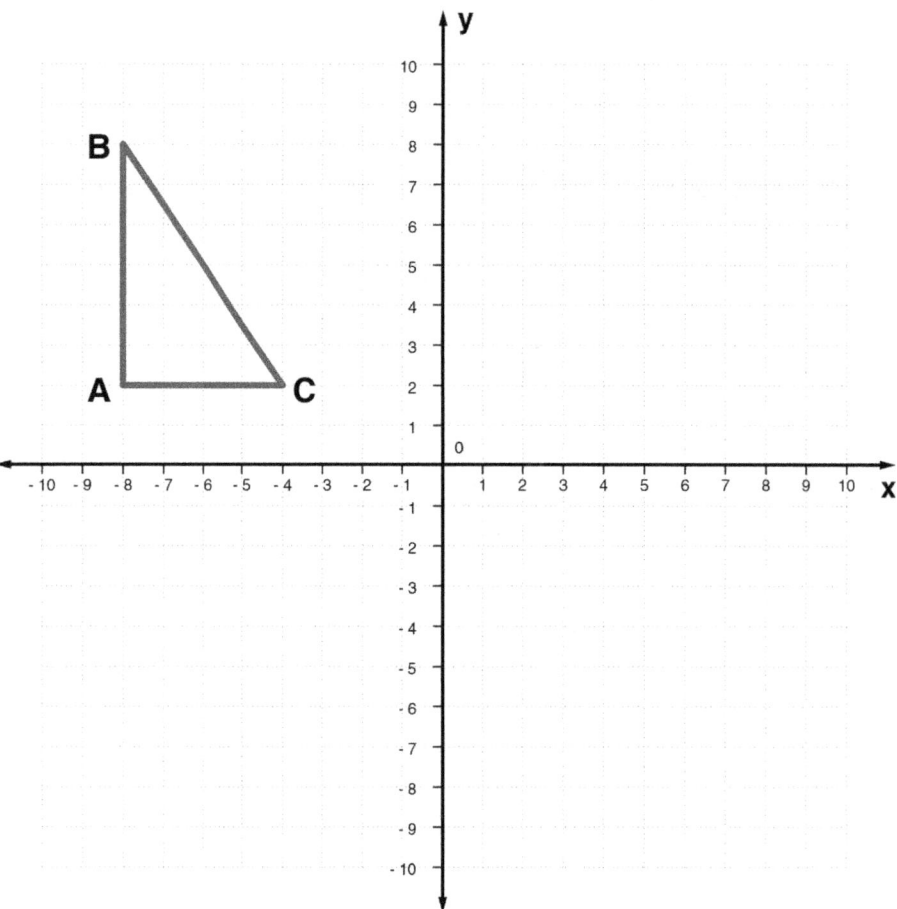

a. $(8, 5)$
b. $(-8, -5)$
c. $(8, 2)$
d. $(8, -1)$

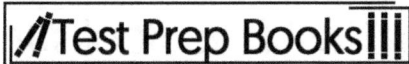

Practice Test #2

Probability and Statistics

1. Five students take a test. The scores of the first four students are 80, 85, 75, and 60. If the median score is 80, which of the following could NOT be the score of the fifth student?
    a. 60
    b. 80
    c. 85
    d. 100

2. Ten students take a test. Five students get a 50. Four students get a 70. If the average score is 55, what was the last student's score?
    a. 20
    b. 40
    c. 50
    d. 60

3. The chart below shows the average car sales for the months of July through December for two different car dealers. What is the average number of cars sold in the given time period for Dealer 1?

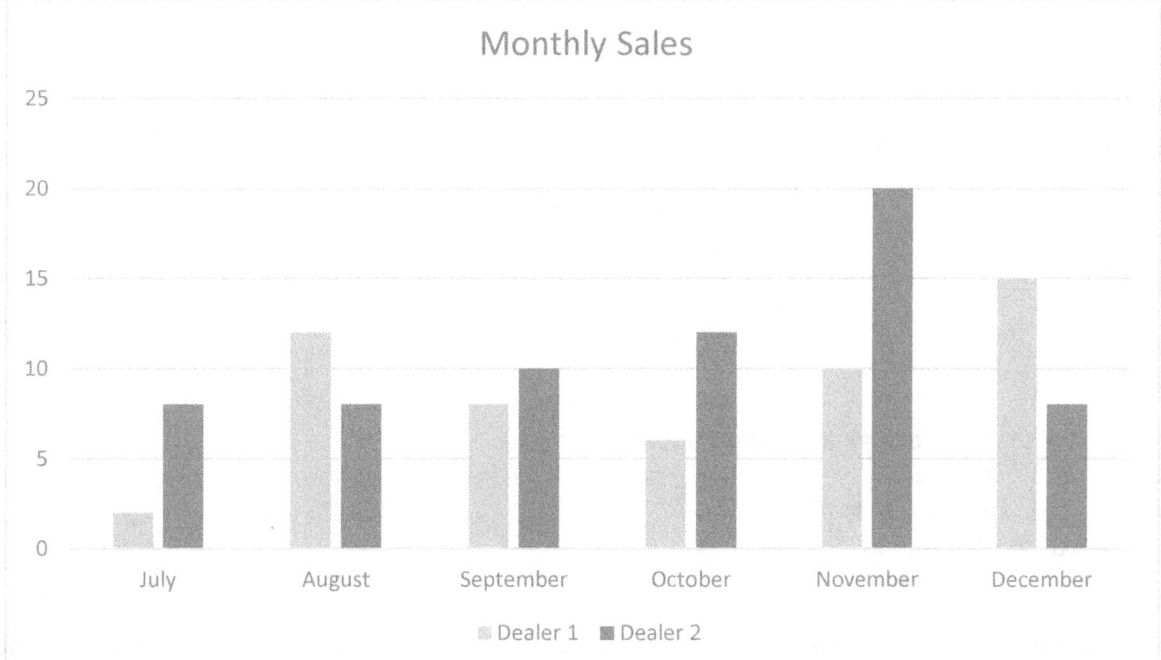

   a. 7
   b. 11
   c. 9
   d. 8
   e. 10

4. Six people apply to work for Janice's company, but she only needs four workers. How many different groups of four employees can Janice choose?
   a. 6
   b. 10
   c. 15
   d. 36

5. Which of the following statements is true about random sampling?
   a. There is a less than equal probability of all units being selected when utilizing random sampling methods.
   b. This method requires extensive information about the population being sampled.
   c. This method can be used when little information is provided about the population being sampled.
   d. None of the above

6. Consider a cashier that averages 50 customers per hour. What is the probability in which the arrival time between customers is less than 1 minute?
   a. 57%
   b. 53%
   c. 100%
   d. 50%

7. Calculate the median of the following data set:

   65, 45, 22, 56, 75, 21, 33, 40

   a. 43
   b. 42.5
   c. 40
   d. 45

8. Which data set has the largest standard deviation?
   a. 1, 4, 7, 6, 10, 13
   b. 100, 101, 102, 103, 104, 105
   c. 10,000, 10,000, 10,000, 10,000, 10,000
   d. 5, 18, 24, 44, 65, 78, 100

9. A bag contains eight blue marbles and four red marbles. Four marbles are chosen at random. What is the probability that three of them are blue? Round to the nearest tenth of a percent.
   a. 33.3%
   b. 11.3%
   c. 45.3%
   d. 65.1%

10. What type of correlation is shown in the following scatter plot?

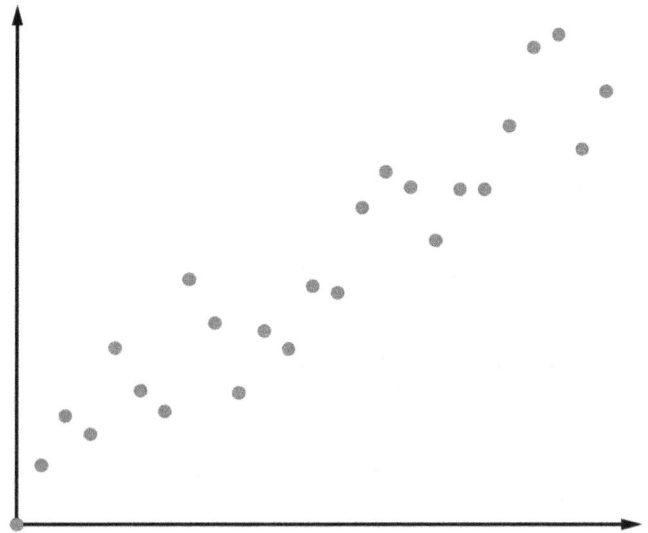

　　a. Strong positive correlation
　　b. Strong negative correlation
　　c. Moderate positive correlation
　　d. No correlation

11. Find the mean of the data set shown in the following stem and leaf plot. Round your answer to the nearest tenth.

Stem	Leaf
0	4
1	0, 7, 8
2	3, 3, 4, 7, 8
3	2, 2, 2, 3, 5, 7, 7
4	0, 0, 1, 1, 3
5	6, 7

　　a. 33.2
　　b. 31.7
　　c. 41.8
　　d. 35.4

12. A coin is tossed 8 times. What is the probability that it lands on tails at least once? Round your answer to the nearest thousandth if applicable.
　　a. 0.125
　　b. 0.003
　　c. 0.5
　　d. 0.996

Practice Test #2

13. Which of the following represents nominal data?
    a. Exam grades
    b. Hair color
    c. Age
    d. Temperature

14. The following data is used to build a least squares regression $y = a + bx$.

x	1	2	3	4	5
y	100	76	54	37	19

Which of the following values is closest to the actual value of b?
    a. -15
    b. 20
    c. -20
    d. -30

Mathematical Processes and Perspectives

1. Carey bought 184 pounds of fertilizer to use on her lawn. Each segment of her lawn required $11\frac{1}{2}$ pounds of fertilizer to do a sufficient job. If a student was asked to determine how many segments could be fertilized with the amount purchased, what operation would be necessary to solve this problem?
    a. Multiplication
    b. Division
    c. Addition
    d. Subtraction
    e. Exponents

2. Which of the following expressions best exemplifies the additive and subtractive identity?
    a. $5 + 2 - 0 = 5 + 2 + 0$
    b. $6 + x = 6 - 6$
    c. $9 - 9 = 0$
    d. $8 + 2 = 10$
    e. $7 + 8 = 15$

3. Write the expression for three times the sum of twice a number and one, minus 6.
    a. $2x + 1 - 6$
    b. $3x + 1 - 6$
    c. $3(x + 1) - 6$
    d. $3(2x + 1) - 6$
    e. $3 \times 2x + 1 - 6$

4. Which of the following equations best represents the problem below?

The width of a rectangle is 2 centimeters less than the length. If the perimeter of the rectangle is 44 centimeters, then what are the dimensions of the rectangle?

a. $2l + 2(l - 2) = 44$
b. $(l + 2) + (l + 2) + l = 48$
c. $l \times (l - 2) = 44$
d. $(l + 2) + (l + 2) + l = 44$
e. $2l + 2(l - 2) = 48$

5. How do you solve $V = lwh$ for h?
   a. $lwV = h$
   b. $h = \frac{V}{lw}$
   c. $h = \frac{Vl}{w}$
   d. $h = \frac{Vw}{l}$

6. What is the radius of the circle $(x - 3)^2 + (y - 2)^2 = 100$?
   a. 100
   b. 10
   c. 3
   d. 25

7. Which of the following represents the area under the curve $y = x^2$ from the values 1 to 2?
   a. $\int_0^1 x^2 dx$
   b. $\int_0^1 2x \, dx$
   c. $\int_1^2 \frac{1}{x^2} dx$
   d. $\int_1^2 x^2 dx$

8. Given the Cartesian coordinates $(1, 1)$, find the corresponding Polar coordinates.
   a. $(\sqrt{2}, \pi)$
   b. $(1, \frac{\pi}{4})$
   c. $(\sqrt{2}, \frac{\pi}{4})$
   d. $(1, \frac{\pi}{4})$

9. Which of the following models would be best suited to fit the following scatter plot?

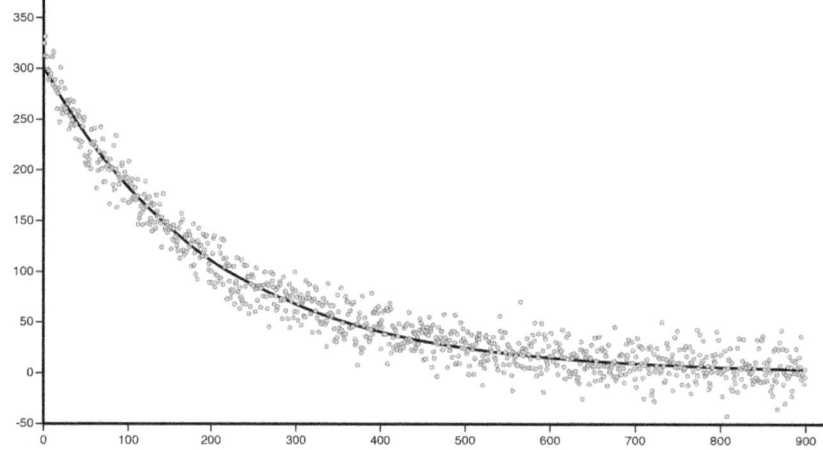

a. Linear
b. Exponential growth
c. Exponential decay
d. Quadratic

10. The exponential model $f(t) = 10.75 \times 1.04^{0.56t}$ represents the population of monkeys in thousands where $t = 1$ corresponds to the year 2001. Find the population in 2022. Round to the nearest whole number.

a. 17
b. 17,050
c. 174
d. 17,428

Mathematical Learning, Instruction, and Assessment

1. Which of the following is NOT true about manipulatives that are used in the mathematics classroom?
    a. They keep students engaged.
    b. They are used by students of all ages.
    c. They are reserved for students falling behind in class.
    d. They support the objectives of the lessons being taught.

2. Which of the following classroom scenarios describes an indirect method of teaching?
    a. Case study
    b. Demonstration
    c. Lecture
    d. Test

3. Which of the following is NOT an example of experiential learning?
    a. Role playing
    b. Storytelling
    c. Building a model
    d. Brainstorming

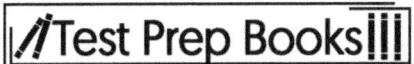

4. Which of the following would be the best type of lesson type on multiplication for a visual learner?
    a. Listening to a song about fractions
    b. Working with a partner
    c. Taking notes
    d. Using flashcards

5. All of the following are components of an inquiry-based learning project EXCEPT:
    a. Exploration
    b. Examination
    c. Conclusion
    d. Discussion

6. Which of the following represents a student who learns better through hands-on processes?
    a. Auditory leaner
    b. Visual leaner
    c. Tactile learner
    d. Verbal learner

7. Which of the following is NOT a formative assessment?
    a. Pop quiz
    b. Opinion poll
    c. Chapter test
    d. Brainstorming

8. Which of the following represents a situation that uses differentiated instruction?
    a. Have all students rotate between stations with various tasks.
    b. Assign both a final exam and a final research paper.
    c. Schedule a quiz for half of the class the day before the other half.
    d. Let some students take handwritten notes while others use computers.

9. Which of the following would be an example of guided math?
    a. Giving a lesson and stopping intermittently to ask questions
    b. Working with groups that have the same level of understanding regarding a math concept
    c. Building learning stations that all students rotate through
    d. Filling out a worksheet that walks students through the new lesson

10. Which of the following is an example of a performance assessment in a geometry classroom?
    a. Taking a chapter quiz over the Pythagorean Theorem
    b. Building a hypothetical garden using geometry calculations
    c. Working through a geometry proof with a classmate
    d. Taking a pop quiz on parallel line

Answer Explanations #2

Number Concepts

1. A: To find the fraction of the bill that the first three people pay, the fractions need to be added, which means finding the common denominator. The common denominator will be 60.

$$\frac{1}{5} + \frac{1}{4} + \frac{1}{3}$$

$$\frac{12}{60} + \frac{15}{60} + \frac{20}{60} = \frac{47}{60}$$

The remainder of the bill is:

$$1 - \frac{47}{60} = \frac{60}{60} - \frac{47}{60} = \frac{13}{60}$$

2. C: It may help to look at this problem as a fraction: $\frac{1.2 \times 10^{12}}{3.0 \times 10^8}$. We can calculate $\frac{1.2}{3} = 0.4$, and using the rules of exponents, we can see that $\frac{10^{12}}{10^8} = 10^{12-8} = 10^4$. This gives us an answer of 0.4×10^4, which is Choice A, but our answer is not yet in scientific notation because the first term, 0.4, is not between 1 and 10. We can rewrite 0.4×10^4, multiplying the first term by 10 and subtracting 1 from the exponent, which gives 4.0×10^3, Choice C.

3. A: The total fraction taken up by green and red shirts will be:

$$\frac{1}{3} + \frac{2}{5} = \frac{5}{15} + \frac{6}{15} = \frac{11}{15}$$

The remaining fraction is:

$$1 - \frac{11}{15} = \frac{15}{15} - \frac{11}{15} = \frac{4}{15}$$

4. B: If 60% of 50 workers are women, then there are 30 women working in the office. If half of them are wearing skirts, then that means 15 women wear skirts. Since nobody else wears skirts, this means there are 15 people wearing skirts.

5. C: $40N$ would be 4,000% of N. All of the other coefficients are equivalent to $\frac{40}{100}$ or 40%.

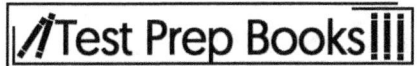

Answer Explanations #2

6. E: Let a be the number of apples, and let b represent the number of bananas. The total number of fruits is $a + b = 10$, and the total cost is $2a + 3b = 22$. To solve this pair of equations, we can multiply the first equation by –3:

$$-3(a+b) = -3(10)$$

$$-3a - 3b = -30$$

Now we can add this to the other equation, and the b terms cancel out:

$$(-3a - 3b = -30)$$

$$+(2a + 3b = 22)$$

$$= (-a = -8)$$

This simplifies to a=8.

7. D: 3 times the sum of a number and 7 is greater than or equal to 32 can be translated into equation form utilizing mathematical operators and numbers.

8. D: If 36 can be divided by a whole number and have no remainder, then that number is a factor of 36. In other words, a factor of 36 is a whole number that can be multiplied by another whole number to make 36. The number 36 equals $1 \times 36, 2 \times 18, 3 \times 12, 4 \times 9$, and 6×6, so it has nine unique factors: 1, 2, 3, 4, 6, 9, 12, 18, and 36.

9. D: This problem can be solved by setting up a proportion involving the given information and the unknown value. The proportion is:

$$\frac{21 \text{ pages}}{4 \text{ nights}} = \frac{140 \text{ pages}}{x \text{ nights}}$$

We can cross-multiply to get $21x = 4 \times 140$. Solving this, we find $x \approx 26.67$. Since this is not an integer, we round up to 27 nights. 26 nights would not give Sarah enough time.

10. A: The relative error can be found by finding the absolute error and making it a percent of the true value. The absolute error is $36 - 35.75 = 0.25$. This error is then divided by 35.75—the true value—to find 0.7%.

11. A: In order to compare the fractions $\frac{4}{7}$ and $\frac{5}{9}$, a common denominator must be used. The least common denominator is 63, which is found by multiplying the two denominators together (7×9). The conversions are as follows:

$$\frac{4}{7} \times \frac{9}{9} = \frac{36}{63}$$

$$\frac{5}{9} \times \frac{7}{7} = \frac{35}{63}$$

Answer Explanations #2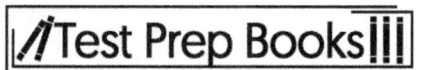

Although they walk nearly the same distance, $\frac{4}{7}$ is slightly more than $\frac{5}{9}$ because $\frac{36}{63} > \frac{35}{63}$. Remember, the sign > means "is greater than." Therefore, Chris walks further than Tina, and Choice A correctly shows this expression in mathematical terms.

12. B: The magnitude of the complex number $a + bi$ is $\sqrt{a^2 + b^2}$. Therefore, the magnitude of $8 - 10i$ is $\sqrt{8^2 + (-10)^2} = \sqrt{64 + 100} = \sqrt{164} = 2\sqrt{41}$.

13. C: There are 6 letters in the word WONDER, and there are no repeated letters. This question asks how many ways 4 letters can be arranged out of 6, which is the permutation $_6P_4$. The formula for a permutation $_nP_r$ is $\frac{n!}{(n-r)!}$. Therefore, the correct answer is $\frac{6!}{(6-4)!} = \frac{6!}{2!} = 360$.

14. A: First, FOIL the complex numbers as you would two binomials: $(3 - 8i)(5 + 10i) = 15 + 30i - 40i - 80i^2$. Collect like terms to obtain $15 - 10i - 80i^2$. Then, use the fact that $i^2 = -1$ to replace $-80i^2$ with 80. Therefore, the correct answer is $95 - 10i$.

Patterns and Algebra

1. A: If s is the size of the floor in square feet and r is the rate on Tuesday, then, based on the information given, $p = \frac{s}{4}$ and $r = \frac{s}{3}$. Solve the Monday rate for s, $s = 4p$, and then substitute that in the expression for Tuesday.

2. C: The quadratic formula can be used to solve this problem. Given the equation, use the values $a = 1$, $b = -2$, and $c = -8$.

$$x = \frac{-b \pm \sqrt{b^2 - 4ac}}{2a} = \frac{-(-2) \pm \sqrt{(-2)^2 - 4(1)(-8)}}{2(1)}$$

From here, simplify to solve for x.

$$x = \frac{2 \pm \sqrt{4 + 32}}{2} = \frac{2 \pm \sqrt{36}}{2} = \frac{2 \pm 6}{2} = 1 \pm 3$$

3. B: To factor $x^2 + 4x + 4$, the numbers needed are those that add to 4 and multiply to 4. Therefore, both numbers must be 2, and the expression factors to:

$$x^2 + 4x + 4 = (x + 2)^2$$

Similarly, in order for both to have $x + 2$ in common, the second expression

4. D: The slope is given by the change in y divided by the change in x. The change in y is $2 - 0 = 2$, and the change in x is:

$$0 - (-4) = 4$$

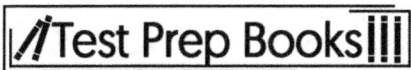

Answer Explanations #2

The slope is $\frac{2}{4} = \frac{1}{2}$.

5. B: Add 3 to both sides to get $4x = 8$. Then divide both sides by 4 to get $x = 2$

6. D: There are two ways to approach this problem. Each value can be substituted into each equation. A can be eliminated, since:
$$4^2 + 16 = 32$$
Choice B can be eliminated, since:
$$4^2 + 4 \times 4 - 4 = 28$$
C can be eliminated, since
$$4^2 - 2 \times 4 - 2 = 6$$
But, plugging in either value into $x^2 - 16$, which gives:
$$(\pm 4)^2 - 16 = 16 - 16 = 0$$

7. B: To simplify this inequality, subtract 3 from both sides to get:
$$-\frac{1}{2}x \geq -1$$
Then, multiply both sides by -2 (remembering that this flips the direction of the inequality) to get $x \leq 2$.

9. D: The slope is given by the change in y divided by the change in x. Specifically, it's:
$$\text{slope} = \frac{y_2 - y_1}{x_2 - x_1}$$
The first point is $(-5, -3)$, and the second point is $(0, -1)$. Work from left to right when identifying coordinates. Thus the point on the left is point 1 $(-5, -3)$ and the point on the right is point 2 $(0, -1)$.

Now we need to just plug those numbers into the equation:
$$slope = \frac{-1 - (-3)}{0 - (-5)}$$
It can be simplified to:
$$slope = \frac{-1 + 3}{0 + 5}$$
$$slope = \frac{2}{5}$$

10. A: The total number of treats distributed will be the number of treats per bag $(4x + 1)$ times the number of bags given out, which can be represented by the variable n. This expression is $n(4x + 1)$. Since this is the amount of treats distributed, set it equal to $60x + 15$. $n(4x + 1) = 60x + 15$. In order to figure out what n is, determine what number times 4 results in 60 ($4n = 60$) and what number times 1 results in 15 ($1n = 15$). In both cases, $n = 15$. Therefore, 15 bags are given out.

Answer Explanations #2

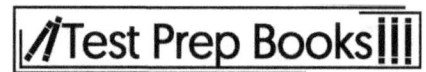

11. C: Each number in the sequence is adding one more than the difference between the previous two. For example, $10 - 6 = 4, 4 + 1 = 5$.

Therefore, the next number after 10 is $10 + 5 = 15$.

Going forward, $21 - 15 = 6, 6 + 1 = 7$. The next number is:

$$21 + 7 = 28$$

Therefore, the difference between numbers is the set of whole numbers starting at 2: 2, 3, 4, 5, 6, 7,...

12. C: For the first car, the trip will be 450 miles at 18 miles to the gallon. The total gallons needed for this car will be:

$$450 \div 18 = 25$$

For the second car, the trip will be 450 miles at 25 miles to the gallon, or $450 \div 25 = 18$, which will require 18 gallons of gas. Adding these two amounts of gas gives a total of 43 gallons of gas. If the gas costs $2.49 per gallon, the cost of the trip for both cars is:

$$43 \times \$2.49 = \$107.07$$

13. C: The situation can be described by the equation $? \times 2$. Filling in for the missing numbers would result in $3 \times 2 = 6$ and $7 \times 2 = 14$. Therefore, the missing numbers are 6 and 14. The other choices are miscalculations or misidentification of the pattern formed by the table.

14. B: The car is traveling at a speed of 5 meters per second. On the interval from 1 to 3 seconds, the position changes by 10 meters. This is 10 meters in 2 seconds, or 5 meters in each second.

15. A: To expand a squared binomial, it's necessary to use the First, Outer, Inner, Last (FOIL) method.

$$(2x - 4y)^2$$

$$(2x)(2x) + (2x)(-4y) + (-4y)(2x) + (-4y)(-4y)$$

$$4x^2 - 8xy - 8xy + 16y^2$$

$$4x^2 - 16xy + 16y^2$$

16. B: Start by squaring both sides to get $1 + x = 16$. Then subtract 1 from both sides to get $x = 15$.

17. A: This amount can be found by plugging $t = 1.5$ into the expression. Therefore, the baseball's altitude is equal to $-16(1.5^2) + 170 = -16(2.25) + 170 = -36 + 170 = 134$ ft.

18. A: First, isolate the radical by adding x to both sides to obtain $\sqrt{16 - x} = x + 4$. Then, square both sides to obtain $16 - x = x^2 + 8x + 16$. This is a quadratic equation, so put it in standard form by adding x to both sides and subtracting 16 off both sides. The result is the equation $x^2 + 9x = 0$. This can be solved by factoring and setting each factor equal to zero. Therefore, $x(x + 9) = 0$ results in the two potential solutions $x = 0$ and $x = -9$. Because the original equation has a radical, these solutions must be checked to see if they are not extraneous. Plugging $x = 0$ results in $\sqrt{16 - 0} - 0 = 4$, which is true. However, plugging $x = -9$ results in $\sqrt{16 + 9} + 9 = 4$, which is not true. The only solution is 0.

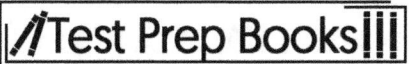

Answer Explanations #2

19. C: The $(3x + 1)$ can be factored to get $(2x − 5)(3x + 1)$.

20. D: Factor the numerator into $x^2 − 6x + 9 = (x − 3)^2$, since:

$$-3 - 3 = -6$$
$$(-3)(-3) = 9$$

Factor the denominator into $x^2 − x − 6 = (x − 3)(x + 2)$, since:

$$-3 + 2 = -1,$$
$$(-3)(2) = -6$$

This means the rational function can be rewritten as:

$$\frac{x^2 - 6x + 9}{x^2 - x - 6} = \frac{(x-3)^2}{(x-3)(x+2)}$$

Using the restriction of x > 3, do not worry about any of these terms being 0, and cancel an $x − 3$ from the numerator and the denominator, leaving $\frac{x-3}{x+2}$.

21. A: The common denominator here will be $4x$. Rewrite these fractions as:

$$\frac{3}{x} + \frac{5u}{2x} - \frac{u}{4}$$

$$\frac{12}{4x} + \frac{10u}{4x} - \frac{ux}{4x}$$

$$\frac{12x + 10u - ux}{4x}$$

22. A: Using the trigonometric identity $\tan(\theta) = \frac{\sin(\theta)}{\cos(\theta)}$, the expression becomes $\frac{\sin\theta}{\cos\theta}\cos\theta$. The factors that are the same on the top and bottom cancel out, leaving the simplified expression $\sin\theta$.

23. D: Solve a linear inequality in a similar way to solving a linear equation. First, start by distributing the −3 on the left side of the inequality.

$$-3x - 12 \geq x + 8$$

Then, add 12 to both sides.

$$-3x \geq x + 20$$

Next, subtract x from both sides.

$$-4x \geq 20$$

Finally, divide both sides of the inequality by −4. Don't forget to flip the inequality sign because you are dividing by a negative.

$$x \leq -5$$

Answer Explanations #2

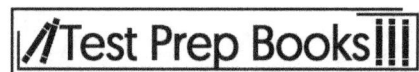

24. B: $\frac{2}{a}$ must be subtracted from both sides, with a result of:

$$\frac{1}{x} = \frac{2}{b} - \frac{2}{a}$$

The reciprocal of both sides needs to be taken, but the right-hand side needs to be written as a single fraction in order to do that. Since the two fractions on the right have denominators that are not equal, a common denominator of ab is needed. This leaves:

$$\frac{1}{x} = \frac{2a}{ab} - \frac{2b}{ab} = \frac{2(a-b)}{ab}$$

Taking the reciprocals, which can be done since $b - a$ is not zero, with a result of $x = \frac{ab}{2(a-b)}$.

25. C: Apply the power rule, to get $2 \times 3x^{3-1} = 6x^2$.

26. D: A horizontal shift of a general function $f(x)$ k units to the left is $f(x + k)$. Therefore, a horizonal shift 7 units to the left is $f(x + 7)$. In this example:

$$f(x + 7) = (x + 7)^3 - (x + 7) + 3$$

$$(x^2 + 14x + 49)(x + 7) - x - 4$$

$$x^3 + 21x^2 + 147x + 343 - x - 4$$

$$x^3 + 21x^2 + 146x + 339$$

27. A: First, rewrite the given line in slope-intercept form to find its slope. Subtracting $4x$ from both side results in $y = -4x + 10$, so its corresponding slope is -4. Plugging the slope and the given point into the point-slope formula gives $y - 6 = -4(x + 4)$, which simplifies into $y - 6 = -4x - 16$ or $y = -4x - 10$.

28. C: To find the zeros of a function, set the function equal to 0. $2x^2 + 5x - 1 = 0$ is a quadratic equation that can be solved using the quadratic formula. Therefore:

$$x = \frac{-5 \pm \sqrt{25 - 4(2)(-1)}}{2(2)} = \frac{-5 \pm \sqrt{33}}{4}$$

29. B: Rewriting this equation in its equivalent exponential form gives $7^3 = 4x + 1$. Therefore, $343 = 4x + 1$. Subtract 1 from both sides and divide by 4 to obtain the solution

$$x = \frac{342}{4} = \frac{171}{2}$$

30. A: A square root of a negative number cannot be computed. Therefore, the radicand must be greater than or equal to 0. In this case, $x^2 + 5x + 25$ is satisfied for any x value. Therefore, the correct domain is all real numbers, or $(-\infty, \infty)$.

31. C: The first derivative of the function is $f'(x) = 3x^2 - 4$, and the second derivative is $f''(x) = 6x$. Possible inflection points (the points in which a function changes concavity) are where $f''(x) = 0$. For this example, the only possible inflection point is $x = 0$. This point splits up the domain into two intervals: $(-\infty, 0)$ and $(0, \infty)$. A function is concave down on an interval when the second derivative is negative. $f''(x) = 6x$ is negative over $(-\infty, 0)$, so this is the interval over which the function is concave down.

32. D: The formula for compound interest is $A = P\left(1 + \frac{r}{n}\right)^{nt}$, where P is the principal, r is the interest rate as a decimal, n is the number of compounding periods per year, and t is the number of years. In this case, $P = 1200, n = 1, A = 1250$, and $r = 0.015$. Plug these into the formula to obtain $1250 = 1200(1 + 0.015)^t$. Divide both sides by 1200 to obtain $\frac{1250}{1200} = 1.015^t$. Taking the natural log of both sides results in:

$$\ln\left(\frac{1250}{1200}\right) = t \ln(1.015)$$

Divide both sides by $\ln(1.015)$ and enter everything into a calculator to find the solution of $t \approx 2.74$ years.

33. B: The sides that are given are 1) the side adjacent to the missing angle (9 cm) and 2) the hypotenuse (11 cm). The trigonometric ratio using cosine can be used to solve for the angle θ because $\cos\theta = \frac{adj}{hyp}$. Therefore, $\theta = \cos^{-1}\left(\frac{9}{11}\right) = 35.1°$ when rounded to the nearest tenth of a degree.

Geometry and Measurements

1. C: The area of the shaded region is the area of the square minus the area of the circle. The area of the circle is πr^2. The side of the square will be $2r$, so the area of the square will be $4r^2$. Therefore, the difference is:

$$4r^2 - \pi r^2 = (4 - \pi)r^2$$

2. B: An equilateral triangle has three sides of equal length, so if the total perimeter is 18 feet, each side must be 6 feet long. A square with sides of 6 feet will have an area of $6^2 = 36$ square feet.

3. D: Denote the width as w and the length as l. Then, $l = 3w + 5$. The perimeter is $2w + 2l = 90$. Substituting the first expression for l into the second equation yields:

$$2(3w + 5) + 2w = 90$$

$$6w + 10 + 2w = 90$$

$$8w = 80$$

$$w = 10$$

Putting this into the first equation, it yields:

$$l = 3(10) + 5 = 35$$

4. B: The figure is composed of three sides of a square and a semicircle. The sides of the square are simply added:

$$8 \text{ in} + 8 \text{ in} + 8 \text{ in} = 24 \text{ in}$$

Answer Explanations #2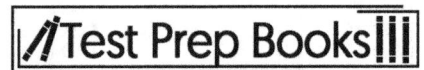

The circumference of a circle is found by the equation $C = 2\pi r$. The radius is 4 in, so the circumference of the circle is 25.13 in. Only half of the circle makes up the outer border of the figure (part of the perimeter) so half of 25.13 in is 12.565 in. Therefore, the total perimeter is:

$$24 \text{ in} + 12.565 \text{ in} = 36.565 \text{ in}$$

The other answer choices use the incorrect formula or fail to include all of the necessary sides.

5. A: The Pythagorean theorem tells us that $8^2 + x^2 = 10^2$, where x is the unknown side. This simplifies to $64 + x^2 = 100$, so $x^2 = 100 - 64 = 36$, and $x = \sqrt{36} = 6$ inches.

6. E: AAA does not prove congruence, only similarity. Choice A is not the correct answer because three congruent sides are not shown. Choice B is not the correct answer because AAA does not prove congruence, only similarity. Choice C is not the correct answer because Angle-Side-Angle is not shown. Choice D is not the correct answer because SSA does not prove congruence

7. B: This can be determined by finding the length and width of the shaded region. The length can be found using the length of the top rectangle, which is 18 inches, then subtracting the extra length of 4 inches and 1 inch. This means the length of the shaded region is 13 inches. Next, the width can be determined using the 6-inch measurement and subtracting the 2-inch measurement. This means that the width is 4 inches. Thus, the area is:

$$13 \times 4 = 52 \text{ sq. in.}$$

8. E: The formula for the volume of a box with rectangular faces is the length times the width times the height, so:

$$5 \times 6 \times 3 = 90 \text{ cubic feet}$$

9. B: The formula for the volume of a cylinder is $\pi r^2 h$, where r is the radius and h is the height. The diameter is twice the radius, so these barrels have a radius of 1 foot. That means each barrel has a volume of:

$$\pi \times 1^2 \times 3 = 3\pi \text{ ft}^3$$

Since there are three of them, the total is:

$$3 \times 3\pi = 9\pi \text{ ft}^3$$

10. D: The volume of a cube with sides of length s is $V = s^3$. Here, $s = 5$, so $V = 5^3 = 125$.

11. D: Parallel lines will never intersect. Therefore, the lines are not parallel. Perpendicular lines intersect to form a right angle (90°). Although the lines intersect, they do not form a right angle, which is usually indicated with a box at the intersection point. Therefore, the lines are not perpendicular.

12. C: The formula for the area of a circle is $A = \pi r^2$. Here, $r = 10$, so we calculate $A = \pi(10^2) = 100\pi$

13. A: The cone has a diameter of 10 inches, so it has a radius of 5 inches (because diameter is double the radius). A cone has a volume of $\frac{1}{3}\pi r^2 h$, so this cone has a volume of:

$$\frac{1}{3}\pi(5^2)(12) = 314 \text{ cubic inches}$$

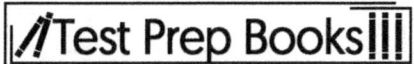

Answer Explanations #2

14. C: The diagonal forms two right triangles within the rectangle. The Pythagorean Theorem can be used to find the length of the diagonal. We have $14^2 + 9^2 = c^2$, where c is the length of the diagonal. Therefore, $277 = c^2$. Taking the square root and rounding to the nearest tenth results in the answer of 16.6 inches.

15. A: The sum of the interior angles of a polygon with n sides is $(n - 2) \times 180°$. An octagon has 8 sides, so the sum of the interior angles is $(8 - 2) \times 180° = 1080°$. An octagon also has 8 interior angles. Divide 1080 by 8 to obtain a single angle measure of 135°.

16. B: The distance between two points (x_1, y_1) and (x_2, y_2) is:

$$d = \sqrt{(x_2 - x_1)^2 + (y_2 - y_1)^2}$$

For the points $(4, -1)$ and $(3, -3)$, $d = \sqrt{(3 - 4)^2 + (-3 - (-1))^2} = \sqrt{(-1)^2 + (-2)^2} = \sqrt{1 + 4} = \sqrt{5} \approx 2.23$.

17. B: The two horizontal lines are parallel, and they are intersected by a transversal line, which creates corresponding angles. The 114° angle and angle y are corresponding angles, so the measure of angle y is 114°. Angles on a straight line add up to 180°. Therefore, the measure of angle x is $180° - 114° = 66°$.

18. D: If this were an entire circle, the area would be $\pi(28)^2 = 784\pi$ cm^2 since the radius is 28 cm. However, this is a segment of a circle. The angle of the sector is 130°, so a proportion can be used. The angle of sector A is found by the following:

$$\frac{130}{360} = \frac{A}{784\pi}$$

Cross-multiply and solve for A to obtain the correct answer of 889.4 cm^2.

19. D: The coordinates of A in the graph are $(-8, 2)$. First, the triangle is reflected over the y-axis, placing point A at $(8, 2)$. Then, shifting it down 3 units moves it to $(8, -1)$.

Probability and Statistics

1. A: Putting the scores in order from least to greatest, we have 60, 75, 80, and 85, as well as one unknown. The median is 80, so 80 must be the middle data point out of these five. Therefore, the unknown data point must be the fourth or fifth data point, meaning it must be greater than or equal to 80. The only answer that fails to meet this condition is 60.

2. A: Let the unknown score be x. The average will be:

$$\frac{5 \times 50 + 4 \times 70 + x}{10} = \frac{530 + x}{10} = 55$$

Multiply both sides by 10 to get $530 + x = 550$, or $x = 20$.

3. C: 9 Cars. The average is calculated by adding up each month's sales and dividing the sum by the total number of months in the time period. Dealer 1 sold 2 cars in July, 12 in August, 8 in September, 6 in October, 10 in November, and 15 in December. The sum of these sales is:

$$2 + 12 + 8 + 6 + 10 + 15 = 53 \text{ cars}$$

To find the average, this sum is divided by the total number of months, which is 6. When 53 is divided by 6, it yields 8.8333... Since cars are sold in whole numbers, the answer is rounded to 9 cars.

4. C: Janice will be choosing 4 employees out of a set of 6 applicants, so this will be given by the choice function. The following equation shows the choice function worked out:

$$\binom{6}{4} = \frac{6!}{4!\,(6-4)!} = \frac{6!}{4!\,(2)!}$$

$$\frac{6 \cdot 5 \cdot 4 \cdot 3 \cdot 2 \cdot 1}{4 \cdot 3 \cdot 2 \cdot 1 \cdot 2 \cdot 1} = \frac{6 \cdot 5}{2} = 15$$

5. C: Random sampling entails randomly drawing an item so that every item drawn has an equal chance of being included in the sample. In other words, there is an equal probability with random sampling. Random sampling is a fairly simple and cost-effective method often used when little information can be obtained about the items in the population.

6. A: The cumulative exponential distribution with $\lambda = 50$ should be used. One minute represents 0.017 hour. Therefore, P(arrival time less than 1 minute) = $1 - e^{-(50)(0.017)} = 0.573 = 57.3\%$. The closest answer is 57%.

7. B: First, place the data values in ascending order: 21, 22, 33, 40, 45, 56, 65, 75. Because there is an even number of data values, the median is the mean of the two middle data values. The mean of 40 and 45 is $\frac{40+45}{2} = 42.5$.

8. D: The standard deviation of a data set measures how much the data varies. In other words, it measures how different the data values are from the mean of the data set. The data set that varies the most from its mean is 5, 18, 24, 44, 65, 78, 100. The other data sets have values that are close together, which means that their standard deviations are small.

9. C: This probability can be found by dividing the number of possible combinations in which three marbles are blue by the total number of combinations. If four marbles are selected and three are blue, that means one marble is red. The total number of combinations of three blue and one red is $_8C_3 \times _4C_1 = 56 \times 4 = 224$. There are 12 total marbles; if four are selected, then the total number of possible outcomes is $_{12}C_4 = 495$. Therefore, the correct probability is $\frac{224}{495} = 45.3\%$.

10. A: A positive correlation exists when the plot shows a linear trend with data that is increasing. The data points are in the shape of a straight line with a positive slope, so the data has a positive correlation. The correlation is strong because the data follows the line closely. A moderate positive correlation would indicate less of a linear shape.

11. B: The stem and leaf plot organizes the data so that the stem is the tens digit, and the leaf is the ones digit. For example, the stem 5 and the leaf 6 create 56. Therefore, the plot lists the following values: 4, 10, 17, 18, 23, 23, 24, 27, 28, 32, 32, 32, 33, 35, 37, 37, 40, 40, 41, 41, 43, 56, 57. Find the sum of the values and divide by the total number of values (23) to obtain the mean. The mean is $\frac{730}{23} \approx 31.7$ when rounded to the nearest tenth.

12. D: The probability of obtaining at least one tails is 1 − P (no tails). The probability of obtaining no tails on 8 tosses is $\left(\frac{1}{2}\right)^8$. Therefore, the probability of obtaining at least one tails is $1 - \left(\frac{1}{2}\right)^8 \approx 0.996$ rounded to the nearest thousandth.

13. B: Nominal data is data that cannot be ordered and has no quantity assigned to it. The only data given that has these characteristics is hair color.

14. C: The values of y are decreasing, so the value of b (the slope of the line) must be negative. Select two values over one increment of x and calculate the average between those values. They all differ by an average of about 20. Therefore, -20 is the correct value. The actual value is about -20.25.

Mathematical Processes and Perspectives

1. B: This is a division problem because the original amount needs to be split up into equal amounts. Although it's not required to answer the test question, we could solve Carey's problem as follows. The mixed number $11\frac{1}{2}$ should be converted to an improper fraction first:

$$11\frac{1}{2} = \frac{(11 \times 2) + 1}{2} = \frac{23}{2}$$

Carey needs to determine how many times $\frac{23}{2}$ goes into 184. This is a division problem:

$$184 \div \frac{23}{2} = ?$$

The fraction can be flipped, and the problem turns into multiplication:

$$184 \times \frac{2}{23} = \frac{368}{23}$$

This improper fraction can be simplified into 16 because $368 \div 23 = 16$. The answer is 16 lawn segments.

2. A: The additive and subtractive identity is 0. When added to or subtracted from any number, 0 does not change the original number.

3. D: The expression is three times the sum of twice a number and 1, which is $3(2x + 1)$. Then, 6 is subtracted from this expression.

4. A: The first step is to determine the unknown, which is in terms of the length, l.

5. B: The formula can be manipulated by dividing both the length, l, and the width, w, on both sides. The length and width will cancel on the right, leaving height, h, by itself.

6. B: The radius of a circle in the form $(x − h)^2 + (y − k)^2 = r^2$ is r. In this example $r^2 = 100$, so the radius $r = 10$.

7. D: The area under a curve $f(x)$ over two points a and b on the x-axis is $\int_a^b f(x)dx$. In this case, $a = 1, b = 2$, and $f(x) = x^2$. The correct answer is $\int_1^2 x^2 dx$.

Answer Explanations #2

8. C: Given Cartesian coordinates (x, y), its corresponding Polar coordinates are (r, θ) where $r = \sqrt{x^2 + y^2}$ and $\theta = \tan^{-1}\left(\frac{y}{x}\right)$. In this case, where $r = \sqrt{1^2 + 1^2} = \sqrt{2}$ and $\theta = \tan^{-1}\left(\frac{1}{1}\right) = \frac{\pi}{4}$.

9. C: The points in the scatter plot decrease quickly initially and then taper off, creating almost a horizontal asymptote at the x-axis. These trends follow the shape of an exponential decay curve. Therefore, the correct option is Choice C.

10. D: When $t = 22$, it corresponds to the year 2022. Therefore, substitute 22 into the function to obtain $f(22) = 10.75 \times 1.04^{0.56*22} = 17.428$, rounded to three decimal places. The output of the function is in thousands, so the answer is 17,428 monkeys.

Mathematical Learning, Instruction, and Assessment

1. C: Manipulatives can be applied to many lessons in math, and they keep the students engaged by providing another way to look at things. They can be applied to lessons ranging from preschool to college, but they are not just for students falling behind in the class.

2. A: An indirect method of teaching is a student-centered way of learning rather than a teacher-led way. Demonstrations and lectures are both teacher-led. Tests are assessments. Since case studies allow students to problem solve on their own, they represent an indirect method.

3. D: Experiential learning occurs when students participate in some kind of student-centered activity. They experience an actual situation in which they use the skills they are learning. Brainstorming is not experiential learning. However, it might occur before one of the other listed learning experiences.

4. D: A visual learner learns best while using visual aids such as charts and images. They prefer items such as flashcards to make sense of the material being taught.

5. B: Inquiry-based learning occurs when students form a question themselves, investigate the answer, and make their own conclusions based on their own exploration. They then discuss their conclusion with their teacher and peers. Examination is not part of this process.

6. C: A tactile learner learns best by using their hands and by physical touch. An auditory learner learns best through sound, a visual learner learns best through sight, and a verbal learner learns best by hearing words or sounds.

7. C: A formative assessment occurs throughout the learning process, not at the end of the learning process. A chapter test would occur at the end of a unit, but the rest of the options would occur throughout the unit.

8. D: Differentiated instruction occurs when a teacher uses various types of instruction to account for the needs and strengths of all students in a classroom. Letting some students take handwritten notes while others use a computer allows students to take notes in the way that is most effective for them.

9. B: Guided math involves instructing small groups based on their needs. Students can be split into these groups based on their understanding levels. Some students need extra help, while others do not. Guided math does not occur when the entire classroom completes the same task.

10. B: A performance assessment involves students completing a task instead of taking a test. A typical performance assessment involves the application of the material learned in lectures to real-world scenarios. Building a garden using geometrical calculations such as area and perimeter is an example of a performance assessment.

Dear TExES Math 7-12 Test Taker,

Thank you again for purchasing this study guide for your TExES Math 7-12 exam. We hope that we exceeded your expectations.

Our goal in creating this study guide was to cover all of the topics that you will see on the test. We also strove to make our practice questions as similar as possible to what you will encounter on test day. With that being said, if you found something that you feel was not up to your standards, please send us an email and let us know.

We would also like to let you know about other books in our catalog that may interest you.

TExES ELAR 7 - 12

This can be found on Amazon: amazon.com/dp/1628459786

TExES Social Studies

This can be found on Amazon: amazon.com/dp/1628459395

We have study guides in a wide variety of fields. If the one you are looking for isn't listed above, then try searching for it on Amazon or send us an email.

Thanks Again and Happy Testing!
Product Development Team
info@studyguideteam.com

FREE Test Taking Tips Video/DVD Offer

To better serve you, we created videos covering test taking tips that we want to give you for FREE. **These videos cover world-class tips that will help you succeed on your test.**

We just ask that you send us feedback about this product. Please let us know what you thought about it—whether good, bad, or indifferent.

To get your **FREE videos**, you can use the QR code below or email freevideos@studyguideteam.com with "Free Videos" in the subject line and the following information in the body of the email:

   a. The title of your product

   b. Your product rating on a scale of 1-5, with 5 being the highest

   c. Your feedback about the product

If you have any questions or concerns, please don't hesitate to contact us at info@studyguideteam.com.

Thank you!